DANGEROUS ESTATE

THE ANATOMY OF NEWSPAPERS

CLASSICS OF 20th CENTURY JOURNALISM

DANGEROUS ESTATE

THE ANATOMY OF NEWSPAPERS

Francis Williams

Foreword by the Rt. Hon. Michael Foot MP

 Patrick Stephens, Cambridge

*First published in 1957 by Longmans, Green and Co.
This facsimile edition published in 1984 by
Patrick Stephens Limited.*

British Library Cataloguing in Publication Data

*Williams, Francis
Dangerous estate.—(Classics of 20th century
journalism)
1. Newspapers—Great Britain—History
I. Title   II. Series
079'.41   PN5118*

ISBN 0-85059-699-8

*Printed in Great Britain on Antique Wove Cream
Vol 18 80gsm, and bound, by The Garden City Press,
Letchworth, Herts, for the publishers, Patrick Stephens
Limited, Bar Hill, Cambridge, CB3 8EL, England.*

CONTENTS

FOREWORD
BY THE RT. HON. MICHAEL FOOT, MP

WHAT makes a great journalist, a great editor, a great newspaper? Curiously, the qualities needed for the three are not identical. They may overlap, but even that is not necessary. Curiously again, the real answers to the questions are hazy, even contradictory. Nobody knows, in particular, what combination of virtues or vices makes a good editor. There are no certainties, no rules, nothing but exceptions.

Partly the confusion arises from the nature of newspapers: are the people who run them engaged in a profession or a trade, a vocation or a business? The balance between the two seems sometimes to be entirely, irretrievably overturned. The pressure for profits and money-making—as, for example, in this era of the 1980s, the age of the Murdoch debasement—becomes all-powerful, sweeping all other factors aside.

Editors or journalists or newspaper managers, if there are such, who dare to insist on serving any other values, are liable to be pushed aside as sentimental misfits or hangovers from a bygone age. And yet even in this wretched period when the Fleet Street Gresham's Law has operated so ferociously, the bad driving out the good, the super-shoddy displacing all feeble attempts to retain any standards at all, it may be that the most remarkable events have been the resistance movements against the destruction of decent journalism successfully conducted in some quarters.

I give three examples from our common Fleet Street experience, although I would happily acknowledge that other good examples could be cited from the newspaper business in the provinces. Here are my three: *The Guardian* in recent years has succeeded in increasing substantially both its circulation and its influence, and it has done so notably in the period when so-called Falklands fever might have seemed likely to make the achievement impossible. *The Guardian* to-day is as great a newspaper as it has ever been, which is high praise indeed, but who can doubt that the commercial pressures and anxieties have been for them at least as severe as anything their founding Scottish fathers had to endure? *The Observer* is another brilliant survivor; who would have expected ten years ago that the *Observer,* on any test of journalistic merit, would have been putting the *Sunday Times* in the shade? And, finally, the *Daily Mirror* and its companion, the *Sunday Mirror.* The most natural result of the Murdoch conquest would have been that the Mirror papers would go under entirely or obediently stoop to the Murdoch depths. The tragedy has not happened. *The Mirror*, created by two inspired editor-managers, Guy Bartholomew and Hugh Cudlipp, and the company of great journalists they assembled around them, retains its individuality, its vitality, its right and capacity to live.

It is good to see that Fleet Street has not lost all its old genial eccentricities, and this unpredictability of the place applies especially to the office of editor. One journalist succeeds with the most unlikely proposition, while another possessing all the talents condemns his charge to sudden or lingering death. Some of the very greatest editors of all time—say, Robert Blatchford of the old Socialist *Clarion* in its most splendid days—could churn out tens of thousands of words a week; others couldn't, or can't, write for toffee. Some are the most exhilarating of companions; for example, Frank Owen, prewar editor of the *Evening Standard* and the best bar none I ever saw in action, inspired his reeling staff from what deceptively looked like a perpetual pub crawl. Others are cold fishes who never drink like one, even in the privacy of their garrets—the place, incidentally, where William Hazlitt said all good editors should be incarcerated, if they were not to be seduced by London society and its dinner tables.

All of which brings me to the case of Francis Williams, an old friend and just occasionally an old rival, but one who fitted into no single category whatever. He was not exclusively a journalist or an editor or manager. He was a newspaper man through and through, to the fingertips. He loved the profession and the business. He knew as much about both as any practitioner of his time which, apart from its intrinsic value, was the reason why this book of his was so widely acclaimed.

If not actually born a journalist, Francis Williams was bred as one by the *Bootle Times*. Liverpool licked him into shape, and he had the good fortune and intelligence to arrive in London just when the soft-hearted and supposedly soft-headed George Lansbury, editor of the impecunious *Daily Herald*, was instructing his millionaire competitors how to recruit the finest crew of writers ever assembled in Fleet Street, and how to run a real campaigning paper.

Often, thereafter, in one branch of journalism after another, Francis proved himself just about the best in the business. He conducted a brilliantly heretical finance column in the *Herald* of the 1930s which compelled even the bankers to study Labour's Own. He ran a column about newspapers themselves, in the *New Statesman* of the 1950s, in which dog ate dog so advantageously that the diet of weekly journalism has been altered ever since.

Other triumphs he could claim without boasting or offence. He was at the San Francisco Conference which established the United Nations in 1945 and at No 10 Downing Street in the subsequent years of the Attlee Labour Government, the perfect public relations officer. He almost invented the role, and it has thereafter appeared indispensable. Those he served most faithfully, Clem Attlee and Ernest Bevin in particular, profited vastly from his exceptional touch and tact. And Churchill did too, although Francis Williams properly revealed how intense was Churchill's anti-Press phobia: during his absurd wartime vendetta against the *Daily Mirror,* he ordered a search of its share register to find out if any shares were held by enemy agents.

But now back to the inscrutable question: is it true that a journalist so superabundantly qualified as Francis could fail as an editor? Appointed to that post on the *Daily Herald* at the age of 32, in 1935, he clashed finally and honourably some five years later with Lord Southwood, the proprietor he had learned to hate. Circulation had soared under his aegis, but Southwood's selling methods had nothing to do with real journalism (they were the 1930s' equivalent of bingo), and even when the *Herald* was the first paper in the country to pass the two-million-a-day total, it was still losing at least £10,000 a week. That was 'peanuts', of course, by present-day standards, but perhaps the proprietors of those days were wiser than their 1980s equivalent. They came to realise how deadly the gamble could be for journalism itself.

No one could say—Francis Williams does not claim—that he had revived the glories of Lansbury's *Herald*. And the same kind of verdict must be passed on a much more modest attempt he made some 20 years later to edit and revive *Forward* on the invitation of Hugh Gaitskell and the Anti-Bevanites. (We on *Tribune* at the time, I recall, had some alternative names for this journal: eg, *The Pink 'Un, The Leek, Slime and Slide, The Old Statesman*.) Anyhow, *Forward* made no progress whatever. The paper which Emrys Hughes (a truly inspired Do-it-Yourself editor) had kept alive for decades, soon collapsed. 'What we needed', wrote Francis Williams, 'was a tycoon; Alf Robens was the nearest to that we had . . .' Yes, later *the* Lord Robens; he lived long after *Forward* had died.

For tycoons cannot run newspapers unless they become journalists, as Beaverbrook did. He was a born editor who had the advantage of being able to appoint his own proprietor. Nowadays, alas, the journalists try to become tycoons. But returning to the mystery, I offer one clue. The great editor loves his newspaper more than any living thing under the sun and stars. To protect and burnish his treasured mosaic, he will, in the last resort, sacrifice friends, wives, lovers, comfort, all normal human relationships. Good natured chaps like Francis Williams should keep clear of that particular branch of the trade, which is what at last Francis so wisely did. Instead he turned his hand and heart to another great newspaper theme: how to learn from the history of journalism. He does it with skill, good humour and a true love for his job. How much healthier the modern trade or profession would be, if the modern practitioners would show the same enthusiasm, the same rejection of cynicism, the same readiness to learn.

February 1984

DANGEROUS ESTATE

The Anatomy of Newspapers

FRANCIS WILLIAMS

TO JESSIE
With Love

I

THIRTY MILLION NEWSPAPERS

No other people on earth are such avid readers of newspapers as the British.

For good or ill, close on thirty million newspapers national, provincial, morning and evening go into British homes on every working day; on Sundays even more. Most of them are read by more than one person, some by three or more. Many of those who read newspapers, although by no means all, read at least two a day—one in the morning, one in the evening—some read more. All in all nearly 90% of the adult population of this island reads regularly at least one national morning paper every day, which means, if statistics of national intelligence are correct, practically all those who can read. No other product of modern civilisation has achieved so complete a saturation of its potential market.

We tend to take this British appetite for the daily written word, this almost universal dependence on newsprint, for granted. Yet it is in fact a comparatively recent development. In the last twenty-five years the population has increased by just over 10%; the readership of national daily newspapers by more than 90%.

Nor is our appetite for newspapers matched by that of the citizens of any other country. The newspapers of the United States are vast in size and penetrating in influence. It can be argued with a good deal of supporting evidence that their place in the historical development of their nation has been, and still is, greater than that of the newspapers of any other country in the world. But they are not read as the British are. Per head of population the British read nearly twice as many of their newspapers as the Americans, nearly three times as many as the French, and many times more than the Russians. In all South-East Asia, so much the battleground of the warring ideologies of East and West, fewer newspapers are read than are disposed of by one London evening newspaper in an afternoon. Nor is there anywhere else in the world anything to approach the individual circulations of the great British newspapers of mass entertainment: nothing within hailing distance of the close on four and three-quarter million copies a day of the *Daily Mirror*, the more than four million of the *Daily Express*, the more than seven million copies of the *News of the World* sold each Sunday.

Neither radio nor television has so far diminished this British appetite for the daily written word although they have affected its character and may do so still more as commercial television develops. The enforced interruption of newspaper reading habits during the newspaper strike of 1955 temporarily halted the ascending spiral and may even have caused some people to ask themselves why they read so many newspapers. Two price increases have brought some slight slackening in demand; it now seems certain that the topmost peak of national daily newspaper sales has at last been passed. But as a whole the habit of newspaper reading remains formidably unshaken. We continue to lead the world with an unwavering fidelity to the products of journalism that is among the most remarkable phenomena of our times.

Yet although the British read more newspapers than any other people on earth they read far fewer individual ones. The United States with three times our population but an average rate of newspaper readership not much more than half ours has eighteen times as many newspapers. France which reads only 240 newspapers per thousand to our 611 has close on half as many newspapers again as we have. So has Sweden with less than one-seventh of our population.

In the thirty-eight years since the end of the First World War much of the political, social and economic pattern of British life has been changed. One of the two great traditional parties of our Parliamentary history has virtually disappeared from effective

Parliamentary life, its place taken by a party which at the end of the First World War was still a small and ineffective minority group but which now commands, it would appear, the settled adherence of at least half the electorate. The trade union movement which at the beginning of that war was still a militant organisation struggling hard and often unsuccessfully for status and recognition has grown into a mighty power accepted as such by employers and Governments of whatever political persuasion.

Over the same period the pattern of incomes in British society has changed out of all recognition and the gap between the richest and poorest narrowed to an extent not to be found in any other major country in the world. A new middle class has emerged bringing with it great changes in the shape of our social structure and our ways of life. The position of women has been so altered and their status in politics, in the professions, and in industry so improved that only by a great effort of the imagination can the struggles of the early suffragettes seem other than infinitely remote and irrelevant to a girl now leaving school. Higher education has been extended to a degree that would once have appeared altogether unrealistic and the trickle of university students from the working classes and the lower groups of the middle classes has swollen to a mighty and powerful stream.

On all the evidence of the past it would have been natural to expect that these vast changes in ways of life and social attitudes would find their reflection in a great development of new newspapers to serve the needs and foster the ambitions of fresh social groups. This has not happened. Existing newspapers have changed themselves vastly in appearance, character and appeal, and some have taken on a new nature to meet the needs of a new mass readership. But during the whole of these more than three and a half decades of peaceful social revolution only two new morning newspapers have sought to establish themselves—one a propaganda paper devoted to the Communist cause, the *Daily Worker*, the other the *Daily Recorder* which, launched on 27 October 1953, never succeeded in securing for itself more than a precarious foothold in the newspaper world and finally collapsed, five months after its birth, with heavy losses. Newspaper readership has more than trebled during the thirty-eight years since the end of the First World War, but instead of new papers coming into existence to meet this expanding demand many famous and long-established daily newspapers, among them the *Morning Post*, the *Daily Chronicle*, the *Westminster Gazette* and the *Daily Dispatch*, have been forced to cease publication— accompanying into the sad limbo of the lost such once influential London evening newspapers as the *St. James's Gazette*, the *Pall Mall Gazette*, and *The Globe* and such once widely read Sunday papers as the *Sunday News*, the *Referee* and the *Sunday Chronicle*.

Great provincial journals of opinion have suffered in even greater number. In scores of towns and cities where once the battle for freedom of news and opinion found its daily reflection in the challenge and counter-challenge of competing morning and evening newspapers with deep roots in local interests and loyalties, the position has so altered that in fifty-six of the sixty-six provincial cities which are still capable of sustaining any sort of daily newspaper press those who wish to read a paper concerned with the social and civic problems of their region must content themselves with what is offered to them by one evening paper only. Nor in this time of vastly increasing newspaper readership, of expanding education, and of town and country planning with its stimulation to civic consciousness, have even the provincial weekly papers, for so long the traditional voices of their communities on matters of local concern, fared any better. At least 225 such papers have been forced to cease publication during these thirty-eight years.

We read more and more copies of fewer and fewer newspapers.

The greatly increased cost of modern newspaper production is often offered as an explanation of this phenomenon of a rising newspaper readership and a declining number of newspapers. It would not seem to be a wholly adequate one. Similar economic conditions exist in many other countries without producing the same effect to anything like the same degree. Even the United States, where the concentration of the traditional functions and responsibilities of the press into fewer and fewer units is also a major feature of the social scene, has not yet gone so far along this road as we have. Economic pressure is one cause. But only one. Despite our pride in British individuality we are subject to a conformity of taste in matters of popular journalism that is not paralleled anywhere else and which presents a somewhat startling picture of the current level of interest of the majority of British people. We seem, indeed, many of us, already to have adjusted ourselves without discomfort, with pleasure even, to being at the receiving end of an anonymous system of mass communication. 'I read it,' we say, 'in *the* paper', as though already there were only one paper and that one gave all that any reasonable man should wish to know about this world.

The development of the press is part of the history of national development. Much more than political constitutions, statistics of economic progress or demonstrations of national unity the state of a country's newspapers discloses which rung of the ladder of civilisation has been reached. This is not only because newspapers reflect, as they must, public taste but because the structure and status of the press show more revealingly than almost anything else the real stage of national development. In a sense even more profound than arises from its nature as a reporter of events the press is the mirror of its age because the degree of authority and independence it is permitted to exercise, or is able to seize for itself, and the nature of its influence on public opinion throw light in a way nothing else quite does on the real balance of power within a society.

From the struggle of the secret presses in the sixteenth century and the emergence of the first newsbooks hot from the booksellers to tempt the taste for scandal of the mob or take advantage of the readiness of politicians to bribe or be bribed in the seventeenth, right down to the modern age of ennobled proprietors and circulations by the several million, the development of journalism offers a guide to the history of Britain. In it there have been, almost from the very beginning, two major themes. The press has been seen as a weapon of freedom, a sword in the hands of those

fighting old or new tyrannies, the one indispensable piece of
ordnance in the armoury of democracy. It has been called, by
Macaulay in honour and by Burke in despair, 'The Fourth Estate
of the Realm', ranking only just, if at all, behind the Lords
Spiritual, the Lords Temporal and the Commons.

But it has also almost always been both more and less than this:
a vehicle of entertainment, a medium for satisfying the common
human appetite for gossip, an answer to the pleasure in news,
not as an aid to forming opinion but for its own sake.

'What would you have, good woman?' asks the Registrar of
the Staple of News in Ben Jonson's play of that name, and the
countrywoman answers in terms that echo down the centuries:

> 'I would have, sir
> A groatsworth of any news, I care not what,
> To carry down this Saturday to our vicar.'

In the history of the British press the *News of the World* and
the *Daily Mirror* have at least as ancient a lineage as *The Times*
and the *Manchester Guardian*. The earliest of the newsbooks
which at the turn of the sixteenth and the beginning of the
seventeenth centuries blazed the trail for the daily and weekly
journals that were to follow were produced to satisfy an interest
as old as the story of Cain and Abel and as new as this morning's
Daily Sketch or next Sunday's *People*; it was of shocking murder
and horrid rape that they told.

Of these two major themes in the history of journalism the
first was perhaps most clearly expressed just over a century ago
in a series of leading articles in *The Times*, then under Delane.
He believed that newspapers had a specific and unique responsibility for the shaping of ideas and the formation of public
policies and exercised, or ought to exercise, a beneficent power
not only separate from any other in the State, and even in a sense
from the State itself, but morally superior to that of the Government.

The occasion was a rebuke levelled against that paper in
February 1852 by Lord Derby, who was shortly to succeed Lord

John Russell as Prime Minister. He had been affronted by what he regarded as the gross irresponsibility of the comments made by *The Times* on the *coup d'état* by which Louis Napoleon made himself Emperor of France and by its outspoken criticism of the character of the new Emperor.

This was not of course the last time a Minister of the Crown was to find himself affronted by the comments of newspapers upon a foreign leader. I remember several repetitions of Lord Derby's protest in the late 1930s when newspaper editors—myself among them—were summoned to Whitehall to be lectured by Mr. Neville Chamberlain, Sir Samuel Hoare and other Ministers of varying authority and clarity of mind on the duty of newspapers to be polite to Hitler. They were not, however, very good lecturers. Nor except, ironically enough, for *The Times* itself, was their audience any more persuaded than Delane had been.

'If in these days', said Lord Derby, 'the press aspires to exercise the influence of statesmen the press should remember that they are not free from the corresponding responsibility of statesmen and that it is incumbent on them, as a sacred duty, to maintain that tone of moderation and respect, even in expressing frankly their opinions on foreign affairs, which would be required of every man who pretends to guide public opinion.'

Although expressed in terms which seem remarkably moderate for an hereditary legislator in the first half of the nineteenth century, this rebuke brought an immediate rejoinder from *The Times*. It was delivered after the most careful consideration by John Walter III, the chief proprietor of the paper, Delane, the editor, Henry Reeve, the leader writer, who actually penned it, and Robert Lowe, another leader writer, who later became Chancellor of the Exchequer in one of Mr. Gladstone's administrations. Its purpose was much more than a mere defence against Lord Derby's charges. In two successive leading articles on 6 and 7 February 1852, Delane and his colleagues sought to set out a complete journalistic creed, a body of permanent principle for the guidance of newspapers.

They began with an examination of Lord Derby's argument that the power exercised by the press was comparable to that exercised by Governments and ought therefore to be governed by the same principles. This premiss *The Times* rejected.

'We cannot admit', it said, 'that its [a newspaper's] purpose is to share the labours of statesmanship or that it is bound by the same limitations, the same duties, the same liabilities as that of the Ministers of the Crown. The purpose and duties of the two powers are constantly separate, generally independent, sometimes diametrically opposite. The dignity and freedom of the press are trammelled from the moment it accepts an ancillary position. To perform its duties with entire independence, and consequently with the utmost public advantage, the press can enter into no close or binding alliances with the statesmen of the day, nor can it surrender its permanent interests to the convenience of the ephemeral power of any Government.'

What then were the duties of the press as *The Times* saw them?

'The first duty of the press', it declared, 'is to obtain the earliest and most correct intelligence of the events of the time, and instantly, by disclosing them, to make them the common property of the nation. The statesman collects his information secretly and by secret means, he keeps back even the current intelligence of the day with ludicrous precautions until [and how topical this sounds remembering Burgess and Maclean] diplomacy is beaten in the race with publicity. The press lives by disclosure: whatever passes into its keeping becomes a part of the knowledge and history of our times; it is daily and for ever appealing to the enlightened force of public opinion—anticipating, if possible, the march of events—standing upon the breach between the present and the future, and extending its survey to the horizon of the world.' What of the duties of the journalist? Of these *The Times* said this: 'The responsibility he really shares is more nearly akin to that of the economist or the lawyer, whose province is not to frame a system of convenient application to the exigencies of the day, but to investigate truth and apply it on fixed principles to the affairs of the world.' And again: 'The duty of the journalist is the same as that of the historian—to seek out the truth, above all things, and to present to his readers not such things as state-craft would wish them to know but the truth as near as he can attain it.'

Even halfway through the nineteenth century when the authority of the press had grown steadily over many years a claim so expressed could not help but seem intolerably presumptuous to most of those with political power. It would, as the official *History of The Times* itself comments, have seemed sheer megalo-mania in the youth of many statesmen then living. Yet for a long period thereafter this claim was to become almost wholly accepted. It was on these terms and by these standards that the press was judged by its readers throughout nearly all the second half of the nineteenth century.

Delane was confident, moreover, that the power of newspapers was only at its beginning. He believed that within measurable time the press would exercise 'a power over the formation of public opinion compared with which its present influence is but slight'.

It is not so easy to share that view today. The principles of independent responsibility upon which Delane rested his case are, it is true, now generally accepted, much more so than in his time. To proclaim the right of newspapers to print all the facts and not merely 'such things as statecraft would wish' was for him an act of challenge: today it is a truism on the lips of every cub reporter. But the result has hardly been what Delane anticipated. His statement of claim makes fine reading. But the readers and in some cases the editors, of many of the most popular of British news-papers—those newspapers which as an American critic in *Time* (not itself the most decorous of journals) recently remarked 'extend by degrees to the wildest and most sensational in the world, and the least informative'—could hardly care less.

We are in the middle of a newspaper revolution more potent perhaps even than that carried through by Northcliffe just over half a century ago or by Barnes of *The Times* three-quarters of a century before that. With the development of mass readership on a scale never previously known the character of much of journalism itself has changed and changed so radically that many former standards no longer apply nor perhaps can ever do so again. Those who seek to sustain these standards find themselves not only in a professional dilemma of the sharpest kind but in the grip of an economic situation in which survival itself depends for many newspapers on the securing of ever larger circulations. Newspapers are today more read than at any time in history—and more criticised. Their popularity is greater than it has ever been—the public esteem in which all but a very few are held, less. They are charged, and very often rightly charged, with irresponsibility, frivolity, sensationalism and the debasement of civilised values. They are accused of prying into private lives, of vulgarising and debasing the most sacred personal emotions; attacked for so acting as to seek to bring into disrepute many of the most honoured institutions of the State—among them the Monarchy. But they are read—how they are read! They hold a mirror to society and appalled and fascinated by what the mirror shows there are many who would like to cut off the hand that holds it.

The editor of a modern newspaper, and particularly of one with a circulation of several millions, is the impresario of a vast entertainment enterprise. He is concerned with a ceaseless search for news that will tickle the palate at breakfast or lift the spirit on the bus journey. His paper is a three-ring circus, daily presenting to its patrons the greatest show on earth; his vocation that of scouring the world for turns that will give the customers a thrill: here a murder, there a political quarrel; on this page a film star in process of falling out of love, on that a rumour of war; in this column a man who has made millions, over the page a man who has lost them; a simple tale of youthful idealism headlined here, a dash of brutality and passion there. There is nothing necessarily to be ashamed of in any of this. The journalist is traditionally an entertainer; he must entertain or find another trade.

But although the popular journalist is compelled by the exigencies of his trade to be a blood-brother to Barnum he still cannot avoid being at least half-cousin to Delane. Whatever their other preoccupations, and they are many, all newspapers must in some measure adhere to the claims advanced by Delane on their behalf if they are to remain newspapers in any true and complete sense.

This dual role of the press, to inform and to entertain, to appeal forever to the enlightened force of public opinion whilst drumming up the largest possible number of paying customers, is not of course solely a modern dilemma. It has always existed. But it has been vastly increased by the enormous cost of producing a modern newspaper: by the fact that each of those thirty million newspapers so avidly read each day by nearly nine out of ten of the citizens of the United Kingdom represents one of the products of a major industry. In this industry shareholders have invested many millions of pounds. It needs for its nourishment the coppers of a vast army of readers, the massed pounds of hundreds of advertisers.

Yet although this dilemma has, along with so much else, been magnified by the conditions of our day, it is inherent in the nature of all newspapers, even the most solemn. Newspapers exist to be read. If they fail in that essential their failure is absolute whatever other merits they may abundantly possess. Not for the journalist is the comfort that sustains the artist. He cannot appeal from the present to the future. He must match his moment. Moreover newspapers are by their nature made at least as much by those who read them as by those who edit and write them. They are as good or as bad as their publics allow, for the greatest newspaper in the world has no future if it cannot get and hold a public. Nor can it, like its peers in the world of literature and art, afford to wait. It lives by and for the day; the present, not the future, is its judge; the tastes of the moment, not those of tomorrow, its support.

To an extent hardly true of any other of the institutions by which society keeps itself going newspapers thus reflect the currently dominant themes in the society of which they are a part; the actual rather than the imagined tastes of those who comprise it. Whether we like the picture they show us or not they mirror our time because they have no life outside or beyond it. Yet although they mirror the present they also derive from the past and cannot be understood except in relation to it. The key to what is in so many ways the most potent and pervasive of all the social forces in our present society lies not only in that society but in the developing history of the press itself. These thirty million newspapers that the British public reads each day are not only carriers of the news, they are news themselves: a current phenomenon; a part of the texture of our history and a portent. If one is to assess them at all one must look to their beginnings.

II

GIANTS TO WRITE FOR IT

THE first daily newspaper ever to be published was issued from an office near Ludgate Hill on 11 March 1702, the year Queen Anne came to the throne. It was called the *Daily Courant* and was made up entirely of extracts from Continental papers several days old. It cost a penny.

There was plenty of news waiting to be reported that year. But not much of it appeared in the *Daily Courant*.

Europe was already torn by war. With a perverse genius for ranging enemies against himself Louis XIV of France had threatened the Dutch by occupying the Barrier fortresses in the Spanish Netherlands, insulted and angered England by recognising the 'Old Pretender' as James III, and menaced the stability of the rest of Europe by insisting that the succession of his grandson Philip to the throne of Spain could not affect his right also to the throne of France.

The War of the Spanish Succession that followed was to last for eleven years; almost the whole of Anne's reign. It was to be marked by a series of great victories under an English general of unparalleled genius, Marlborough, whose military achievement was to grow sonorous with the names of the most dazzling victories, Blenheim, Ramillies, Oudenarde. And, finally, there was to be added to that roll a name so drenched with blood as to make even the most bellicose ready to contemplate peace—Malplaquet.

But the readers of the *Daily Courant* found in its pages no first-hand account of any of these. The day of the war correspondent and the diplomatic correspondent was not yet. The

Daily Courant confined itself to reprinting extracts from Continental news-sheets several days old, its boast as it made its bow to the public was that it made 'no pretence of Private Intelligence' nor aspired to explain the significance of events by 'Comments or Conjectures'. With a self-denial rare in its successors it declared that it 'supposed other People to have Sense enough to make Reflections for themselves'.

At home the years that broke the military supremacy of France in Europe and established Britain's leading role in the Continental balance of power saw the Act of Union between England and Scotland and the end of antagonisms that had lasted since Edward I. And finally with the defeat of the House of Lords by the peace party and Marlborough's political fall, his military glories still thick about him, they ushered in a decisive chapter in the constitutional struggle that had gone on since the Restoration, making the transfer of political power to the House of Commons a permanent reality.

In such matters the first daily newspaper in England did not meddle.

The British daily press had been born. The newsbooks and newsletters that preceded it had bowed themselves off the stage seven years before when the long struggle to end the licensing of printing was finally successful and the great principles of freedom enunciated by Milton in the *Areopagitica* half a century before were at last accepted. The first of the thirty million was on its way. But the *Daily Courant* took no risks with this new liberty. It kept to second-hand news and avoided opinion. It was to the periodical and the pamphlet, not the newspaper, that was left the task of showing just how powerful an instrument of public opinion this new free press could become.

The press was fortunate in its first freedom. It had giants to write for it: Defoe, Swift, Steele, Addison, Prior: seldom in any period of journalistic history have there been such names to conjure with. It was a golden dawn.

Great political issues moved the country. The struggle of Whig and Tory and the debate between those who would push war to the extreme and those who would end it convulsed public opinion. This public opinion was well served by the new journalism of the pamphleteers and the periodical writers.

In British political history there has probably never been any single piece of journalism, with the exception of *Eikon Basilike*, to compare in immediate effect with Swift's pamphlet attacking Marlborough and the Whig Ministers: *The Conduct of the Allies*. The first edition was exhausted in two days. It had to be reprinted seven times. Nor was Swift, although pre-eminent, alone among the political controversialists of the time, either as a pamphleteer or as a polemical journalist writing regularly for the Tory *Examiner*. The *John Bull* pamphlets of Dr. John Arbuthnot, the newspaper writings of Matthew Prior and others, all these had a profound effect on political attitudes.

Yet curiously it is not in such political writings that the journalistic flavour of this time is most correctly to be found, or for that matter the true ancestors of the modern press to be discovered. England was at war and was to be so for eleven years. She was in the throes of a political development which if less violent than those that had preceded it was hardly less significant. Yet despite the victories that illuminate the reign of this most unremarkable and easily forgotten Queen and the political intrigues that perpetually revolved around her and her favourites, the formidable Sarah Churchill and Abigail Hill, the reign of Anne was above all else an age of content. It ushered in a period of commercial expansion, political moderation and intellectual freedom—'that adorable eighteenth century', as Clive Bell called it, which although it lacked the amenities of existence awaiting anguished birth in the industrial revolution yet commands our admiration by accounting the virtues of reason, tolerance and intellectual curiosity among the supreme qualities of civilisation.

It was these virtues—so contrary to those found in the scattered newswritings of the previous half-century—that found their expression in the mode of journalism most characteristic of this age. Upon this mode three men above all others stamped their imprint: Defoe, Steele and Addison.

It was an age of the sharpest contrasts. The high civility of aristocratic society cast something of its radiance on to the social levels immediately below but it did no more than throw into blacker shadow the teeming life of crime and poverty, violence, bravado and mock elegance that Defoe depicted in all its horrific zest and vigour in *Moll Flanders*, and that Gay enlivened with wit and gaiety in *The Beggar's Opera*. Yet it is also true as Buckle said in his not now perhaps very highly regarded *History of Civilisation* that 'one of the leading characteristics of the eighteenth century, and one which pre-eminently distinguished it from all that preceded, was a craving after knowledge on the part of those classes from which knowledge had hitherto been shut out'.

It was the craving for knowledge that first found expression in the new periodical press of the time just as it was to do nearly two centuries later in the revolution in popular reading habits produced by Newnes and Pearson and Harmsworth.

Among the earliest of the periodicals designed to meet this demand was one of which Defoe himself was a casual reader, the *Athenian Gazette*, later renamed the *Athenian Mercury*, which began life in 1690, a decade, strictly speaking, before the eighteenth century was born. Its purpose according to its publisher, John Dunton, was to provide 'those curious in philosophical and recondite matters with matters of interest'. But it also provided what must be the first personal advice service ever provided by a periodical—an interesting evidence of how far the roots of popular journalism run. 'I have lately', wrote one reader, 'courted a young gentlewoman and she is now in mind to marry me. Lately died a relative and left me £100 a year, on condition, moreover, that I never would marry the aforementioned lady. Query, whether to take the lady and leave the money, or take the money and leave the lady.' Faithful to principles that were to continue to animate popular journalism the *Athenian Mercury* came down on the side of romance. And then there was the *Gentleman's Journal*, founded a year later and published in the form of a monthly 'Letter to a Gentleman in the Country'. Its primary purpose like that of the glossy weeklies of our own time was to convey to country squires and their ladies such anecdotes of the great world as would, if occasion offered, enable them to feel at home in society. But it also published verse, offered information on history, philosophy and literature, and printed the words and music of currently successful songs, a feature adopted at various times since by many popular periodicals.

It is, however, with the launching of Defoe's *Review* in 1704 that the new journalism truly begins to take its characteristic shape. Defoe was by then forty-five, somewhat late in life even in our longer-lived age to begin a new and successful career in journalism. But there are no rules to be applied to this remarkable man who was, in so far as any single man can be said to be, the founder of modern journalism; just as fourteen years later, changing course at fifty-nine, he became, so far as any man can be said to be so, the father of the English novel, writing *Robinson Crusoe* in four months.

Defoe was born on the eve of the Restoration—thirty-one years after Bunyan. And if, as Dr. Trevelyan has said, Bunyan may properly be put down on the great roll of English literature as the 'last of the Puritans', Defoe may no less properly be regarded as the first of the dissenters—a non-conformist but a practical commonsensical one, a tradesman, not a visionary. Before he launched his *Review* he had already, having been made bankrupt several times, turned his pen to a popular verse satire *The True-Born Englishman*. It is typical of him that when its successor, *The Shortest Way with the Dissenters*, landed him, to his terror and horror, in the pillory he did not take to denunciation or self-pity but set to work instead to establish an organ that was to become a model of straightforward journalism and strike a new note of reason and moderation in the discussion of political and ecclesiastical affairs.

The *Review* marked a total break with the violent partisan journalism that had characterised most of the short-lived broadsheets and pamphlets of the previous century. It was not only very characteristic of Defoe himself but ideally suited to the needs of the time. That Defoe should combine his editing of it with employment as a secret agent for that oddly Baldwinian character, the Tory Robert Harley, may seem to modern eyes a dubious marriage of interests. In fact it was a conjunction of jobs that not only suited Defoe but served the new journalism admirably.

As he travelled the country on secret business for his patron he observed with those keen reporter's eyes of his every facet of the changing national life. He described these changes for the readers of his *Review*, at first once a week, then twice a week and finally, for more than seven years, three times a week. Each issue contained articles on political, commercial and social matters and there were from time to time a number of supplements. The whole of it Defoe wrote single-handed and without outside help. To the task he brought an unexampled genius for plain writing and a superb never surpassed talent for the accumulation of significant detail. In so doing he not only established what journalism at this stage most needed—a tradition of responsible popular reporting—but also provided a pervasive antidote to the fierce partisanship that had earlier held almost undisputed dominance in the world of periodical journalism. He cultivated moderation. In matters of opinion his purpose was not to scarify but to persuade, a purpose so unusual as to seem almost eccentric. Like Swift he cast aside the pretentious journalism of the past and with it the dialogue form that had until then been almost the only mode for periodical writing.

'If any man was to ask me', he said, 'what I would suppose to be a perfect style of language, I would answer, that in which a man speaking to five hundred people of all common and various capacities, idiots or lunatics excepted, should be understood by them all.' That is a precept which any junior reporter starting out this morning to cover his first police court or mayoral reception could not do better than make his own.

Defoe had to an extreme degree one other quality essential to the good reporter, the capacity to be all things to all men. He was at home wherever he found himself. Only when he turned to irony—ever a dangerous tool for those who write for the

English—did he misjudge the capacity of his public. In 1712 he found himself in prison again, this time for a satirical pamphlet *Reasons Against the Succession of the House of the Hanovers* which he intended as a blast against the Jacobites but which was read as a defence of them.

His imprisonment ended the *Review*. It was far from ending Defoe. Released, he at once launched a new periodical, the *Mercator*, to support the interests of the commercial classes in general and defend the principle of Bolingbroke's Treaty of Commerce in particular.

But journalists must live. When the death of Anne brought the moderate Tories on whose patronage he relied tumbling from office he trimmed his course accordingly and took secret service with the Whigs. Henceforth, although he continued to write for Tory newspapers, he did so as a Whig agent until at the end of his life he who had mixed so much among enemies, hiding his true employments under a whole series of disguises and often in daily risk of death, as in Edinburgh during the negotiations for Union ('He was', wrote Clerk of Penicuik, 'a spy among us but not known to be such, otherwise the mob of Edinburgh had pulled him to pieces'), suddenly grew terrified and went into hiding under the name of Moreton declaring that 'relentless enemies' were on his track.

'He was', says Sir Harold Nicolson on the evidence of his letters to Harley, 'a nasty spy and an unattractive man.' I cannot feel so. It is enough for me that he had an endless curiosity and a passion for facts, and was faithful to what he saw. He used his eyes and described what they told him without bias and without rancour. His uncalculating love of liberty shines through all he wrote. What more can one ask of any reporter? What reporter among us would not be proud to share one-half his qualities or need be ashamed to hail him, with all his imperfections, as the father of our craft?

Defoe was a genius with a talent for vivid reporting. Steele and Addison, it has been well said, were writers of talent who rose almost to genius because they instinctively collaborated with

the spirit of their age. It was because of this instinctive collabora-
tion, more complete even than Defoe's because less crippled by
constant financial worry, that they had an even larger part than
he in shaping the new pattern of journalism.

Defoe was the man of business, the dissenter, the homespun
man busy with affairs. Steele and Addison spoke for those who
were moving out of the middle classes of commerce into society,
taking with them their own good sense and sober morality to
replace the wit and profligacy of the Restoration.

The fireworks were over. Lechery, although still, no doubt, a
private pleasure, was no longer a public virtue. Bravado had had its
day. Urbanity had become the mode and in the bookshops and
coffee-houses new periodicals of many kinds competed for the
attention of this new society. There were political journals, social
journals, literary journals, *Mist's Weekly Journal*, *Read's Weekly
Journal*, the *Craftsman*, for which Bolingbroke wrote, and the
Grub Street Journal; these and others competed for the attention
of the politically minded. The best and the liveliest of them were
Tory—not because journalists are so by nature—some are, some
are not—but because opposition is ever a piquant sauce and
attack comes more readily than official propaganda to journalists
of an independent temperament.

Steele and Addison made a contribution to the history of
journalism larger than the publishers of any of these competing
political journals, lively though many of them were, because to a
greater degree than any others they responded to the unpolitical
but basic needs of the time.

The *Tatler*, which Steele founded in April 1709, owed in its
original form a good deal to Defoe's *Review*. Like the *Review* it
came out thrice weekly to catch the country mails and, like it,
contained a number of essays on varying subjects. But its mood
was different. It was concerned neither with business nor politics
but with guidance in the ways of civilised living. Its purpose was
comment on all matters of breeding, taste and chivalry; a task for
which Steele, himself, was ideally suited since he encompassed in
his own character the old world and the new. He was a man of

the Restoration, an Irishman, a soldier, a wit and a rake. But he
was also a moralist who had begun to tire of Restoration values
and become aware of the promptings of his higher nature, although
fortunately when he gave way to them he did not, as so often
happens in such cases, throw out wit with his vices. The coffee-
houses provided him with his public—his public and most of his
sources of information. By the time the *Tatler* began there were
already close on five hundred of them, each with its own intimate
clientèle. There was White's Chocolate House in St. James's
Street for the fashionable, the Cocoa Tree Chocolate House for
the Tories, the St. James's Coffee House for the Whigs, Will's
near Covent Garden for the poets and critics, Truby's for the
Clergy, the Grecian for scholars, Lloyd's in Lombard Street for the
merchants, the Windsor at Charing Cross for those who sought
early intelligence of foreign affairs (it advertised chocolate at
twelve pence the quart and the translation of the *Harlem Courant*
as soon as the post came in) and a host of others for every kind
and manner of men, shopkeepers, shipbrokers, politicians,
dandies, Dissenters, Papists, Quakers, Jacobites. There was no
interest that could not expect to find its home in some coffee-
house or other.

But if Steele primarily appealed to those who frequented coffee-
house society in which, although rank and position counted, it
counted much less than elsewhere, it was not to them alone. He
had an instinctive awareness of the change that was beginning to
come in the status of women and of the increasing importance of
the family in the new society that was now developing. He set
himself both to reflect and promote this change, putting down his
purpose with an encouraging flourish of wit in his first number
on 12 April 1709.

Left to himself Steele would have been a cheerful moraliser
and good-humoured gossip, a journalistic innovator full of
abundant ideas but without the capacity to develop them all.
But soon after the *Tatler* began he had the great good fortune to
find the ideal collaborator in an old school friend at Charterhouse
who had begun to make some noise in the world as a poet and

politician. This was Addison, a man of the same age sharing many of the same interests but with a polished urbanity of style that Steele could not rival, a power of irony and an understanding of character superior to his. Where Steele was adventurous and impulsive, Addison was reserved and careful; a contemplative man. Steele owes a great deal to him, including, perhaps, his immortality. But it is no less true, as Steele himself said, that 'the public owes Addison to Steele'. Under Addison's influence the *Tatler* rapidly changed form.

It had begun as a thrice-weekly with news, advertisements, notices of new books and plays, anecdotes and original poetry. After Addison began to contribute to it, it developed into a series of essays, one to each issue, on manners, morals and social conventions. So acceptable to the public was the change that when the Whig Government was driven out of office—a victim as much to Swift's journalism in the *Examiner* as anything else—and Addison found himself without either his Chief Secretaryship for Ireland or even his Fellowship at Magdalen the two friends turned their minds to a more ambitious project: a daily journal.

It is a remarkable episode in the history of British journalism and an even more remarkable tribute to the reading habits of the eighteenth century that the second daily paper to appear in Britain should be not a newspaper at all but a literary journal of surpassing excellence. We are very fine people these days and avid readers of journalism indeed, but who can imagine for one moment that room would ever be found among our 30,000,000 newspapers a day for such a journal as Steele and Addison's *Spectator*, or even for that matter among the declining number of our weeklies?

It was published by Sam Buckley at The Dolphin in Little Britain. Buckley was also publisher of the *Daily Courant*, which he took over after its tenth issue, but the new journal had nothing else in common with that pedestrian production. It was not a newspaper in any true sense, nor even, as the *Tatler* had been at its inception, a critical journal dealing in each issue with what was current in the world of foreign and domestic politics, literature, learning and entertainment. It was 'a sheetful of thoughts every morning', their purpose to bring 'philosophy out of closets and libraries, schools and colleges, to dwell in clubs and assemblies, at tea tables and in coffee-houses'.

The design was Addison's and he set it out very clearly in the first issue when he described the character and qualification of 'Mr. Spectator'—a gentleman of the middle kind, 'born to a small hereditary estate, which, according to tradition of the village where it lies, was bounded by the same hedges and ditches in William the Conqueror's time that it is at present, and has been delivered down from father to son, whole and entire, without the loss or acquisition of a single field or meadow, during the space of six hundred years'; a man well suited to be the guide and confidant of the new society that was growing up around him.

But Mr. Spectator was no ordinary stay-at-home country squire. He was a man of the world, travelled and cultured: a quiet man who at the university had distinguished himself by 'a most profound silence' but who also applied himself with such diligence to his studies 'that there are very few celebrated books, either in the learned or the modern tongues, which I am not acquainted with' and who thereafter had allowed an insatiable thirst after knowledge to carry him into all the countries of Europe: 'nay, to such a degree was my curiosity raised, that having read the controversies of some great men concerning the antiquities of Egypt, I made a voyage to Grand Cairo on purpose to take the measure of a pyramid . . .'.

In London there was no place of general resort into which he did not go. 'Sometimes I am seen thrusting my head into a round of politicians at Will's and listening with great attention to the narratives that are made in these little circular audiences. Sometimes I smoke a pipe at Child's and while I seem attentive to nothing but the Postman, overhear the conversation of every table in the room. I appear on Sunday nights at St. James's coffee-house, and sometimes join the little committee of politics in the inner room, as one who comes there to hear and improve.

My face is likewise very well known at the Grecian, the Cocoa-
tree and in the theatres both of Drury Lane and the Haymarket.
I have been taken for a merchant upon the exchange for about
these ten years and sometimes pass for a Jew in the assembly of
stock-jobbers at Jonathan's. . . .'

As conceived by Addison Mr. Spectator was, indeed, the very
pattern of journalism : a man who knew everything and everyone ;
an eighteenth-century exemplar of all the modern columnist would
wish to be and does his best to persuade his readers he is.

Moreover, although Addison and Steele were men of some
political ambition, they sensed, as Defoe in his plainer way had
done before them, that in spite of its public brutalities and the
fierceness of its party controversies the true spirit of this age was
one of moderation and reason.

'I never espoused any party with violence', wrote Mr.
Spectator, 'and am resolved to observe a strict neutrality between
the Whigs and Tories unless I shall be forced to declare myself
by the hostilities of either side.' It was, indeed, one of the great
merits of the *Spectator*, and one of the prime causes of its success,
that it rigorously excluded everything of a party nature and
sought instead to serve the need for unity that existed deep within
this rapidly developing new society. To entertain their readers
while doing what they could in a small way to combat ignorance
and affectation, folly and impurity, this was the modest objective
Steele and Addison had in mind. They were concerned not with
one particular sort of man but with mankind, and they knew—
it is the one essential piece of knowledge a journalist must never
forget—that in such a study no triviality is so small as to be
unimportant.

The club society Steele invented to provide the proper setting
for Mr. Spectator was equally cunningly devised to catch light
from every facet of the comedy of manners and spread the appeal
of the paper in the widest possible way, as one easily sees from
its composition.

Consider it. First there is that immortal Worcestershire
gentleman Sir Roger de Coverley : 'A gentleman that is very

singular in his behaviour, but his singularities proceed from his good sense and are contradictions to the manners of the world only as he thinks the world is wrong.' He is followed in the Club's esteem by a member of the Inner Temple, 'but one who knows Aristotle and Longinus better than Littleton or Coke and is better known at the play than at the Courts'. Then Sir Andrew Freeport, a merchant of great eminence in the city 'who has made his fortune himself and says that England may be richer than other Kingdoms by as plain methods as he himself is richer than other men'. Next to Sir Andrew is Captain Sentry, a soldier of courage, understanding and modesty now retired to a small estate in the country, 'one who holds it is a civil cowardice to be backward in asserting what you ought to expect, as it is a military fear to be slow in attacking when it is your duty'. Then there is Will Honeycomb, the ageing but still admirably pre-served gallant, ever ready 'at that sort of discourse with which men usually entertain women', one 'who knows the history of every mode and can inform you from which of the French King's favourites our wives and daughters had this manner of curling their hair, that way of placing their hoods, whose frailty was covered by such a petticoat and whose vanity to show her foot made that part of the dress so short in such a year'. And finally—although a less regular attender than the others—there is a clergyman 'a philosophic man, of general learning, great sanctity of life, and the most exact good breeding'.

It was thus a group ideally designed to reflect the main themes in early eighteenth-century society and allow potential readers of almost every kind and taste to feel at home. Moreover, although Defoe had been ahead of Steele and Addison in recognising the importance of the commercial middle class in post-Restoration society, the bourgeois—that class which was to assume such importance in English society as the century lengthened—appears for the first time as a serious figure in English literature in the character of Sir Andrew Freeport.

The *Spectator* was an immediate success. Within less than two weeks Addison, writing of 'the *Spectator* and Its Purpose', was able to announce that it was already selling 3,000 copies a day. Before long the figure was 4,000. For some issues it was very much higher—even as high as 20,000 on some special occasions. Moreover, since not all those who wanted to read the paper could afford to buy it daily, it was collected and bound periodically. A first printing of 10,000 copies of the bound volumes was usual and further printings were frequently called for.

A sale of 4,000 copies a day may seem very small beer to a modern newspaper proprietor. But the population of England and Wales when Queen Anne came to the throne was no more than five and a half millions, less than an eighth of what it is today. The number of educated adult people able to read and in the habit of doing so was only a small part of this. According to a Treasury statement when the first newspaper stamp tax was imposed, the total sale of all newspapers and periodicals in 1711, the year of the *Spectator's* birth, was, indeed, something less than 7,500 a day, excluding Sundays: 2,250,000 for the whole year.

'To have the *Spectator* served up every morning with the bohea and rolls' was, as Macaulay says in his essay on Addison, 'a luxury for the few'. Even those copies bought privately were as a consequence passed on to many others, especially in the country, and read by perhaps as many as ten or twenty people before they were done with. Those bought by coffee shops and other establishments had an even larger readership. Although its paid sale was 4,000 copies a day the *Spectator's* actual daily readership was far greater. It may have been ten times as much, or even more. The readership of particular issues was sometimes much greater than this.

Indeed in relation to the size of the reading public of the time, and without seeking to press the analogy too far, the *Spectator's* popular success in its own day is not altogether without comparison with that of, say, the *Daily Express* in ours, an interesting reflection of the difference between our two societies. Of the 555 numbers in its year and ten months of existence Addison wrote 274 and Steele 236. The rest were contributed by various other writers, among them Hughes, Budgell, Tickell and Phillips—

none of them names of much importance now. It was Addison and Steele who made the *Spectator*. They did so by a consistent quality of writing and invention without parallel in daily journalism for what they wrote was not only read eagerly as it came off the press but is hardly less entertaining and enlightening now. Upon the social customs and conventions of their own age their impact was truly remarkable.

'It is', said John Gay, writing of Mr. Spectator, 'impossible to conceive the effect his writings have had on the town; how many thousand follies they have either quite banished or given a very great check to; how entirely they have convinced our fops and young fellows of the value and advantage of learning.'

There are many journalists today who wield forceful pens, or fancy they do, especially on Sundays. But even in these days of great press power of how many of them can as much as a quarter of this be said? This influence Addison and Steel achieved not by a high solemnity or a constant preoccupation with great affairs, but by the exercise of their pens on an infinite variety of subjects. 'Popular Superstitions', 'Ladies' Head-Dresses', 'French Fopperies', 'Fans', 'Difference of Tempers in the Sexes', 'Lottery Adventurers', 'Female Orators', 'Dissection of a Coquette's Heart', 'Dreams', 'Inconstancy', 'Gardens', 'The Value of Exercise', 'Coffee House Politicians': one would not be surprised to find similar articles on the feature pages of any morning or evening paper of today.

The *Spectator* offers, in fact, a supreme example of one of the most profound of all journalistic truths—that whosoever would influence the public must first learn to entertain it. Swift might sneer in a letter to Stella, 'I will not meddle with the *Spectator*, let him *fair sex* it to the world's end', but its two editors had no doubts. They were as conscious of the need to hold the interest not only of men but of women as the editor of any modern paper with a circulation of several millions. They never forgot their obligation to amuse. And because they kept it ever in mind they were able to influence the manners and social climate of an age.

III

CONTRIBUTION OF A RAKE

IN 1712 when the *Spectator* was the rage of London society the press seemed well on the way to becoming a settled force in public life. Seventeen years of freedom from licensing then lay behind it. Addison and Steele had made it an accepted and acceptable influence in the improvement of manners, Defoe had given it a seriousness of reportage well suited to the inclination of the commercial classes, Swift and Bolingbroke in the *Examiner* had shown how potent a political power it could exercise, had demonstrated indeed a truth that becomes more significant as time passes, that politics cannot work at all except on the most unsophisticated authoritarian level without an independent press capable of expressing in pungent language the divergences of public opinion. The air rang with the cries of Mercuries offering ever new journals to meet the public taste.

Why then did not journalism continue to advance in status and influence instead of becoming, as it shortly did, a byword for venality and corruption? The answer is to be found in the fact—as true and topical today as then—that new powers do not arise without evoking jealousy in old ones. So long as the press used its freedom to interest and amuse the propertied classes or lent itself to the support of 'the Establishment' it was tolerated as a luxury that might serve a useful purpose. But the habit of reading was growing. New papers were extending their appeal even to the lower strata of society: a French visitor to London, Montesquieu, was soon to note that the deplorable habit had spread so far that the very slaters had newspapers brought to them on the roofs while they worked. In relation to its population the England of

Queen Anne managed with rather less than half as many news-papers as does the Belgian Congo to-day. But to those who ruled in Britain this number seemed heavy with mischief for the security and well-being of the State.

The newspaper history of the next one hundred and fifty years reflects the ruling class's fear of what might happen if newspaper reading were allowed to become general. It was from this fear of the masses that the stamp tax on newspapers derived, first im-posed at the rate of 1d. a sheet in 1712, then progressively increased to 4d. a copy by 1815 and not finally abolished until 1855. So did the advertisement taxes which were imposed at the same time and remained in force until 1853, and the paper duties which lasted until 1861.

Their purpose was to keep the press on a leash, to tame it if it could no longer be suppressed and to ensure that if all else failed the price of newspapers should at least confine their circulation to the 'responsible' middle and upper classes where they could perhaps do no great harm. The first effect of the taxes was all their sponsors could wish.

'Grubb St. is dead and gone last week. The *Observator* is fallen, the *Medleys* are jumbled with the *Flying Post*, the *Examiner* is quite sick. . . . No more ghosts or murders now for love or money', reported Swift to Stella. Even the *Spectator* shortly closed its doors. Yet these taxes did not in fact achieve their purpose of permanently reducing the circulation of newspapers. The forces seeking expression through an expansion of the press were too strong. Trade was increasing and with it the size and power of the commercial classes. The development of industrial-isation made necessary a more educated artisan class. Population rose: by the end of the century it was to be nine million com-pared with five and a quarter million at the beginning. Every-where the habit of newspaper reading was increasing. Within forty years the circulation figures anxiously noted by Queen Anne's Ministers had trebled.

Nevertheless the taxes on newspapers had the most dire consequences. They could not reverse the rising demand for

newspapers although they could limit it. What they could and
did do was to take away from all but the very strongest the
possibility of economic, and thus of political, independence.

It is possible that even if there had been no taxes on newspapers
the press of the eighteenth century would have been corrupt.
This was an age of political corruption, and the press reflects its
age. It had become natural for a gentleman who lacked other
fortune 'to get his bread by voting in the House of Commons',
and for one of the main preoccupations of all Governments to be,
as the Duke of Newcastle, the great master of political bribery,
remarked, that 'of finding pasture enough for the beasts that they
must feed'. The one great question of principle that had divided
the country, that of Hanoverians or Stuarts, was no longer a
political issue. Mob passions were stilled, public opinion had little
to excite it. It remained quiescent although still capable of sudden
eruption. The House of Commons so far from being what it was
later to become, both a representative and a disciplined body,
consisted at one extreme of Court placemen and Civil Servants
who automatically supported the Government of the day, and
at the other of the country gentlemen who acted independently
of all Governments except when it was made to their advantage
to do otherwise. In between, the political factions contended for
power. There were Whigs and Tories but no party organisations.
Such organisations would, indeed, have been regarded by all
shades of opinion as treasonable conspiracies. Governed neither
by great principles nor a Party Whip many Members by accepted
custom sold their votes to the highest bidder. It would have been
odd, indeed, if even an untaxed press had stood apart from the
natural climate of the times.

It was given no chance to show whether it could. To clamp
economic shackles on the press was almost a necessary part of
the machinery of Government. Only if denied the hope of
economic independence could the press be intimidated and
bribed, changed from a potentially dangerous instrument of
public opinion into the servant of Governments and factions: a
tamed animal. Once tamed it became, as those bred for freedom

often do in captivity, sour and mangy. As a consequence the history of the press throughout most of the eighteenth and early part of the nineteenth centuries is mainly that of a journalism corrupted by bribes and subsidies, usually partisan to the extreme, mostly ill-conducted, almost always easily intimidated and still more easily bought.

There was hardly a newspaper in those years that was not in receipt of secret subsidies of one kind or another. Walpole, a master of political management in all its forms, was found by the Committee of Secrecy appointed in 1742 to inquire into his conduct to have paid out over £50,000 of secret service money to pamphleteers and Treasury newspapers in the last ten years of his administration. According to Professor Aspinall's detailed researches in his admirable study *Politics and the Press 1780–1850* the short-lived Shelburne Ministry spent £1,084 on bribing the press in the nine months from 10 July 1782 to 5 April 1783, and at the end of that time still owed £800 on the commitments it had entered into with editors. To secure public support for unpopular India Bills the Coalition Ministry of Fox and North bribed the newspapers of all sides.

Even Pitt, despite his public popularity, found it necessary to buy direct support from at least five newspapers in the first twelve months of his administration: the *Public Ledger*, the *London Evening Post*, the *Morning Herald* and two tri-weeklies the *Whitehall Evening Post* and the *St. James's Chronicle*. He spent at least £1,238 on such subsidies and employed various go-betweens—including the proprietor of the Covent Garden Theatre, Mr. Harris, and Mr. Longman, bookseller and early member of the publishing firm which issues this present volume—to pass the money to the editors concerned. At least £5,000 a year was distributed among newspapers by the Government at the time of the French Revolution, some nine of the most respectable being on a regular annual allowance, including the *Morning Herald* and the *World*, which got £600 a year each, and *The Times* which got £300 a year. Sums at least equal to this total of £5,000 a year were also almost certainly passed regularly to friendly newspapers in concealed subsidies paid in the form of official advertisements. In addition, a considerable number of journalists and writers of varying degrees of ability and respectability were on the Treasury pay-roll at sums which ranged from a few guineas for individual articles or paragraphs to a regular salary amounting in at least one instance to £500 a year.

To such a pass was the press, which had seemed as the eighteenth century opened to be on the verge of the highest achievements, brought by the economic measures used to tame it that political independence ceased to have even the force of a distant aspiration to most of those engaged in it. They took their money and did what they were told as though the long struggle for freedom throughout the sixteenth and seventeenth centuries had never taken place. Most of them were wholly worthy of the contempt in which all of them came to be held. The age got the press it deserved.

From history, however, we learn little. Measures of the same kind for controlling and taming the press are still in existence over much of the world, including a good deal of the democratic half of it. Part, indeed, of the interest—if a somewhat melancholy one—of studying the relations between Government and newspapers in eighteenth-century England is to note how little change there is in the attitude of autocratic, corrupt and politically retrogressive Governments, and even of some that proclaim themselves democratic, towards this dangerous power of a free press and how much the means chosen to cripple it stay the same. A report published by the International Press Institute in January 1956 listed no fewer than forty-two self-governing countries in what is loosely described as the free world from which it had received detailed evidence of attempts to control or intimidate the press in varying measure by one or other of the following means: penal laws, direct and indirect political pressures, discriminatory practices and such methods as the refusal of official advertisements, the denial of newsprint supplies, the withholding of information, charges of breach of privilege, bribes and secret subsidies and, in the more extreme cases, the suspension of newspapers and the imprisonment of journalists without fair trial. It noted, moreover, that so far from opening out since the end of the war the freedom of the press has, on the whole, diminished over a large part of the world. So far from being confined to countries new to political democracy in which conditions of national instability make anxiety about the exercise of full press freedom natural enough, the pressures upon the press have spread to several countries that are democratic in tradition and have a long history of political freedom behind them.

The idea that one may apply the experience of the past to the problems of the present or learn anything other than knowledge of the particular circumstances of a particular period from the study of history is now unfashionable.

Yet it is interesting to visit a Middle East capital such as Baghdad—to mention one neither better nor worse in this respect than many others in the Middle East and elsewhere —and feel oneself, so far as the press is concerned, almost bodily transported to eighteenth-century London. There is the same proliferation of political journals, rootless and short of life, existing always in the shadow of official fear and distrust, threatened and bribed by turn; the same lack of responsible reporting or untainted opinion; the same constant struggle to exist under the threat of suppression on circulations of no more than a few hundreds, the same contempt by authority for the press and the same justification for it in the press which authority itself has made.

For if it is a principle spanning the centuries that wherever there are Governments which rule without the full assurance of popular support or which fear the light of public interest on their activities there are attempts to curb, control, suborn and intimidate the press, it would appear to be a principle no less universal and subject to distinction neither of time nor place that a controlled or subsidised press is always a bad press. Whatever the danger there is in the matter of newspapers no real alternative to freedom.

All experience, indeed, makes it clear that the only way to have good newspapers is to have independent ones. The only way to have independent newspapers is to have economically strong ones. And the only way to have economically strong newspapers is to have newspapers that are solely dependent for their survival on the approval of readers, expressed in their willingness to buy them, and of advertisers, expressed in their willingness to pay for space in them.

Before it could break the hold of bribery and intimidation and reach out to economic independence and through it to political independence the press of the eighteenth century had to establish its right of access to information of public interest. This was the one key that could open the door of its prison.

It had one advantage over the press of some countries of the modern world—it was not subject to censorship. It is, indeed, a curious evidence of the ambivalent attitude of the eighteenth century to journalism that although the attempt to control and corrupt the press was scarcely disguised the belief that its freedom was one of the three great principles upon which the superiority of the British constitution over all others depended— the other two being the right to petition Parliament and the right of public meeting—was so strong that at no period of crisis, even that of the Napoleonic wars, was any attempt made to re-impose the censorship abolished in 1695. But this negative freedom from censorship, although vital, was not in itself sufficient to pave the way to independence, any more than it is today. For that the positive right of access to news and information was necessary. Only through freedom to report could newspapers hope to win such public interest and circulation as would make economic independence possible.

The struggle that went on for three-quarters of the century for access to information, and particularly for the right to report Parliamentary proceedings, is for this reason a key struggle in the development of newspapers. Although a good deal of the Parliamentary insistence on secrecy was rooted in the fact that secrecy had become a valuable, indeed an essential, adjunct to Parliamentary corruption and a shield to those private bargains by which Ministers made eighteenth-century politics work and

Members made them pay, there were not wanting, as always in such cases, more respectable reasons for opposing the right of the press to report. Many honestly believed that, as Windham later declared had actually happened, the publication of its debates could not but lower the dignity of the House and by increasing Parliament's dependence upon popular opinion tend to rob it of its independent and representative character and make it the servant of the mob. It is interesting to compare the arguments of these sincere eighteenth-century opponents of the press reporting of Parliament with those now used to defend the ban on independent discussion of matters still before Parliament by the B.B.C. and Commercial Television. The political animal does not change much.

In 1771 the pertinacity of John Wilkes and the independence of the City of London were to turn this issue into one of the most decisive in the struggle for Parliamentary democracy in Britain, and one of the most decisive also in the fight for an independent press. But until then the conflict between Parliament and press had to find its reflection in a series of skirmishes in which, although the heavy armament was always on the Parliament side, the tactical victories went for the most part to the press.

The early eighteenth century was still primarily an age of the periodical, not of the daily newspaper. Roads were being gradually extended and improved—four hundred Road Acts were passed in the first half of the century, sixteen hundred in the second half—but communication was for the most part still slow and hazardous. Heavy coaches dragged by six horses bumped their laborious way in summer along narrow roads pitted with pot-holes and in winter often had to give up altogether as the slow trains of pack horses reduced all movement to a walking pace. The lighter stage coach drawn by four horses was not to come until halfway through the century, the mail coach not until 1784. Postal services were inefficient, costly and irregular. Daily papers were confined to the Metropolis; none of them could hope to organise distribution beyond a very limited range, even if the newspaper stamp tax had not effectively kept them from a large public. The periodical, however, could command a country as well as a town circulation. It did not matter if it arrived days or even weeks late. Because of its longer life it could command a price that offered some chance of economic independence.

In the first half of the century it was therefore to the periodical that those who wished to influence the public turned. And it was from one such periodical, the *Gentleman's Magazine*, founded in 1731 as a monthly digest of home and foreign news, commercial happenings, and literary and other events, that the first successful challenge to Parliament on the issue of reporting came.

It is interesting to recall the various stages of that challenge, for it was by persistence in overcoming repeated obstacles to freedom of reporting that the press established its independence. It is by similar persistencies that it must even today defend it at a time when, as *The Times* remarked in a recent leading article, 'the fear of publicity; the huddle into which all concerned hurriedly go when there is any potential difficulty, difference of opinion or likelihood of trouble; the evasions of the Press conference; the reticence of the hand-out, all these are now the stock-in-trade of too much of our public administration and enterprise'.

Edward Cave, the founder and editor of the *Gentleman's Magazine*, made use of a reporter on his staff named Guthrie who possessed to a high degree that attribute of all good reporters, an excellent memory. Cave was well aware that if instead of having to rely, as other newspapers and magazines did, on hearsay and rumour he could find some means of obtaining reliable reports of what was said in Parliament they would be of intense interest to his readers. By judicious bribery of the doorkeepers he managed to get Guthrie smuggled into the House of Commons. Once inside Guthrie's phenomenal memory enabled him to secure a substantially accurate record of the main subjects debated, the names of the Members taking part, and the chief arguments advanced on either side.

The danger of prosecution for a breach of Parliamentary privilege remained. Cave sought to avoid this by delaying publication of Guthrie's material until the end of the Parliamentary session and by publishing only the initials of Members. To modern taste reports of Parliament weeks or months late must seem very cold porridge. But such was the extraordinary demand for news of Parliament at this time that Guthrie's reports created an immediate sensation. So great was the interest created that not only were they read with intense excitement in London and the great provincial centres and pored over in country houses and village rectories, they were also translated and reprinted on the Continent. The *London Magazine* and the *Scots Magazine*, journals similar in their general appeal to the *Gentleman's Magazine*, followed Cave's example with equal success. So did others.

For eight years their ingenious circumventing of the letter of Parliamentary privilege by restricting publication until Parliament had risen kept these journals out of trouble, without, such was the appetite for politics, diminishing the demand. But by 1738 the evidence of increasing public interest in Parliamentary affairs brought back by Members from the country so disturbed Parliament that the matter was raised in the House. It was there treated as a grave issue of privilege. The publication of reports was expressly prohibited under the most serious penalties not only during Parliamentary sittings but at any time thereafter.

Cave was a man of great journalistic ingenuity. He was not prepared to relinquish so valuable a feature of his magazine if he could by any means avoid it. He paid higher bribes to the Parliamentary doorkeepers and smuggled Guthrie into the House as before. Instead, however, of publishing the material as a Parliamentary report he now presented it in fictitious shape as a record of the proceedings in the Senate of Lilliputia and provided the various speakers either with Roman names to suit their characters or with fictitious ones in the form of anagrams of their real names.

Guthrie was a pertinacious and reliable news gatherer. But he used a prose style unsuited to the classical tradition. Cave therefore engaged a sub-editor to give his writings polish; an impecunious scholar from Lichfield who had advertised his Academy for the teaching of young gentlemen in the Latin and Greek languages in the columns of the *Gentleman's Magazine* a couple of years earlier. At the age of twenty-nine Dr. Johnson was newly come to London. He had a high opinion of the *Gentleman's Magazine*, the sight of whose offices when he first laid eyes upon them filled him, he told Boswell, 'with reverence', and one of the first things he did when he arrived in the Metropolis was to write to Cave enclosing some Latin verses in praise of the journal. These much gratified its editor, who decided that their author was just the man to add polish to Guthrie's rough notes and assist generally in the rewriting of articles for the magazine.

Thereafter for a good many years employment as a sub-editor on the *Gentleman's Magazine* provided Johnson with his main source of income—not the first nor last time that a man of letters has found it necessary to keep the wolf from the door by anonymous hack-work. Under his hand, the Parliamentary reports were transformed, so much so that Cave soon decided that instead of simply rubbing the rough edges off Guthrie's copy Johnson should edit the feature entirely, continuing to receive notes from Guthrie and other informants but treating them as he wished. For three years from 19 November 1740, Johnson became, in consequence, entirely responsible for the Parliamentary reports which appeared regularly in the *Gentleman's Magazine* under the Lilliput disguise, often, as he told Boswell, having little more to go on than the names of those who had joined in a debate and the side they had taken.

The story of Johnson's methods as a Parliamentary reporter is well known from the excellent account given by one of his early biographers, Murphy. He was dining with Johnson one evening in the company of Foote, the actor, and Dr. Francis, the translator of Horace, when the conversation turned to oratory. Dr. Francis remarked that a speech by Pitt in one of the debates towards the end of Walpole's administration was the best he had ever read. Foote and Murphy agreed and quoted passages of the speech from memory as evidence of its superiority. Johnson remained silent until the tributes were ended and then astonished the company by remarking, 'That speech I wrote in a garret in Exeter Street.' When they expressed their amazement and asked for an explanation he went on: 'Sir, I wrote it in Exeter Street. I never had been in the gallery of the House of Commons but once. Cave had an interest with the doorkeepers. He, and the persons employed under him, gained admittance, they brought away the subject of discussion, the names of the speakers, the side they took, and the order in which they rose together with notes of the arguments adduced in the course of the debate. The whole was afterwards communicated to me, and I composed the speeches in the form which they now have in the Parliamentary debates.'

After recovering from their surprise the others praised Johnson not only for his inventive genius but for his impartiality, remarking that he had dealt out reason and eloquence with an equal hand to both parties. But this Johnson would not have. 'I saved appearances tolerably well,' said he, 'but I took care that the Whig dogs should not have the best of it.' In fact he was better than his claim; the reports in the *Gentleman's Magazine* justify on the whole the praise for impartiality bestowed on them by Foote and Francis. When, however, Johnson discovered that many people regarded them as genuine he refused to continue with the work. He would not, he said, 'be accessory to the propagation of falsehood'. Yet whether he wished it or not they stand, in fact, among the only records available of the Parliamentary proceedings of that time. As such they appear in Hansard's predecessor, the *Parliamentary History* which Cobbett edited. Many M.P.s have had cause at many different times to be grateful to reporters for translating their stumbling sentences into passable English with a beginning, a middle and an end. The Commons of Walpole's day are, however, the only ones to have the felicity of appearing before posterity clothed to a man in sonorous Johnsonese. It is a pity they were not more conscious of the privilege.

Yet despite the ingenuity of Cave and his fellow magazine

editors the real battle for freedom of Parliamentary reporting could not be won by such means. The campaign could be kept alive by guerrilla engagements in which publishers, pitting their ingenuity against a Parliament determined to treat every report as a breach of privilege, were repeatedly censured, committed to Newgate or otherwise punished, only to start doing it all over again as soon as they were free. But it could not be ended in this way. For that it was necessary that the whole force of popular opinion should be aroused.

It was an age in which it seemed no more unnatural for the tribulations of politics to be sweetened by the profits of patronage than it still does throughout a good deal of Asia and the Middle East or, for that matter, in many American cities. Those in power looked after their friends; the public conscience was not much put out by corruption so long as it did not manifestly set Parliament apart from the general sentiment of the nation. Under Walpole, who was a master of bribery, and Pitt, who left it to Halifax as much as he could, it had not done so. Both were well aware that in order to govern successfully they must govern not only as the management of Parliament made possible but as the main current of middle opinion outside Parliament would approve. They did not make the mistake of forgetting that, as Defoe had counselled Harley, 'a man can never be great that is not popular, especially in England'.

It was only when this safeguard of popular leadership passed with the accession of George III and the downfall of Pitt that a condition of popular anger came into existence which made a frontal attack on Parliamentary secrecy not only possible but inevitable as part of a general movement of political reform.

Battered and disreputable as the measures to tame and bribe it had made most of the press, it remained in such circumstances the one tribune of public opinion to which the progressive and mercantile classes could turn. As they did so the press itself was emboldened to take on a more independent and purgative role.

This independent spirit found its first vigorous expression in the famous 'Letters of Junius' in the *Public Advertiser*. Than

'Junius' few men in the history of journalism have been blessed with a bolder or more biting pen: none with a publisher, Henry Sampson Woodfull, more ready to stand behind him. Not only by their brilliance and force of argument but by their regularity of publication the 'Letters of Junius' made public opinion a genuine force in politics. It is an evidence of their success in this respect that despite the virulence of their invective the authorities only once found the courage to risk a prosecution against Woodfull for publishing them. And even this failed because of the sturdy refusal of a London jury to convict despite the judge's direction to them to do so.

'Let it', wrote 'Junius', celebrating this legal victory in an article potently expressing the new journalistic temper of the times, 'let it be impressed upon your minds, let it be instilled into your children, that the liberty of the press is the palladium of all civil, political, and religious rights of an Englishman, and that the right of juries to return a general verdict, in all cases whatsoever, is an essential part of our constitution, not to be controlled or limited by the judges, nor in any shape questionable by the legislature. The power of King, Lords and Commons is not an arbitrary power. They are the trustees not the owners of the Estate.'

Woodfull was a greater newspaper man than Wilkes, 'Junius' a finer writer and a more profound political thinker. But in the house of the press there are many mansions, not all inhabited by such as the guardians of morality and social propriety would approve, nor even for that matter by men wholly committed to journalism. In the cardinal issue of the right to obtain and publish the Parliamentary information without which the freedom to criticise was bound to be crippled—and to obtain it not in driblets and by subterfuge, as Cave and Johnson had been forced to do, but openly and in its entirety—it is to John Wilkes, the rake turned politician and politician turned journalist, that the major credit must go.

It does so because he succeeded to an extent that even 'Junius' did not, in rallying public opinion to his side and in attracting to his own person, disreputable, flamboyant and egotistical as it was, the popular enthusiasm for reform. The *North Briton* which he founded to attack his enemy Lord Bute matched the popular mood from its first number in the violence of its denunciations of the Government and its Ministers, but it was issue No. 45 of the journal that turned Wilkes himself into a popular hero. It did so not so much because of what he wrote, although that was popular enough, as because of the events that followed, and more especially because of the skill he showed in turning the apparatus of the law—so often used to break the small fry of printers and publishers—against the Government itself.

It cannot have been much surprise to Wilkes himself that a general warrant for the arrest of all those concerned in its writing, printing and publishing should follow when, in an attack on the King's Speech in this issue, he wrote that George III had been 'brought to give the sanction of his sacred name to the most odious measures and to the most unjustifiable public declarations', and concluded 'I wish as much as any man in the Kingdom to see the honour of the Crown maintained in a manner truly becoming royalty: I lament to see it sunk even to prostitution.'

For this 'infamous and seditious libel tending to influence the minds and alienate the affections of the people from His Majesty and to excite them to traitorous insurrections against his Government' forty-eight persons, printers, proof readers and newsvendors, were arrested in addition to Wilkes himself. That was no great matter for remark. It was common enough. What followed was far from being so. That Wilkes, who had paid £7,000 for the pleasure of representing Aylesbury in the House of Commons, should claim privilege as an M.P. and refuse to answer questions was also no great cause for surprise. When, however, he went further and challenged the legality of a general warrant that merely specified the offence but did not name the persons charged with it he was striking at one of the most formidable and frequently used of the weapons employed to intimidate the press. It was inevitable that he should become a popular hero when, with an independence of the Crown unusual among members of the Bench in his day, Chief Justice Pratt not only upheld Wilkes's plea of Parliamentary immunity but ruled that the general warrant under which the others had been arrested was contrary to the law of the land and awarded them large damages for wrongful arrest.

He remained so even when a few weeks later he fled to France, badly wounded in a duel to which he had been provoked by a Government M.P. and temporarily intimidated by the strength of the forces against him as the Government carried motions of censure in both Houses of Parliament and brought a new and more skilfully drawn charge against him in the King's Bench Division. He was still a popular hero when he returned five years later to offer himself to the electors of Middlesex in defiance of the outlawry imposed on him. The effect of 'Number Forty-Five' was then seen to have carried farther and lasted longer than anyone could have dreamed possible.

Benjamin Franklin, noting that there was 'not a door or window shutter to be found in the City that was not marked with the figures "45"' and that 'this continued here and there quite to Winchester which is sixty-four miles', expressed the well-known view that if Wilkes had had a good character and George III a bad the King would have been turned off his throne at that moment. And indeed, as Parliament four times declared Wilkes's repeated election for Middlesex invalid, the public temper grew to such an extent that it seemed for a time possible that Wilkes and the City Merchants who had given him their support and who elected him an Alderman of the City might really lead a nation-wide radical movement for Parliamentary reform. Perhaps they would have done so if communications had been better. But although Wilkes organised public meetings and petitions and gained some support in the country he could not reach the majority of those in the provinces and his cause remained primarily one backed by the citizens of London and based on a precarious and temporary alliance of city merchants and London workers. 'In St. James's', said a Wilkes pamphlet, 'Mr. Wilkes's enemies are forty-five to fifteen; in the City his advocates are forty-five to fifteen and in Wapping his staunch supporters are forty-five to none at all.' In the end this radical campaign was destroyed in the reaction against the Gordon riots, for which, ironically enough, Wilkes had no responsibility at all; indeed, with remarkable personal courage he did his best at the head of a small band of volunteers to stop the looting and burning while the Government still vacillated.

But if the wider radical movement which it seemed at one moment Wilkes might lead came to nothing, he managed to provoke the one reform that the press most needed for independence when he defied the ban on Parliamentary reporting in the *Middlesex Journal* and persuaded others to do likewise.

He was, of course, far from being the first to make such a challenge—the conflict was already old when he came to the field. But the provocation was so open and came in a climate of opinion already so heated that it was bound to bring the issue to a climax. When that climax came he had at his disposal through his alliance with the commercial interests of the city and his own authority as Alderman a weapon that others who had defied the ban had not possessed. He used it with all the ingenuity and bravura that had long made him the idol of the London crowd. It was before Wilkes himself that Whebble, the printer of the *Middlesex Journal*, was brought at the Guildhall when, having refused a summons to appear at the Bar of the House, he was arrested by a fellow printer following a Royal Proclamation calling for his apprehension in the King's name. A second printer, R. Thompson of the *Gazetteer*, arrested on a similar charge, was brought before Wilkes's close associate, Richard Oliver, at the Mansion House. A third, John Millar of the *London Evening Post*, arrested under a Speaker's Warrant, was brought before Wilkes, Oliver and Crosby, the Lord Mayor, also at the Mansion House. All three printers were at once discharged by Wilkes and his fellow magistrates. In order to leave no possibility of doubt as to their intentions they committed those who had arrested them to trial on charges of assault and wrongful arrest.

What followed was no less considered. Summoned as Members

of the House to answer for a breach of its privileges Oliver and Crosby refused to apologise. They were committed to the Tower, whereupon the London crowds came out into the streets, stoned Ministers and wrecked Lord North's carriage in default of finding the Prime Minister himself. But for the fortunate fact that the prorogation of Parliament came quickly on the heels of their committal and both men were thereupon released there would probably have been more serious disorder. Wilkes whom the House, despite his fourfold election for Middlesex, refused to recognise as a Member was summoned to appear at the Bar. He replied with his customary effrontery that since the summons had not been correctly addressed to him as a Member it was impossible for him to obey it. The summons was repeated. Again he ignored it. Again it was repeated.

By now, however, the temper of popular opinion was such that the Commons dared no longer ignore it. It chose an oddly incongruous path of retreat. On this third occasion the summons was made for a day when Parliament was not sitting and there the matter was allowed to rest. Nominally the rule against Parliamentary reporting continued in force. In fact it was never again employed.

Formidable difficulties still remained in the way of those who wished to secure a full and accurate report of debates. Not until 1803 were reporters allocated seats in the public gallery, not until after the fire of 1834 was special provision made for their accommodation, yet another fifty-four years had to pass before the rules for the admission and exclusion of strangers were placed on a rational footing. But after 1771 the right of newspapers to report Parliament was never again denied. Wilkes had won a lasting victory, no less decisive because by default. By so doing he had not only made a politically free press possible but had made political reform itself inevitable.

The right to report Parliament did not, of course, stop newspaper bribery at once, any more than it ended political corruption overnight. Even as late as 1834 the *Standard* offered to sell its services to Peel when he became Prime Minister and the

Observer continued to take secret service money up to 1840. But after 1771 the bribery of the press came to be less and less of a factor in public life. The established sale secured by the demand for Parliamentary reporting made papers of character no longer open to bribery. The only ones prepared to sell themselves were, as Lord Liverpool advised his cabinet colleagues in 1815, not worth buying.

The establishment of the first great independent English newspapers dates from Wilkes's victory. He was never himself a journalist except in so far as journalism gave him a whip to beat his political enemies with and he played no part in the newspaper developments he made possible. But he cleared the path for all others. Because of him the press was given the means to play a commanding part in the development of British society.

IV

HERESY OF FREEDOM

POLITICALLY the press was now free. Wilkes, 'Junius', and Woodfull and others less able and less remembered but by no means always their inferiors in courage had won for it the right to report and the right to criticise—to criticise, if they were so minded, even the King's Ministers and the King himself. But between the right to report and comment and the independence to use it there is a wide gap.

The ruling class deeply suspicious, as was to be expected, of the potential challenge of this new power had been forced to retreat a little. But its hostility was unimpaired. For the next seventy years the history of newspapers was to be largely the history of this hostility, and of the various means tried by Governments and party rulers to prevent newspapers from seizing the opportunities for greater circulation and public influence given by victory in the battle for the right to report Parliament.

Men like Wilkes and 'Junius' might, as guerrilla fighters do, disrupt the settled order of things for a time and even score a few major victories but the press as a whole was still subservient. To keep it so, to prevent the development of independent and, above all, of popular newspapers, was from now on one of the primary objectives of the ruling class whether Whig or Tory.

That this should be so is no matter for surprise. Established powers, as has been said earlier, cannot be expected to welcome the advent of new ones. Nor need resistance to the development of an independent press be regarded as evidence of an especial malevolence on the part of those who feared and hated it, any more than is the current Parliamentary dislike of television and

radio discussion. Their view was shared by many of the most
able and disinterested men in public life as well as by some
of the worst, for it threatened to call in judgment against them
those whom the whole context of the age made them regard as
ignorant, licentious and low and to place in the hands of classes
they regarded as altogether ignorant of the necessities of statesmanship the power to criticise and perhaps to shape it. To Burke
the press appeared as the grand instrument for the subversion of
order, morals, religion and the social system; to Windham as the
distributor of a poison that spread its venom every twenty-four
hours to the extremity of the kingdom. Southey complained that
newspapers 'inflamed the turbulent temper of the manufacturer
and disturbed the quiet attachment of the peasant', and even as
late as 1829 Sir Walter Scott could write to Lockhart: 'Your
connection with any newspaper would be a disgrace and
degradation. I would rather sell gin to poor people and poison
them that way.'

To many of the best minds of the age as well as to those
opposed to all reform the great need of the time came to be the
restriction of newspaper circulations to limit the harm they could
do. But a counter-interest was also at work, that of political
groups anxious to use newspapers as instruments of propaganda.
From their point of view independence not circulation was the
danger. Kept in control newspapers could have their uses, merit
employment in much the same way as a paid bully or a hired
informer—and be held in the same contempt.

From both these points of view the newspaper stamp duties
were peculiarly valuable. They ensured that those attracted to
the dubious trade of journalism would be in no financial position
to ignore their betters. And they made it impossible for them to
offer their wares at a price the lower classes could pay. For any
who kicked against the pricks the Government had other
weapons to hand in the Post Office, which was the sole agent
for distribution at home and abroad and controlled the entry of
all newspapers into the country. Distribution of those papers
regarded as dangerous could be held up, as Cobbett alleged the

distribution of his daily paper the *Porcupine* and his famous weekly the *Political Register* frequently was; the foreign journals upon which newspapers relied for most of their foreign news could be delayed or lost—as *The Times* repeatedly declared to happen to those addressed to it.

Heavily taxed, hampered in distribution, his supply of foreign news interrupted, cut off from the official intelligence made available to those acceptable to the Treasury and the Foreign Office, denied the regular payments from secret service funds that went to his rivals, the journalist who dreamed of independence had little to encourage him in his fantasy. Nor were such secret or overt means of bringing him to his senses as these all he had to contend with. The law was a sword waiting to strike. Until Fox's Libel Act of 1792 restored to juries the right to decide upon every indictment for libel whether the defendant was guilty or not guilty newspapers were at the mercy of judges who often scarcely bothered to conceal their readiness to act as agents of Ministers. Nor, even after the Act of 1792, was the journalist's position much better in those matters which the Government regarded as affecting its interest. The Attorney-General had the right to require that any press prosecution he conducted be tried by a special jury. Such juries, composed for the most part of civil servants and magistrates, commonly did what he asked them.

This weapon of prosecution was not allowed to grow rusty with disuse: there were seventy press prosecutions in the first thirty-one years of George III's reign. Sentences were savage. For publishing a paragraph that annoyed the Russian Ambassador one printer was sentenced to imprisonment for a year and sent to the pillory. For the same offence another was sent to gaol for eighteen months and fined £200, and two others imprisoned for a year and fined £100 each. One, but only because she was a woman, was let off with six months' imprisonment and a fine of £50. Moreover the Attorney-General had a further privilege well adapted to the intimidation of newspapers of too independent a spirit. He had the right to file ex-officio information for libel and dispense with a preliminary hearing before a Grand Jury: an instrument of coercion as Professor Aspinall remarks in *Politics and the Press 1780–1850* well suited to terrify journalists into 'compromise, compliance and servility', for by its means the threat of proceedings could be kept hanging over the heads of recalcitrant newspapers for months or even years. At one time more than half the newspapers published in London had such threats of prosecution hanging over their heads—although not one of the charges was ever brought to court. Moreover the mere filing of such ex-officio information involved newspapers in heavy costs so that the Attorney-General could in effect inflict a large fine on any journalist or newspaper proprietor he did not like. No wonder John Almon, publisher of the *London Magazine*, declared: 'A man had better make his son a tinker than a printer. The laws of tin he can understand but the law of libel is unwritten, uncertain and undefinable. It is one thing today and another tomorrow. No man can tell what it is. It is sometimes what the King or Queen pleases, sometimes what the Minister pleases, sometimes what the Attorney-General pleases.'

Yet even so there were forces at work too strong for any deterrent to be effective. Public opinion with its need for information was on the move.

'Give me the liberty of the Press', declared Sheridan in the House of Commons in 1810, 'and I will give the Minister a venal House of Peers, I will give him a corrupt and servile House of Commons, I will give him the full swing of the patronage of office, I will give him the whole host of ministerial influence, I will give him all the power that place can confer upon him to purchase submission and overawe resistance and yet, armed with the liberty of the Press, I will go forth to meet him undismayed. . . .'

And there was still another force at work no less important— commercial development. It was this that was in the end to give the press the means to freedom for as commerce developed and became more profitable it brought with it not only the demand for reliable information but the possibility of economic independence through advertising revenue despite the penal advertisement taxes. It is not accidental that of the nine newspapers published daily in London twelve years after Wilkes's victory five were primarily advertisement sheets: the *Daily Advertiser*, *Public Advertiser*, *General Advertiser*, *Public Ledger*, and *Public Gazetteer*, while of the remaining four the *Morning Post* carried the subtitle of *Cheap Daily Advertiser*, and the *Morning Chronicle*, the *Morning Herald* and *Citizens' Morning Post* devoted at least half and usually more of their space to advertisements.

The dangerous dependence of newspapers upon advertisements has often been the theme of newspaper reformers—usually from outside its professional ranks. But the daily press would never have come to existence as a force in public and social life if it had not been for the need of men of commerce to advertise. Only through the growth of advertising did the press achieve independence.

What were they concerned with, these daily papers launched for the most part to satisfy the advertising needs of the syndicates of businessmen who founded them? By the very nature of the news-gatherer's trade and the political and social compulsions of the time, they could not avoid becoming something much more than instruments of commercial exchange. The editor as such hardly yet existed although he was soon to become an increasingly important figure. Nor did the leader-writer. Those newspapers that concerned themselves with politics and public questions commonly employed for their hazardous excursions into criticism and comment the medium of a letter 'To the Printer'. It was thus that 'Junius's' letters appeared.

The normal format was a single sheet of $24\frac{1}{2}$ inches by $18\frac{3}{4}$ inches folded once to produce a four-page paper in folio $12\frac{1}{4}$ inches by $18\frac{3}{4}$ inches. Each page was made up in four columns printed solid with the minimum of headings. The news offered consisted normally of summaries of Parliamentary debates, foreign intelligence copied from Continental papers, Court intelligence, reprints of the *London Gazette*, brief reports of decisions in the law and police courts and a certain amount of commercial intelligence. In addition as general readership grew there might be a medley of gossip paragraphs about those in the public eye, a column of jokes and epigrams on social follies, notices of new plays, some verse and a 'Letter to the Printer'.

Apart from the morning papers there were some ten tri-weekly papers published in London on Tuesday, Thursday and Saturday in time to catch the mail to the provinces. These carried more news and fewer advertisements than the dailies. And although it was still illegal to sell anything but milk and mackerel on a Sunday and those found hawking newspapers were subject to a fine, Sunday papers had already begun to make their appearance. They appealed to a more popular and less educated public than did the dailies and were peculiarly the subject of official anxiety as 'vehicles of treason'. Over and above these daily, tri-weekly and Sunday newspapers there was a varied, shifting and steadily expanding concourse of political, literary and social journals and periodicals which—if only because they could exist on smaller resources than could the dailies or tri-weeklies—were responsible for some of the most vigorous and critical journalism of the time. It is thus a lively enough picture that the press presents in the closing years of the eighteenth century, despite all the efforts of the ruling classes to cage the dangerous animal.

Sales were, of course, still small. This was so not only because of the difficulties of distribution, the primitive communications, the illiteracy of large masses of the population and the obstacles placed in the way by Ministers but also because the technological conditions necessary to the development of a mature newspaper industry were still lacking. Until 1814 when *The Times* shot ahead of its rivals with the introduction of steam-driven machinery capable of printing 1,100 sheets an hour all newspapers were printed by hand. The maximum number of sheets they could run off in an hour was no more than 250 and often in practice considerably less. Even a daily print of 2,000 or 3,000 was a long-drawn-out and difficult operation.

In every aspect, political, legal, economic, the trade of journalism was a hazardous one. But it was also a lively and expanding one responding to the deep compulsions of the time and it did not fail to attract to itself men of diverse character with motives as varied as their personalities.

Among them four stand out as making a particular impact upon the journalism of their time: John Bell, James Perry, David Stuart, John Walter. These are the ancestors of the men who produce the 30,000,000 newspapers of today.

Bell brought to the journalism of the second half of the eighteenth century gifts that it badly needed: lightness and entertainment, appeal to the eye as well as to the intellect, ranging curiosity about a great many things. He had already established himself as a successful bookseller and a publisher with a flair for hitting fashionable taste before ever he turned to journalism: one of his books was the famous *Apology for the Life of George Anne Bellamy* whose dazzling career as mistress of half the aristocracy had set the town talking. This work he advertised in a manner to fill the circulation manager of a modern Sunday paper with envy. It would, he promised, disclose the hitherto unsuspected secrets of every well-known man about town in London. As a publisher he had made it his ambition to be recognised as the finest typographer of his age. He brought the same interest in good appearance to journalism and exercised upon the make-up of the newspapers of his time somewhat the same effect as the *Daily Express* has exercised on ours. He was one of the syndicate of twelve that, along with the founders of Christie's and Tattersall's, launched the *Morning Post* in 1772. But it is not on the *Morning Post*, in which he was never more than a minority shareholder, that his reputation rests but on the *World and Fashionable Advertiser*, started fifteen years later, and on a host of subsequent papers and periodicals to which he brought an energy and a flair that give him the right to be regarded as one of the great innovators and impresarios of the press, the Northcliffe of his day.

His partner in the *World* was Captain Edward Topham, a gentleman of means who wished to promote the career of a Drury Lane actress, Mrs. Wells, who had shown her affection for him by bearing him four children. But it was Bell who made the paper. The *World* was something new in journalism. Light-hearted, sophisticated, knowing, concerned with the gossip of the fashionable world rather than with great principles, and vastly superior in type and lay-out to anything that had been seen before, it permanently altered the conception both of what a newspaper should look like and what it should write about—the first swallow that presaged the summer of popular journalism. Within a year it had reached a circulation of between 3,000 and 4,000 a day. It would probably have gone on to a much larger figure if the two partners had not quarrelled and if Topham had not, as Bell publicly proclaimed, 'rashly and unhandsomely' withdrawn the contract for printing from him. Topham continued the paper for another five years with a secret Treasury subsidy of £600 a year to help him, and Bell launched another paper, the *Oracle, Bell's New World*. It was, however, in the field of magazine and Sunday journalism that he made his next great impact on the press of the time. In 1770, a year after starting the *Oracle*, he launched what one can hardly avoid describing as a lush magazine for women, *La Belle Assemblée; or Bell's Court and Fashionable Magazine, addressed particularly to the Ladies*.

It was not the first specifically woman's magazine. That had appeared nearly a hundred years before in 1693 in the form of a broadsheet called the *Ladies Mercury* which contained excellent advice on a range of matters from whitening the teeth to the moral dilemma of a young lady of quality who having earlier suffered the calamity of being 'so seduced as to give up the very Soul of Beauty, My Honour, to a lewd and infamous rifler' had since married a rich and worthy man and wanted to know whether she should tell him. The *Ladies Mercury* said 'No'. But although Bell's magazine was far from being the first to appeal exclusively to women it set, as the *World* had in daily journalism, a new standard in presentation, offering excellent coloured fashion plates and drawings along with a great variety of reading matter. Six years later Bell hit on an even more successful idea, a Sunday magazine called *Bell's Weekly Messenger* for those wanting to be 'informed or amused at the Sunday Breakfast table'.

Again Bell was the adapter, not the inventor. The first Sunday newspaper had been published sixteen years before by a woman, Mrs. E. Johnson. It had evoked a fine crop of imitators, among them the *Observer* which was already five years old when Bell came along with his *Messenger*. But whereas these earlier Sunday papers were primarily weekly newspapers he invented a formula that still draws the millions to popular Sunday newspapers more than a century and a half later. His *Messenger* gave a summary of the news of the week but its real appeal lay in feature articles catering for every sort of taste from sport, politics and scandal to the latest theatrical and literary events. It had an immediate and enormous public success and became one of the most emulated periodicals in the history of journalism.

Bell was not much concerned with principles. He was an entertainer and populariser, not a prophet: a pathfinder for the popular journalism of the future. But he has a place in the struggle for the freedom of the press larger than that of some more serious-minded men because he showed the way to that popular appeal upon which such freedom rests. 'He possessed', says Leigh Hunt of him in his autobiography, 'no acquirements, perhaps not even grammar; but his taste in putting forth a publication and getting the best artists to adorn it was new in these times, and may be admired in any. . . .' Bell's son, with whom he quarrelled, founded the *News of the World*.

If Bell may be described as the first of the popular press proprietors, Perry, 'a pleasant man with a dash, no slight one either, of the Courtier' according to Charles Lamb, was the first of the great editors in the modern mode—or rather in a mode now passing. It is, indeed, from him that the idea of the importance of the editor first comes.

Wilkes's victory was twelve years old when, at the age of twenty-seven, Perry was invited to manage the *Gazetteer*, an unimportant advertisement sheet just turned into a general newspaper. Earlier as a reporter on the *General Advertiser* he had

made a name ıor himself by his vivid account of the court-
martial of Admiral Keppel and it was to an improvement in the
news reporting of the *Gazetteer* that he first applied himself.
The most influential and widely read paper in the country was the
Morning Chronicle. This position it held largely because of the
excellence of its Parliamentary reports and Perry made up his
mind to surpass them. The *Chronicle's* leadership in Parliamentary
reporting depended primarily upon one man: its editor, William
Woodfull, younger brother of that Henry Sampson Woodfull of
the *Public Advertiser*, who had published the 'Letters of Junius'.
Woodfull was possessed of a phenomenal memory, far exceeding
even that of that earlier Parliamentary reporter, Guthrie of the
Gentleman's Magazine. He regularly produced from memory
reports of debates up to seven columns or more in length. It
was these reports, unequalled elsewhere, that sold the paper.

Perry could not hope to emulate Woodfull's feat as a memory
man. Instead he organised a corps of Parliamentary reporters—the
first in newspaper history. Each of them was instructed to follow
the debate for a short stretch and then with memory still fresh
write out his report while another took over, to be succeeded in
his turn by a third, a system still in operation among Parliamentary shorthand reporters. By the standards of the time it was
a very expensive method of getting a Parliamentary report. But
it paid. The *Gazetteer* was able to come out with a much longer
report than the *Chronicle* and one produced at greater speed and
with more accuracy.

The moment was propitious. Lord North's Government had
fallen, crushed by Cornwallis's surrender to Washington's
forces at York Town and by the loss of the North American
colonies. George III was forced to accept what he had so long
resisted, a Whig administration determined not only to stop the
war but to end the royal domination of Parliament. An era of the
liveliest public interest in Parliamentary affairs was opening.
Moreover a new star of the first magnitude was rising in the
Parliamentary sky—the younger Pitt. When Perry had been
managing the *Gazetteer* for a year the elections of 1784 brought

Pitt to the premiership in a House of Commons which if not in any full sense representative, for that was not possible without reform, was yet for almost the first time since the Commonwealth the result of a genuine uprising of public feeling. The issues with which this Parliament had to deal, including as they did the impeachment and trial of Warren Hastings, were of a nature to keep popular interest at fever point.

In his determination to have the best Parliamentary reports in the country Perry was therefore guided by one of the basic maxims of successful journalism in any time and place—that it is virtually impossible to give your readers too much of a really big story. His policy paid. Indeed it paid so much that it almost put the *Chronicle* out of business. That paper suffered the penalty that lies in wait for all newspapers that fall behind in the sheer technique of their trade, it lost circulation rapidly to its more enterprising rival. Woodfull was not prepared to adopt Perry's methods. He could not bring himself to believe that his wonderful memory had had its day. When his partners demanded that he do as Perry did he left the paper in a huff. Within six years of Perry's innovation the *Chronicle*, fallen in circulation and prestige, came on the market. Perry bought it with a loan of £500 from his bank, an investment of a similar amount from a schoolmaster friend at Charterhouse with journalistic ambitions, and the promise of financial backing from Bellamy, the doorkeeper of the House of Commons who was also a prosperous wine merchant—the eighteenth century was favourable to dual roles.

He revived it by the same methods as had enabled the *Gazetteer* to ruin it, spending what was for the time the extraordinary sum of between £2,000 and £3,000 a year on what he wryly described as 'these disgusting though necessary reports of Parliamentary chattering'. At the same time he greatly improved its news coverage in other directions: he spent a year in Paris during the French Revolution organising reports of what had become the greatest news of the day. But he did not confine himself to improving the paper's news service only. He also attracted to his service as contributors the most eminent writers he could find:

Sheridan, Coleridge, Lamb, Thomas Moore, Ricardo, all wrote regularly for him and Hazlitt became his dramatic critic. He remained editor of the *Chronicle* for twenty-eight years, its principal owner until his death in 1821, and to a degree that had not formerly been the case even in its greatest days he made it far and away the most influential and widely read paper in the country, one that, as that stern critic Cobbett said, 'discovered a spirit of independence rarely to be met with and a degree of talent that does great honour to the Press of this country'.

Perry, taking over the *Morning Chronicle* when it had become a shadow of its former self, raised it to a new level of authority and esteem by recognising and catering for the public demand for news. Although he was succeeded as editor by a journalist of parts who had served under him—John Black who gave Dickens his first chance as a reporter—the independence he had won for it soon disappeared after his death. When its circulation fell to less than a third of that in his day it lost its economic freedom and became a Government mouthpiece—'What the heads of the party desire to be inserted is immediately published', said Roebuck; 'the Treasury sends its missives and they must be obeyed.'

What Perry did for the *Morning Chronicle* Stuart did for the *Morning Post*—only for it also to follow the same path to party subservience after he left it: striking evidence of a truth uncongenial to some newspaper proprietors who change their editors more frequently than they do their cooks, that great newspapers are made by great editors.

The *Morning Post* had been founded, some twenty-three years before Stuart acquired it, to catch the raffish taste of fashionable and would-be fashionable London. It was at first remarkably successful in doing so under the editorship of a dissolute young clergyman, Henry Bute, whose penchant for public brawling made him popularly known as 'The Fighting Parson'. Its first number included the offer for sale of a complete, up-to-the-minute list of the names and addresses of 'those ladies of the town to be found at home in or near Piccadilly' and until Bute landed himself in prison for libelling the Duke of Richmond it was the favoured reading of most of the young bloods of the town. After that it hired itself to the Treasury as a whip to beat the Prince Regent with but switched sides when the Prince offered its manager a thousand guineas and £350 a year to keep quiet about Mrs. Fitzherbert.

In 1795, when Stuart bought it, it had lost the last shreds of its reputation in a sensational libel action and was known only as an insignificant and wholly contemptible mouthpiece of Carlton House. Its circulation was down to 350 copies a day. This derelict and disreputable publication, Stuart, then twenty-nine, bought for £600 and turned within little more than a year into one of the most admired and successful journals in the country with a circulation of over 4,500: evidence, said Coleridge, 'that genuine impartiality with a respectable portion of literary talent will secure the success of a newspaper without the aid of party or Ministerial patronage'.

His success was built on a combination of editorial talent and shrewd business sense. It was rooted in the belief (some modern editors seem to imagine that it was they who invented it) that although public affairs are important to be successful a newspaper must be 'cheerfully entertaining, not entirely filled with ferocious politics'; a dictum that the Victorian age was almost entirely to forget. One part of his formula for success, a formula that echoes like a familiar Fleet Street story across the centuries, has been agreeably described by Charles Lamb, who was one of Stuart's regular writers at sixpence a paragraph:

'The chat of the day—scandal, but, above all, dress—furnished the material. . . . A fashion of flesh, or rather pink-coloured hose for the ladies, luckily coming up at the juncture when we were on our probation for the place of Chief Jester to S's Paper established our reputation in that line. Then there was the collateral topic of ankles. What an occasion to a truly chaste writer like myself, of touching that nice brink, and yet never tumbling over it, of seemingly ever approximating to something "not quite proper"; while, like a skilful posture-master, balancing betwixt decorums and their opposites, he keeps the line, from which a hair's breadth deviation is destruction. . . .'

Journalistically Stuart's great achievement and the true basis of his success was to show the world that a readiness to entertain was not incompatible with literary quality or responsible reporting or serious political purpose. He made the *Morning Post* sell by giving its readers plenty of variety and by providing a paper that men and women of many differing tastes could both enjoy and respect. He learned a good deal from Bell, as did every other journalist of the time, but he turned Bell's technique to more public-spirited purposes and he kept a constant eye on advertising revenue.

He was one of the first to see that in addition to being essential to economic and political independence advertisements were also highly attractive to readers in their own right.

'Advertisements act and re-act', he said. 'They attract readers, promote circulation and circulation attracts advertisements.' He would have found wholly incomprehensible the lordly contempt of the editorial staff for the advertisement department that characterised Victorian journalism. Not only as a proprietor but as editor he regarded advertisement revenue as a matter of his most intimate concern. It was what gave him freedom from the party managers and he set himself to encourage it by every means in his power, holding small advertisements (classified advertisements as we should now call them) to be particularly valuable to a paper because 'the more numerous the customers, the more permanent and independent the custom'.

Bell, Perry, Stuart, each in their several ways, planted signposts for other newspapers to follow and demonstrated that even in an era when the press was continually subject to threat or bribe independence could be won by producing a paper that satisfied the public taste. Yet oddly enough the credit for making independence not merely the luxury of an outstanding editor but a settled principle of newspaper organisation must go to a journalistic dynasty founded by a man infinitely smaller in journalistic stature than any one of these three—John Walter I of *The Times*.

John Walter was not a great journalist, nor even a particularly high-minded or honest one. Nor did he embark on newspaper publication out of any natural feeling for news. He did so merely because, having failed as an underwriter at Lloyd's and being disappointed in his expectation of some post under the Government, he found himself at the age of forty-five compelled to look around for something new to do, his 'business sunk by hasty strides, and the world to begin afresh, with the daily introduction to my view of a wife and six children unprovided for and depending on me for support'. In the course of thus looking for something new he became interested in a patent for an improved system of typography invented by a London printer, Henry Johnson. With the assistance of two City friends, a merchant and a solicitor, he bought the rights in it and acquired a disused printing works in Printing House Yard, Blackfriars, formerly belonging to the King's Printer. This done he set forth with energy and fortitude to rebuild his fortunes.

A daily newspaper was no part of his original plans. His modest ambition was to print books and pamphlets and set himself up in business as a bookseller. Only as an afterthought did he add to these activities those of a daily newspaper and for the first seven years of his new career it was the effort to establish himself as a publisher and bookseller that occupied most of his energies. Nor had he any very high ambitions for his *Daily Universal Register*, as *The Times* was called for the first three years of its life, when the first number was published on 1 January 1785. His main purpose in producing it was to advertise his printing patent and provide a cheap means of publicity for the books he published. He sold it at $2\frac{1}{2}d.$, a halfpenny less than the normal price, but it was inferior to the rest of the daily press in its news service and literary quality although, until Bell came along with his innovations, superior to most of them in appearance. Its main strength, such as it was, lay in its commercial service and in its reports of market prices and the movements of ships. Certainly there was nothing about it to suggest that it would, within a generation, become paramount among all the newspapers of the world, or that its circulation would become several times greater than that of all other British morning newspapers combined.

The strange heresy of press freedom stirred no such response in John Walter's businesslike breast as it did in those of Perry and Stuart as he embarked upon newspaper proprietorship. He supported the Government and expected to be paid for it like anyone else, contracting for a fee of £300 a year to publish any paragraphs that came to him with the private mark of Thomas Steele, the Joint Secretary of the Treasury. As it turned out this was an unfortunate bargain. Within three years two of the paragraphs thus sent to him were held by the Court of King's Bench to be criminal libels on the Prince of Wales and the Duke of York, and poor Walter, after refusing, very honourably, to divulge the source of his information, found himself sentenced to two years in Newgate. He got no particular credit from his paymasters for his reticence, receiving, as he complained to Lord Hawkesbury, 'no tidings to relieve my anxious moments nor the least comfort of any other nature but am abandoned to ruin, disgrace and infamy as far as the Sentence of the Law can convey the Idea, torn from my Family, my business left to mercenaries, my Health suffering from Confinement in a noxious Prison where I am lock'd in every night at 8 o'clock'. 'And all', as he declared with understandable bitterness, 'without a Sixpence for the extraordinary Expenses I am at.' But though he complained he did not quarrel with his paymasters. He had too sharp an understanding of their power for that. He continued to draw his £300 a year and do as he was bid until they, not he, decided to end the bargain eight years later.

Nor was a secret Treasury subsidy the only means embraced by Walter to cushion himself against the financial perils of newspaper publishing. He adopted a practice still followed very profitably in many parts of the Middle East and among the less reputable scandal sheets of Hollywood of offering to those in the public eye the privilege of paying him not to blacken their reputations. It was a rewarding sideline. Mrs. Wells, Topham's former mistress, records in her memoirs that after her second marriage she and her husband both found *The Times's* interest in her disconcerting. Thereupon her husband invited Finney, the 'editorial conductor' of *The Times* under Walter, to call upon him and 'pulling out from his escritoire a large parcel of notes handed over a packet to him saying "Will that be enough?"' To this Finney devoutly replied: 'Give me a few more and by St. Patrick I'll knock out the brains of anyone in an office who dare even whisper your name.'

'Suppression fees', 'contradiction fees', payments for puffs, all were grist to the mill of the first John Walter as he set about his unintended task of establishing the greatest newspaper in the world and the first to become wholly and permanently independent. He was, said Crabbe Robinson who served him and was for a time editor under his son, 'as dishonest, worthless a man as I have ever known, at least among those who preserved appearance'. And William Combe, author of the *Tour of Dr. Syntax*, whom he employed for a time as a writer on *The Times*, declared of him that 'he never did an honest act in his life' but established his fortune by 'the vilest arts—extortion of money through calumny etc.'

All this no doubt is true. With one or two exceptions like Perry and Stuart the same could be said of most of those who practised the same profession at the same time. This was the soil in which the journalism of the eighteenth century was nurtured: a soil natural to the age and no more sour than that in which most of the century's politics and a good deal of its social life were rooted.

But John Walter I had one quality more important in the perspective of time than any of these defects. And he had one remarkable piece of good fortune. The quality was tenacity. With it went good sense. Starting as the producer of a mediocre commercial sheet he recognised more quickly than most the implications of the revolution in newspaper production brought about by Bell's innovations and reorganised his paper accordingly. Under its new and handier title of *The Times*, the *Daily Universal Register* brightened both its appearance and style, taking on new writers for the purpose. Nor did it hesitate to outstrip even the *World* in the provision of scandal and innuendo. But Walter had the wit quickly to recognise the changing public taste brought by the French Revolution. Gossip and scandal had served well. Now, as at all times of great crisis, what newspaper readers wanted was hard news. With every new day interest in public affairs mounted, touching every level of society. The era of journalistic flippancy that Bell had inaugurated and that Walter had been delighted to exploit was over.

Although deeply involved in his own personal difficulties, for he was in the midst of preparing his unsuccessful reply to the charge of libelling the Royal Dukes, John Walter bent all his energy to the task of organising a news service from the Continent, laying in the process the foundations of that pre-eminence in the field of foreign reporting that was later to give *The Times* its great authority. Moreover he was quick to recognise that events of such magnitude required wholly new treatment in space and typographical display and on the very eve of his imprisonment completely reorganised the make-up of the paper, bringing out—odd though it now seems to think of *The Times* in this guise—a paper with headlines larger and more sensational than had ever been seen in any newspaper before: the *Mirror* of its time. Nor even in prison did he allow his own misery to interfere with his awareness of the needs of his paper. During the whole of his enforced stay in Newgate he continued to exhort his staff to fresh efforts in securing news sources abroad.

It is doubtful whether, even so, *The Times* would have survived all the other journals of the time or John Walter I be remembered except as a minor name in the history of eighteenth-century journalism had not good fortune come to his aid. He was a business man, not a journalist. His luck lay in the fact that although his eldest son was neither, his second son, John Walter II, was not only a better business man than his father but possessed, what he did not, a burning integrity and a passion for independence. It was to this second son that John Walter I passed the management of the paper when he himself returned to his real interest, the printing buisness. Yet even so the father scarcely deserved the luck that made him the founder of the most famous newspaper dynasty in history. He quarrelled with his son and cut him off in his will with only a tiny minority interest in *The Times*, a mere three-sixteenths of the shares instead of the full possession his son had been led to expect. However, even in anger he was at least enough of a newspaper-man to realise that 'the conduct and interest of a newspaper concern requires the most absolute power in the persons carrying on the same in making allowance and payment at their discretion'. Although he refused to leave to his second son the financial control he hoped for he made it a condition of his other bequests that 'my son John continue to have the sole management'.

By these means the future of *The Times* was secured. John Walter I founded it. But it was John Walter II and the remarkable editor, Thomas Barnes, whom he had the good fortune to discover and to whom he gave an editorial freedom such as no other employee of a newspaper had ever possessed, who made it great. In so doing they won independence not only for *The Times* but for the whole of the British press.

V

FEELING OF THE COUNTRY

IN the seventies of the eighteenth century the cause of political and Parliamentary reform although unsuccessful (perhaps, indeed, for that reason) was fashionable.

It ceased to be so after the French Revolution. The French aristocracy had no doubt invoked if not entirely deserved its fate. Unready to offer even the most casual of genuflections to the spirit of liberalism, it had become expendable. When the Bastille fell Charles James Fox could remark without obvious excess, 'How much the greatest event that has happened in the world', and add without a tremor, 'and how much the best'.

But it soon became plain that French revolutionary zeal did not end there. Not content with cutting off the heads of their own lords and ladies the French masses were ambitious to help other nations who wished to 'recover their liberty' to do the same for theirs. When a French Minister talked of landing 'fifty thousand caps of liberty' in England to help the British radicals, reform began to take on the smell of treason.

The change in the pattern of British life brought by the beginnings of the Industrial Revolution could not in any event have done other than impose the severest social and political strains on British society. To these were now added the effects of the fear of revolution followed by twenty years of war. Repression became the ruling passion of political policy and Britain a nation in which it was 'safer to be a felon than a reformer'. Progress, said Cobbett, 'is marked by gaols ten times as big as formerly: houses of correction; treadmills, the hulks and a country filled with spies of one sort and another'.

It was in this haunted atmosphere of anti-Jacobinism, culminating in the notorious Six Acts of 1819—'the high water mark', as Professor Aspinall has said, 'of legislation restricting the freedom of the press'—that newspapers learned not only to be politically independent but popular. It was in this atmosphere too that the radical and anti-authoritarian tradition that has played so large and ebullient a part in the history of the British press, and from which it always departs at its peril, put down its strongest roots.

The measures taken by the ruling classes to prevent the influence of the press reaching down to the ordinary mass of people, those Commons of England who under the impact of the Industrial Revolution were to become no more than 'the lower orders', were of the most extraordinary and far-reaching kind. The means adopted by editors and publishers to defeat them were not less so.

The great weight of repression did not this time fall first on the daily newspapers. As men of property their conductors were for the most part as fanatically anti-Jacobin as the Government itself and in any event the newspaper stamp tax ensured that their journals should cost too much to be bought by the mob. It fell on the periodical press.

Never has there been such a flowering of periodical and pamphlet writers as at this time, never before or since, I think, such an impact of printed matter upon the thoughts and actions of ordinary people. William Cobbett stands out, of course, above the rest: a crotchety, self-opinionated, homespun, radical-anarchist of a man with a towering genius for putting things plain that had not been equalled since Defoe and was not to be even distantly approached again until Robert Blatchford.

But there were others: Leigh Hunt and his brother John, both of whom went to prison for two years for attacking the Prince Regent in the *Examiner*; Henry Hetherington who enthusiastically defied authority with his unstamped *Poor Man's Guardian*, 'established contrary to "Law" to try the power of "Might" against "Right"'; the journeyman printer Thomas Jonathan

Wooler who published the *Black Dwarf* and escaped prison on the ingenious plea that although the indictment accused him of writing a libellous article he composed in type without a manuscript; William Hone, the parodist of the *Reformist's Register*, who made a fool of the Attorney-General when he was prosecuted on his ex-officio informations; and most indomitable of all, Richard Carlisle, British publisher of Thomas Paine's *Rights of Man*, who suffered altogether nine years' imprisonment in his fight for freedom of publication. There were others more obscure than these but not less stalwart, like Gilbert Macleod, editor of a Glasgow radical paper, who was transported for five years.

Passed from hand to hand, read in public houses and even to crowds assembled in the open air, these radical periodicals reached an enormous public. The stamped copy of the most important of them, Cobbett's *Political Register*, which cost 1s. 1½d. a copy, was, in fact, read so widely by groups gathered for the purpose in public houses and elsewhere that the authorities were driven to the intimidation and victimisation of innkeepers who bought it for the convenience of their customers. Many were warned that the magistrates would withdraw their licence if they continued to do so. Cobbett's reply was an unstamped 2d. edition of his *Register* containing comment but no news in order to keep it outside the legal definition of a newspaper and cheap enough for his readers to buy for themselves: his 'Twopenny Trash' as his enemies called it until he triumphantly took over the title and turned it to his own advantage.

The unstamped *Political Register* could not, of course, be sent through the post—the only generally available means of newspaper distribution. Cobbett overcame this difficulty by inviting small shopkeepers in every part of the country to become his selling agents. He arranged for parcels to be delivered to them by coach at a wholesale price of 12s. 6d. a hundred, reduced to 11s. a hundred if 1,000 copies or more a week were regularly ordered—a discount sufficient, as he pointed out, to give a man enough profit on the sale of a few hundred to support a small family. A display placard was sent with each bundle.

By these means Cobbett achieved the then stupendous sale of between 40,000 and 50,000 copies a week. Soon, as Samuel Bamford the Lancashire reformer notes in his *Passages in the Life of a Radical*, there was hardly a cottage hearth in the manufacturing districts of South Lancashire, Leicester, Derby and Nottingham and in many of the Scottish manufacturing towns, also, where the *Political Register* was not read aloud each week. The same was true of many of the rural areas. Some issues, indeed, sold far more than 40,000 to 50,000. Sir Robert Wilson writing to Lord Grey in November 1816 anxiously advised him that Cobbett's paper 'is circulating with wings through the country'. He had, he declared, evidence that of one issue one bookseller alone had sold 40,000 copies and that the total distribution could hardly be far short of half a million. This must either have been quite exceptional or the exaggeration of a very badly frightened man. But even with a normal weekly sale of between 40,000 and 50,000 copies, each one of which was regularly read to a score or more people, Cobbett achieved in relation to the population of the time a readership comparable to those of the mass circulation Sunday papers of today. He achieved it, moreover, solely by hard-hitting political comment, without any of the modern aids to distribution and without leaning on sex, crime, competitions, salacious serials, sport, strip cartoons or pictures of ladies in lingerie. A remarkable man—and a remarkable reading public.

Not, of course, that sex, crime, sport and other such weekday and Sunday delights did not have their place in the reading opportunities of the age. The Sunday paper had not yet found its full vocation, the horror comic still lay squirming in the womb of time. But the broadsheets on the streets did their work with no less relish and with an appetite for murder, rape, execution and mutilation that any American horror comic editor might envy. Public taste may not have risen very much in the last 150 years but we need not think it has fallen greatly. As for sport not only were reports of famous horse-races and great prize-fights awaited with the most intense interest and eagerly devoured by people of almost all classes, but they contain some of the best plain writing and vivid description that journalism has ever known. Then as now sports writers could often teach their more sophisticated brethren on the leader page a thing or two about the handling of words.

Not even Cobbett's forced flight to America in 1817 on the suspension of the Habeas Corpus Act, nor the 'gagging bills' rushed through Parliament to prevent 'seditious' meetings, speeches or publications on pain of death could destroy the influence of the *Political Register*, although Cobbett was much criticised for his American journey by those radicals like 'Orator' Hunt who held their ground. A hot fighter when he had a chance of success, Cobbett, as Mrs. Cole has commented in a brief but penetrating study of his life, had no taste for martyrdom. He knew very well that whoever else escaped arrest under the new Act he certainly would not. Fed by his writings from the New World, the *Political Register* continued to appear: he was an absentee editor whose words lost none of their pungency on a transatlantic voyage. Nor could the Six Acts of 1819 that followed the massacre of Peterloo destroy the *Register*, although one of them, the Newspaper Stamp Duties Act, compelled him to raise the price of his unstamped edition and eventually to discontinue it. This it did by deliberately altering the definition of a newspaper to include all papers and pamphlets issued more than once a month at a price of less than sixpence in order to 'restrain the abuses arising from the publication of blasphemous and seditious libels'. Even so when Cobbett was prosecuted unsuccessfully in 1831 for publishing a seditious libel inciting labourers to violence the Attorney-General had to admit that despite the forced rise in the price of the *Register* to a shilling the labouring classes in every part of the country still contrived to read it, clubbing together and sitting 'in great societies' for the purpose, so that it had a 'prodigious effect'. Even the fining, imprisonment and flogging of some of those who sold it did not stop it from circulating.

Between Cobbett and *The Times*, 'the bloody old *Times*', 'that cunning old trout' as he called it, there was, as between him and the rest of the 'respectable press', a continuous feud. Yet Cobbett's influence upon *The Times* and through it upon other newspapers was profound. He forced them to recognise the existence of a popular opinion far larger even than the public opinion of the middle classes whose advocates they had become and whose views they had, often at considerable risk to themselves, forced on the attention of Governments. He did so—although the comparison may seem odd and even irreverent to some of his latter-day admirers—because he was a master of the secret that has helped to bring the *Daily Mirror* its immense success in our own times: that of making radical politics as sensational and attractive as sex or crime. It was a secret that Robert Blatchford also discovered and made use of at the turn of the nineteenth century and it is no coincidence that in William Connor, 'Cassandra', the *Daily Mirror* possesses the only modern columnist whose sustained power of indignant writing can stand any sort of comparison with theirs. Like all the great natural radicals, Cobbett was a man in a constant passion. Negligible as a creative political philosopher it is not so much what he was for that matters as what he was against. He was a blustering, bullying egotist of a man thrown into a frenzy by disagreement and he changed his mind over and over again, travelling all the way from extreme right-wing reaction—the *Political Register* began as a bitter opponent of republicanism and of all nonsense about the rights of man and as a strong supporter of bull-baiting and the slave trade—to a burning, violent radicalism that made him the bogey of the rich and the hero of the landless labourers and industrial workers. He changed because although his political theory was often dubious his eyes were wide open. He recognised injustice when he saw it. When he recognised it he hated it. And whatever he hated he attacked with a corroding invective that made what he wrote more exciting than a prize-fight. He put new life into politics and new heart into common men.

Because he possessed this immense ability to make politics come alive he did more than any man to disclose the power and strength of popular opinion. He gave the mob a voice. It was because Barnes of *The Times* heard this voice and understood its meaning in newspaper terms better than others that *The Times* found the key to one of the most significant newspaper revolutions in our history and to a public authority greater than any Cobbett himself was ever able to command. It achieved this greater authority not because it knew public opinion better than Cobbett, which it did not, nor because its political understanding of the practical was greater, which it was, but because it was a newspaper and Cobbett's *Political Register* was not. It was therefore able to build upon the insatiable appetite of men and women for news and by so doing to command a wider audience than even Cobbett's superb commentary could of itself permanently attract.

The means by which *The Times* rose to a position of authority never before or since equalled by any other newspaper is fascinating to the journalist and of continuing significance to present-day newspapers. Both John Walter I and his greater son, John Walter II, originally conceived of it as a paper supporting the party in power. They thought of it as, if not quite the semi-official spokesman of the Government of the day that it later for a time became, at least its friendly counsellor and ally.

By the time Thomas Barnes was appointed editor in 1817— the first great editor to be solely a professional journalist without having, as Perry and Stuart had, the advantage of financial control of the paper he edited—*The Times* had achieved a considerable, although not yet unique, position. This arose not from any outstanding independence of judgment in its opinions but from the excellence of its foreign news service—it was, for instance, far ahead of all rivals and Government couriers with news of the Battle of Trafalgar—and the superiority of its business management and printing facilities. It moved forward from this respectable reputation to a position of unparalleled journalistic power because Barnes saw much quicker than anyone else the growing force and size of public opinion and determined to make *The Times* its independent voice.

By background and education a moderate reformer—he was a

close friend of Leigh Hunt and as a young man kept the *Examiner* alive when Leigh Hunt and his brother were in prison—he recognised as no other daily newspaper editor did the strength of the popular interest in reform that Cobbett had called into being. He decided to challenge Cobbett for its leadership.

He succeeded because John Walter II neither wished, as many subsequent newspaper proprietors have done, to make his paper the vehicle of his personal views nor imagined himself possessed of God-given powers as an editor by the mere fact of his share-holding. A business man and a printer he acted on the self-effacing assumption that journalism is best left to journalists. Having once made Barnes editor he endowed him with complete authority over the paper's contents. The revolution that carried *The Times* to a position of power such as no other paper has ever reached before or since was an editorial revolution, not a pro-prietorial one. It of course rested on, and could not have been carried through without, Walter's commercial skill in manage-ment and the technological lead he gave to *The Times* by his printing innovations from the introduction of steam printing in 1814 onwards. These things made the revolution possible. They gave *The Times* the commercial strength and mechanical facilities by which it was able to take advantage of the popular demand for the paper that Barnes's policy created. But the revolution could not have been produced by them alone. It was made by Barnes.

Barnes joined the paper as a young man from Cambridge. He served it as dramatic critic, Parliamentary reporter and leader writer and had already given good evidence of his quality when he was chosen editor in 1817 at the age of thirty-two—a year younger than Perry when he acquired control of the *Morning Chronicle*, and three years older than Stuart when he took over the derelict *Morning Post*. Slowly at first and then with ever-increasing vigour Barnes set himself to put into effect editorial principles new not only to *The Times* but to every newspaper. Perry and Stuart before him had sought, and sought successfully, to produce a daily paper free of the trammels of subservience to a party machine. Barnes's purpose was larger than this. It was, as the official *History of The Times* says, 'to foster, to guide and to ally himself with the feeling of the country', to make *The Times* not, as other newspapers had been, the voice of one man or party or Government, but of public opinion itself. He was the first man to put steadily into practice the thesis that the press is a separate power required by its nature to act independently of all Governments, even of those it approves, owing responsibility to none but the general body of the public. Like his successor Delane he held that it cannot be subject to 'the same limitations, the same duties, the same liabilities as the Ministers of the Crown' or be ancillary to any interest however worthy other than that which is peculiarly its own.

In these days it is sometimes thought to be disreputable in a newspaper to follow public opinion—as though the virtue of a journalist were to be judged primarily by the depth of his contempt for his readers. Barnes, a man of strong principles, suffered from no such conceit. He went where popular opinion led him because he regarded public opinion as the only valid authority a newspaper should admit, even if this week it took him in a different direction from that of last week. To those who accused him of inconsistency and nicknamed *The Times* 'The Turnabout' he replied contemptuously that what mattered was not what the paper had said in the past but 'whether what we say *now* is true and just and to the purpose *now*'.

His only consistency—which was also his unique journalistic quality—was to believe that public opinion must always be taken into account and that it is a newspaper's duty to search it out and express it plainly with as much 'devil' as possible. He had no patience with 'ifs and buts'. Like Cobbett he thought opinions should be spoken plainly, not wrapped in cotton wool. No doubt, as those who do not like a good deal of modern journalism claim, he and other great editors of the past would raise at least one eyebrow at some of the activities of the 'popular press' of today. But I cannot help thinking the dignified rotundities of some modern *Times* leaders would be hardly more to his taste. He made *The Times* a national institution not by conducting it as if it were one but by never forgetting that it was a newspaper. When he was accused of being violent and offensive he took it as a compliment, for he was both by deliberate intent. Newspaper writing was, he said, 'what brandy is to beverages'.

The two John Walters had established for the paper an unrivalled network of foreign correspondents. Barnes set to work to do the same thing at home, not only for purposes of news but even more in order to have at his command the best possible intelligence on the state of public opinion in every part of the country. He was determined always to be in a position to know which way it was moving and his local correspondents were instructed to keep him constantly posted on the views of shop-keepers, landlords, paupers, squires, bishops and industrialists.

He was equally determined that what the public had to say for itself should be adequately reported.

Perry had revolutionised Parliamentary reporting by organising a corps of Parliamentary reporters. Barnes now revolutionised the reporting of demonstrations of public opinion by obtaining for *The Times* the service of the best shorthand writers of the day and organising them into teams to cover great public meetings in all parts of the country. One of his reporters, a Mr. Tyas, was on the platform with 'Orator' Hunt when the cavalry charged the crowds at Peterloo and sabred nearly a hundred peaceable demonstrators. He was arrested but despite arrest managed, as a good reporter should, to get back to his paper the first full account, subsequently made available for reproduction all over the country. Similarly, when the inquest on a number of those killed at Peterloo was held at Oldham, Barnes sent his reporter John Ross to cover it and despite official obstruction obtained from him reports that occupied column after column of *The Times* throughout October 1819. As a result of such reporting of unpleasant facts *The Times* was, like many newspapers since, accused by Ministers of dangerous radicalism. Barnes replied that there was no falsehood however glaring the 'servile adherents' of Ministers would not swear against the paper because 'there is nothing which they so much dread as a free journal, unattached to any other cause than that of truth, and given to speak boldly of all parties'. And this indeed was the heart of the matter and expresses in a couple of dozen words or so the basic principle on which Barnes conducted his paper.

The attempt to suppress all movements of reform that culminated in the savage charge on the Lancashire demonstrators at Peterloo and in the Six Acts that followed it drove Barnes, swayed as he was by the reports he received on popular feeling, more and more away from the previous *Times* tradition of automatic support for the Government of the day. But appropriately enough in the light of the then position of *The Times* as the leader of popular journalism it was the public reaction to a Royal scandal that first showed him how large a factor support for a popular cause could play in providing newspapers with the means to economic and political independence.

In January 1820 George III died and the Prince Regent became King. He immediately repudiated his Queen, Caroline. On 9 July an Act was introduced to deprive her of her position and dissolve the marriage. Cobbett, closer by instinct than Barnes to popular feeling, all his sense of chivalry aroused, rushed to defend her. Barnes moved more cautiously. He was well aware, as Cobbett was not, for he refused to listen, of the formidable case that could be made against the Queen and the damaging evidence that might be brought against her at her forthcoming trial. But his instinct was to go with public opinion and a fall in the sale of *The Times* when it had criticised Queen Caroline on an earlier occasion made him anxious not to take sides against the popular cause. So soon as it became clear from the reports of his agents in the country that this was one of those issues that transcend politics and arouse popular emotions to a degree that political questions in themselves rarely can, Barnes did not hesitate. His principle of action was that newspapers should speak for the public: when the popular sympathy for the Queen became clear *The Times* cast aside its private doubts and became Queen Caroline's chief champion.

In so doing Barnes alienated almost all those on whom *The Times* had previously depended—the Court, the party leaders, the most solid of its own subscribers—and cut the paper off from many of its most valuable sources of information. The reward outweighed the loss. By supporting the Queen *The Times* doubled its sales: within a week or two the sales of the paper jumped from 7,000 to over 15,000 a day. Many of the readers thus attracted bought a newspaper for the first time. They represented not the transfer of subscribers from one journal to another but the tapping of a whole new reading public brought into existence by the passionate popular interest in Queen Caroline's cause and the feeling that a shocking travesty of justice was about to be perpetrated.

Moreover, sympathy for the Queen formed a rallying point for all other anti-Ministerial sentiment. It thus provided the basis for a development of public opinion that could not help but give *The Times* as its chief spokesman an unprecedented position of influence. Keeping pace with the popular movement of opinion as shown in its rising circulation *The Times* became the most forcible advocate of Parliamentary reform, promoting Political Unions in the great provincial centres to advocate it and broadcasting their activities through the length and breadth of the country by means of express reports. With every new development of the public opinion it thus fostered and reported, and to which its leading articles gave a powerful regular voice, the circulation of *The Times* increased. In March 1832 it was able to report that it had sold 4,328,025 copies in 1831, an increase of nearly 1,000,000 on the previous year and more than seven times the sales of the chief Conservative newspaper and principal opponent of Reform, the *Morning Post*. As always advertisements followed circulation. They were soon reaching *The Times* in such numbers that special supplements had to be printed to accommodate them.

Barnes deliberately chose the role of the first of the great popular journalists. More constantly even than the editor of a mass circulation newspaper of today he kept his ear to the ground for news of every movement of public opinion. The public he was interested in was not of course the same as theirs. Much of theirs did not then exist, even potentially, as newspaper readers. Nor was it Cobbett's public of the industrial workers and landless labourers that he catered for—for which reason Cobbett always angrily denied *The Times's* claim to speak for the British people. It was the public of the mercantile middle classes. Barnes was against aristocracy and inherited privilege, but for property, and especially for property acquired by individual initiative. He was not a Utopian but a man of his time, concerned, as every successful daily journalist must be, with the immediately possible.

Because he was a popular journalist he did more than any man to give to his own newspaper, and eventually through its example to others, the status and influence of a separate and independent power. So successful a popular journalist was he, indeed, that within five years of becoming its editor he had raised the circulation of *The Times* not merely to the largest in the country but to nearly as much as that of its two nearest competitors combined and by the time of his death was selling twice as many as any three of his rivals put together. Within another ten years *The Times* was to achieve on the foundations he laid a sale nearly three times as much as that of the whole of the rest of the daily press, dominating the newspaper scene to such an extent that for close on forty years the history of *The Times* is to all intents and purposes the history of the British press.

Never before or since, although the fact is sometimes overlooked, has there been so successful an example of popular journalism as *The Times* under its two greatest editors. Not Northcliffe, nor Beaverbrook, nor Bartholomew could have taught Barnes and Delane anything of the business of catering for public demand. They did not cater for it by being correct, respectable and discreet, or by loyally supporting the 'establishment'. 'The press lives by disclosures', declared *The Times* in its famous rejoinder to Lord Derby. It meant what it said.

Both Barnes and Delane lived according to that principle. They employed all their enterprise and spent large sums of money on getting the news before anyone else. And when they got it they printed it, however uncomfortable it might be or however inconvenient to authority. There has never been an editor more adept at the organisation of a news service than Barnes, never one more expert in uncovering confidential information than Delane, who followed the excellent precept that if you want to get at secrets you must 'stick close to the centre of them'. There are few modern editors—or proprietors—whether of 'serious' or 'popular' papers, who could not even now learn a good deal from both of them, whether it be in the importance they attached to news, their consistent enterprise in going out after it, their courage in publishing it, or their forthright way with those in authority who tried to suppress it. Or indeed in the plain English in which they expressed their opinions.

'The rubbish must be wheeled away to the last barrowful before any sure foundation can be laid for a new building', wrote Barnes when he demanded the reorganisation of a Cabinet. 'Good God! Are we to have another downright fraud passed upon the rightful expectations of the country?'

The great lesson that Barnes learned and that he taught to a newspaper press not overwilling at first to receive it and to a ruling class that hated the very idea of it was that the true foundation of a newspaper's strength lies solely in its own quality as a newspaper.

In recognising the importance of public opinion and in insisting that it was on this opinion and not on the views of the Court or of Ministers or of any kind of official authority that newspapers must depend, Barnes was not only a great innovator: he laid down the only sound principle for a newspaper in any age. But he not only followed and interpreted public opinion, he sought also to inform and shape it. Above all he gave it knowledge of its own power. He found the middle classes who made up the public to whom he directed himself nervous and irresolute, without votes or steady political power. 'He taught, urged and thundered their duty to them in his daily articles', as the *History of The Times* justly records, 'until they recognised themselves as the largest and most coherent body in the State'.

VI

THAT VILE TYRANT *THE TIMES*

To secure the independence of the press was of the first importance. To establish the principle that the powers of Government and press are 'constantly separate, generally independent, sometimes diametrically opposed' and that it is in the public interest that they should be was of no less importance. But what now began to be posed in an extreme form by the extraordinary position secured by *The Times* was the question— still relevant in our own day—how far the power that resides in newspapers can be concentrated within narrow areas of control without itself becoming, as Lord John Russell declared the power of *The Times* to be, tyrannical.

In spite of the temporary lodgments won by Perry and Stuart and the marauding victories of Wilkes, 'Junius' and Cobbett, the power of the press before Barnes had been as thistledown when set against that of Ministers and of the complex of social and other forces available to the defence of the 'Establishment'. Barnes and John Walter II corrected this balance. Delane and John Walter III not merely maintained the new position, they tipped the balance too much the other way. In this they were aided by a combination of commercial and political circumstance that to a unique degree served to concentrate newspaper power very largely in their sole hands, and by Delane's exceptional talent for acquiring the most confidential information.

'There has grown up, and is still growing, an influence over the conduct of members so imperious that the Speaker, instead of demanding from the Sovereign freedom of speech, had much better ask it from *The Times*.' So wrote John Wilson Croker,

Secretary to the Admiralty, to Lord Brougham at the beginning of the Crimean War. And at the end of that war, in the course of which the influence of *The Times* increased enormously, Lord John Russell wrote to the Earl of Clarendon: 'For me who have had my full feast of office it does not much matter, but if England is ever to be England again, this vile tyranny of *The Times* must be cut off.' It was a view shared by many of the most powerful and able in public life.

It is, of course, usual for politicians to dwell on the menace of the press when they find themselves opposed by it. But there was a good deal more in these anxieties. *The Times*, in fact, was in a position not only to influence but often to make or break political leaders and even Governments.

Its power rested in the first place on its extraordinary circulation position at a time when the relationship between circulation and political influence was greater than it had ever been or could be now. Barnes had helped to make the middle classes the largest and most coherent body in the State. It was among this body, exercising since the passing of the Reform Act of 1832 a power of political influence that no Government could ignore, that the main body of newspaper readers was to be found. With its vast excess of sales over all other newspapers *The Times* was thus daily read by nearly all the most politically interested and active people in the country.

Its position was further strengthened by the lowering of the tax on advertisements a year after the passing of the Reform Bill and by the reduction in the Newspaper Stamp Duty from four-pence to a penny a copy three years later. Although the newspaper owners, early demonstrating a habit of restrictive combination in trading practices that persists to this day, jointly agreed not to pass the full tax relief on to their readers but to lower the price of newspapers by only 2*d.* instead of 3*d.*—from 7*d.* to 5*d.*—the reduction brought with it a considerable increase in the number of newspaper readers. Of this increase *The Times*—contrary to the hope and expectation of those who had urged a reduction in the stamp duty—obtained the lion's share. It did so not only because its prestige was a natural attraction to new readers but because by reason of John Walter's commercial acumen it manifestly offered better value for money than any other paper—more pages, normally twelve or sixteen to their eight, and a free advertisement supplement three or four times a week.

Advertisements were at this time charged for at the same flat rate for all newspapers. The cost of an insertion in *The Times* was the same as for one in the *Morning Post*, which had only a tiny percentage of its sales. The days of advertisement rates linked to circulation figures were still distant. So was the development of display advertisements. The supplement did not itself, therefore, yield a profit; at best it merely covered the cost of its paper and printing. But it brought rich rewards to *The Times* in increased circulation. By 1842, six years after the reduction in the stamp duty to 1*d*., sales had more than doubled. In the next eight years, between 1842 and 1850, they doubled again, although in the same period those of the *Morning Herald* fell by a third and those of the *Morning Post* and the *Morning Chronicle* by a half.

It was thus to a newspaper already holding a massive superiority over its rivals and steadily increasing the gap between them that John Thaddeus Delane succeeded as editor at the age of twenty-three and of which John Walter III became chief proprietor six years later in July 1847. Building on this foundation they provide an example of the height to which press power can rise such as no subsequent editor or newspaper proprietor has come within hailing distance of.

Although it was the pre-eminence of *The Times* in circulation and commercial prosperity that provided the basis for its political power the journalistic exploitation of this commercial strength was due very largely to Delane's personality as an editor. After 1850, in fact, *The Times* made no further effort to increase its circulation although in the judgment of Mowbray Morris, its manager, it could easily have again doubled its sales in the course of the next two years if it had wished. Its unique public authority was such that increased sales were no longer of any interest to it, certainly not sales which might have to be achieved at the expense of either the quality or quantity of the news it offered to its readers.

Delane, unlike Barnes, was not a writing editor. Indeed among the great editors of newspaper tradition—Barnes, C. P. Scott, J. A. Spender, H. W. Massingham, J. L. Garvin, the almost legendary possessors of political influence at its journalistic greatest—he stands curiously aloof, more akin in some ways to a modern managing editor than to them.

It is sometimes complained, I have so complained myself, that the modern popular newspaper gives too much influence to the sub-editor, the re-writer and polisher-up of other people's copy. The excellence in news presentation achieved for example by the *Daily Express* depends to no small extent upon the fact that its editor for the last twenty-three years, Arthur Christiansen, is the most brilliant technician and make-up man in modern journalism, presiding over his journalistic team not as a remote deity brooding on matters of high policy but as a working editor wielding a sub-editorial pencil with superb professional sophistication.

When such editorial methods were introduced into the office of the *Express* and other modern popular newspapers they seemed to many journalists of an older generation to portend a sad change in editorial function: the replacement of the informed weigher of policy by the technician. But unlike some of his successors in the tradition of 'serious journalism' Delane, I suspect, would have found himself wholly at home in a modern news-room. He would certainly have thought it natural that the editor should lead his troops in person during the hottest skirmishes of the nightly battle. It was the practice he himself followed.

He wrote little himself but he supervised not only the leaders but every article and news story, indeed almost every sentence, that appeared in his paper. 'I believe', he wrote once, 'not a column has been published in *The Times* which has not some of my handwriting in the margin.' It is indeed a remarkable picture not only of a 'great editor' in the popular, traditional sense of the term but of a superb professional working journalist that emerges from the detailed study of his regime in the second volume of the *History of The Times*, from the biographies written by his nephew Arthur Dasent and Sir Edward Cook, and from contemporary records. It was this professionalism that helped to make *The Times* superior to all its rivals not only as an organ of opinion but as a general newspaper.

Of another great editor, C. P. Scott of the *Manchester Guardian*, a close colleague and successor as *Guardian* editor, W. P. Crozier, once wrote that on almost any other paper he would have been sacked; 'he had such ideas about news values'. No one would ever have thought that of Delane. He was, as the *History of The Times* says, 'the living personification of the news sense . . . awake to one aspect only of the events of his exciting world; wars, the discoveries of science, movements in literature, painting and music, the catastrophes of Nature, railway disasters, crime, famine, the fall of dynasties interested him little and only in so far as they needed recording in *The Times*'. Nor, although it was upon the reporting and analysing of the major themes in national and international affairs that he concentrated the full force of his journalistic interest, did he disregard anything that might entertain his readers. 'That was a good murder you had last week', he wrote approvingly to his assistant editor when he was briefly away from the office. His partner in the organisation of the paper, Mowbray Morris the manager, complained to the paper's Vienna correspondent, 'Do the Viennese never commit murder or rape? Does no merchant prince ever forge or levant with other people's money or break disreputably—does nobody in Vienna or elsewhere in the Austrian dominions ever do anything amusing or exciting?'

He had—perhaps it is an essential qualification of the supremely successful editor—no major interest in life other than his paper, and very few minor ones. He was seen everywhere, knew everyone, attended every important function—but only in the interests of his paper. He had, he said, 'the bad taste not to greatly admire the society of Dukes and Duchesses', but he put up with their company a good deal on his paper's behalf. He did not dance but there was hardly a fashionable ball or reception at which he was not to be found. In such gatherings each subtle variation in the temper of the social world could be gauged, each rumour that might point to the shape of future events in politics overheard. He spent his entire life 'thinking of *The Times*'.

Barnes had been an anonymous editor in the completest sense, confident that those whose information or judgment he valued would seek him in his own office, content to be unknown to others. The first occasion on which his name appeared in the paper that he made great was when he died at the age of fifty-six and even then the event was merely noted briefly in a two-line entry in the births, marriages and deaths column without reference to his connection with the paper. Delane sought news wherever it was to be found; a busy, gregarious man known to everybody. He was a professional newspaperman every moment of his life: 'all his other senses in abeyance to his journalistic sense'. Perhaps because of the tragic nature of his domestic life—his wife had a serious mental illness a few years after their marriage and lived apart from him under medical care—he had virtually no private life nor ever seemed to want any: Barnes on the other hand lived in quiet domestic bliss with a mistress.

It was his habit to arrive at Printing House Square at ten o'clock each evening and remain until five o'clock in the morning. He rose at noon and after eating a combined breakfast and lunch went for a ride in the Park—a duke, as was remarked on one occasion, walking on each side of him as he rode. Afterwards he spent two or three hours at his desk in his chambers in Serjeants Inn not far from *The Times* office, reading documents, dealing with correspondence and dispatching precise instructions to his leader writers so that they should be well ahead with the work of preparation by the time he arrived at the office. In the evening he would usually look in at several social functions or dine privately with a leading member of the Cabinet in pursuit of that exclusive confidential information that gave *The Times* under him its extraordinary reputation. Having arrived at his office at ten he at once took over detailed control of every department of the paper, reading the Parliamentary and all other news reports, letters to the editor (they averaged 200 a day and he had finally to pass to an assistant some of the work of picking those to be published), dispatches from foreign correspondents, special articles and literary reviews (he had little liking for poetry other than that of Lord Tennyson and dismissed a reviewer's request to be allowed to write on Shelley with the remark: 'Excrement! Excrement!'). He directed and supervised leaders, dictated policy, issued instructions to the staff; revised, rewrote and sub-edited, while at the same time concerning himself ceaselessly—although not in this department with any great originality—with the lay-out and presentation of the paper and with 'those devils of printers' who were, he said, constantly trying to save a quarter of a column by taking out leads at 'the expense of disfiguring the whole paper'. At five o'clock in the morning, the last edition having gone to press, he would leave the office and walk to Serjeants Inn and so to bed—seeing in the course of his life, as he once re-marked, more sunrises than almost any man alive.

Other great editors have often held themselves aloof from the daily turmoil of news-getting and news-presentation. He never did. He was as much a working executive as the editor of any modern popular paper.

But he was, of course, much more than an extremely competent managing editor, although if he had not been that *The Times* would not have been the paper it was. He was also a journalist of extreme courage and integrity with a most penetrating and independent political judgment and with a superb sense of the duty of a newspaper to report, inform and guide public opinion and to allow no one to stand in the way of its doing so. And he was perhaps the best political correspondent that ever lived.

There was no important political or diplomatic secret of his time, however confidential, that he did not possess himself of, and, having secured, print: for he continued to hold throughout his life, in face of the harshest accusations and the sharpest pressures, the belief that 'the Press lives by disclosures', that its first duty is to obtain 'the earliest and most correct intelligence of the events of the time and instantly, and by disclosing them, to make them the common property of the nation'.

Discretion 'in the public interest', and particularly in the public interest as seen by Ministers, is a journalistic virtue much practised in modern times. It was a principle for which Delane had no sympathy in any circumstances whatever. He belonged to, or perhaps it would be truer to say he founded, a tradition that is today practised at its most absolute only on the other side of the Atlantic.

Only the *New York Times* among modern newspapers can invite comparison with *The Times* of his day in the publishing of confidential Cabinet decisions and State documents, not as an exceptional accident but in the ordinary line of business. It is able to do so for somewhat the same reasons. Early nineteenth-century British Cabinets were, like modern American Administrations, not so much cohesive bodies governed by party loyalties and strict internal disciplines as loose alliances of politicians who thought it natural to advance their particular interests in whatever way seemed best to them. Cabinet secrecy was no more than a convenience to be set aside when expediency prompted.

Because he moves in somewhat the same kind of world Mr. James Reston, head of the *New York Times* Washington Bureau, shares in our day something of the advantages of Delane in his— together with something of Delane's aptitude for persuading politicians to disclose their minds to him. No British journalist does or could. The detailed newspaper disclosure of the most confidential Cabinet decisions and 'top secret' international documents has, as a result, come in these days to be regarded as a peculiarly American custom to which other Governments are required to accustom themselves with what diplomatic stoicism they can. Delane would have considered it a peculiarly British custom vested as of journalistic right in the editor of *The Times*.

'Our most secret decisions are made public [in *The Times*] ... somehow or other this evil should be corrected', complained Aberdeen to Clarendon in February 1854, and Lord John Russell wrote to Queen Victoria that: 'The degree of information possessed by *The Times* with regard to the most secret affairs of State is mortifying, humiliating and incomprehensible.'

The occasion for these particular protests was the advance publication by *The Times* of the news that an ultimatum had been dispatched to the Tsar of Russia by the British and French Governments, despite the most extraordinary precautions to keep it secret until the ultimatum itself had been presented to the Tsar. But the same complaint is to be found repeated again and again during most of Delane's editorship up to 1865. After that the development of stronger party discipline following Palmerston's death altered the situation to his disadvantage.

Delane, in fact, established such a position of ascendancy and commanded so many and so varied confidential contacts with Ministers who were anxious to secure his goodwill that there was practically no State secret of which he was not informed within a few hours of its disclosure to the Cabinet.

'I don't much care to have "confidential" papers sent to me at any time,' he complained to Sir John Rose, 'because the possession of them prevents me using the information which from one source or another is sure to reach me without any such condition of reserve.' And indeed so many people in high places were ready to disclose official secrets to him that he could be independent of any one of them. He was rarely, if ever, under the necessity to pay for information with editorial support. Nor, although Delane was the major channel through which such information reached *The Times*, was he the only one. For fifteen years from 1840 to 1855, at first under Barnes and then under Delane, the paper had in its employ the Clerk of Appeals to the Privy Council, Henry Reeve. The offices of the Privy Council were then much more intimately involved in the daily machinery of Government than now. Partly because of this but still more because of his remarkable aptitude for making friends in high places—when he was only twenty-six he was able to report proudly to his mother that he found himself on terms of close intimacy with the whole Cabinet with the exception of Lord Melbourne and Thomas Baring—Reeve was able over a long period of years to provide *The Times* with intimate knowledge of the most confidential affairs. His sources of information were second only—and sometimes not even that—to Delane's own.

This almost uninterrupted flow of confidential information to *The Times* did not of course go unchallenged. There were repeated attempts to end it and set up in its stead an agreed system passing exclusive confidential information only to those newspapers that were either already known as Government organs or were prepared—which *The Times* never was—to promise support in return for information. Indeed ever since the press had begun to be troubled with ideas of independence some means of replacing the haphazard individual betrayal of secrets by Ministers by an office for taking approved journals into the Government's confidence had repeatedly been considered. Government public relations services are not just a modern naughtiness. A Government Press Bureau managed by the Treasury and fed with selected secrets from each Department for passing to reliable newspapers with 'a hint of the line which it is wished should be taken' was contemplated in 1809. Twenty years later Wellington was still exercised by the problem. He went for advice to Croker, who suggested that a Cabinet Minister should be made responsible for 'instructing' friendly newspapers.

'In a Cabinet like ours', said Croker, 'surely there might be one person who could find leisure for this sort of supervision, if not for some more direct cooperation. If anything of this kind were practicable it ought to be done in the most profound secrecy and every possible precaution against even a suspicion should be taken and the Minister who should undertake it . . . should throw in, here and there, such a slight mixture of error or apparent ignorance, as should obviate suspicion of its coming from so high a source.' Croker, who has some claim to be regarded as the first and certainly one of the most talented of the now all-pervasive family of public relations officers (he was much envied when Secretary to the Admiralty for what Lockhart described as his 'invisible predominance over the Tory daily press'), went on to urge that 'the times are gone by when statesmen might safely despise the journals, or only treat them as inferior engines which might be left to themselves or committed to the guidance of persons wholly unacquainted with the views of the Ministry'.

'The day', he declared, 'is not far distant when you will (not *see*, or *hear*) but *know* that there is someone in the Cabinet entrusted with what will be thought one of the most important duties of the State, the regulation of public opinion.'

Although neither of these proposals came to much, other efforts to break the lines of communication between *The Times* and the Ministries were not wanting. In 1845 Peel urged upon Aberdeen the need to punish the paper by 'the discontinuance of all communications from the Foreign Office'. When Clarendon was his Foreign Secretary Lord John Russell repeatedly asked him to see that when news was given to *The Times* it was also given to the *Daily News* and the *Morning Chronicle*. The *Morning Herald* continuously protested that despite its own loyalty to the Administration *The Times* was given secrets that the *Herald* was not given, and in 1841 the *Morning Post* was given such firm promises of exclusive information that it boldly announced itself to be 'the ministerial medium for early information'. Eleven years later the *Post* was again promised confidential news withheld from *The Times*, Lord Derby considering this the best means of securing its support 'in the cheapest possible manner'.

All these attempts to cut out *The Times* failed. They did so because, as Lord Clarendon wrote frankly to Reeve, 'I don't care a straw what any other newspaper thinks or says. They are all regarded on the Continent as representing persons or cliques, but *The Times* is considered to be the exponent of what English public opinion is or will be, and as it is thought that whatever public opinion determines with us, the Government ultimately does, an extraordinary and universal importance attaches to the views of *The Times*.'

This hold on public opinion was further strengthened by the part played by *The Times* in the war with Russia, a war which, as the second volume of the *History of The Times* points out, its enemies claimed it made and in which victory was secured by the Crimean campaign for which it was largely responsible. In the course of the war it destroyed a Ministry, forced the removal of the Commander-in-Chief, raised public opinion to the need for the most thorough overhaul of the Army medical services and, indeed, of the whole Army, linked itself closely in the public mind with the idolised Florence Nightingale and raised a great fund for the relief of the sick and wounded. The dispatches of its brilliant war correspondent W. H. Russell—chosen for the assignment by Delane almost at random—brought the war home to the British people as nothing else did. They left all other sources of war news, including the official, far behind, becoming with their graphic writing and exclusive information the one record accepted by the vast majority as authentic.

The Times had in truth reached, as Reeve after quarrelling with it in 1855 and going off to edit the Edinburgh Review, declared, 'an extraordinary and dangerous eminence'.

This eminence did not leave its controllers unscathed: they were no more immune than modern press lords from the corrupting influence of their own sense of power. Egomania is an occupational hazard of successful newspapermen. They did not escape it. They came to regard The Times as so much superior to all other human institutions as to be above criticism even when it was wrong; subject to none of the common obligation to justify itself by facts.

When Mowbray Morris was called before a committee of the House of Commons to substantiate insinuations published by The Times that all the Irish Members were in receipt of bribes, he acted very much like the editor of a modern tabloid called before the Press Council. The press—or at any rate The Times— had, he indicated, the right to do whatever it chose and was required to explain to no one. He was asked if he extended his idea of the privileges of the press to facts as well as to opinions. He replied briefly, 'To everything whatever.' To the question whether he was willing to offer any explanation or justification of the charges brought against the Irish Members, he answered shortly, 'I am not.' After which as the Manchester Guardian, then a bi-weekly, but a vigorous one, commented, 'the gentleman bowed, retired and went home to dinner, convinced no doubt that the Czar of Russia, the Member for Bucks [Disraeli] and *The Times* newspaper can defy the whole of mankind'.

It was an attitude that could not but add fuel to the fire of those who accused *The Times* of 'despotism' and contempt for truth and who had begun to feel, as the *Manchester Guardian* remarked, in a phrase still pertinent to the newspaper situation, that to extend Delane's claim for newspaper independence so far as to include 'the liberty to declaim and depreciate without the attestation of facts is to sink its position, not to exalt it'.

'No apology is necessary', said the first issue of the *Saturday Review* 'for assuming that this country is ruled by *The Times*. We all know it, or if we do not know it, we ought to know it. It is high time we began to realise the magnificent spectacle afforded by British freedom—thirty millions of *cives Romani* governed by a newspaper.' Nor was this reputation and the power that went with it confined to the United Kingdom. It extended all over Europe where the resident correspondents of the paper, whose numbers had been much increased by Delane and Mowbray Morris, were treated almost as ambassadors. Although they did not yet include anyone quite so courted by the great as the fabulous Henri de Blowitz of a few years later they were frequently invited to share more freely in the secrets of confidential diplomatic transactions than were their Government's representatives. Indeed this reputation went far beyond Europe. 'The London *Times*', said Lincoln, welcoming its famous war correspondent W. H. Russell to Washington on the eve of the Civil War, 'is one of the greatest powers in the world—in fact I don't know anything which has much more power—except perhaps the Mississippi.'

This power had been achieved primarily by the excellence of the paper itself, by the commercial ability of its chief proprietors and of Mowbray Morris (the manager appointed by John Walter III) and by the genius of Barnes and Delane. None but itself had given the paper the position of near monopoly that it possessed.

Nevertheless this power, although sometimes, no doubt, exaggerated in the attacks of its enemies, had become too great to be allowed to continue unchecked.

To reduce it, to provide in the words of Queen Victoria to Palmerston in one of her many letters of complaint at its 'atrocious articles' some 'check on the reckless exercise of that anomalous power the danger of which to the best interests of the country is so universally admitted', had become—understandably and even correctly—one of the prime preoccupations of many of the most eminent in public life.

Characteristically the Queen's own remedy was that 'the Editor, the Proprietor and the Writers of such execrable publications' should henceforth be excluded from the circles of 'higher society', a course which she felt would 'mark fitly disapproval of their acts'. She had, indeed, long found it difficult to understand why journalists should be received socially and was little persuaded by Palmerston's explanation that although there was 'no doubt some inconvenience in the admission of editors and writers of newspapers into general society', yet if they happened 'to be in a position in life which would naturally lead to their being invited, it would not be easy to exclude them merely on account of their connection with a newspaper'.

However, to curb *The Times*, something more was needed than the loss of a few dinner invitations.

This extraordinary concentration of press power in the hands of one paper John Walter III used with a self-effacement to which the press lords of the twentieth century have lost the key. He never tried to use it for his own purposes or even directly to administer it, handing it over instead to salaried employees to use according to their judgment of the truest public interest. When one looks back on this power Delane seems to stand out pre-eminently as its embodiment and expression. Yet despite the immensity of his contribution to the paper's political position his influence was only the tip of the iceberg above the water. What lay below the surface was even more important: the trading position of the paper. It was this that made the absolute dominance of *The Times* possible and it was this that had to be dealt with if there was to be any thaw in a press structure so solidly frozen as to make impossible the emergence of any real rival to *The Times*—just as today, although from different causes and with less extreme consequences, the current trading position in the newspaper industry effectively prevents the launching of any new national daily newspapers.

There is a certain poetic irony about the choice of the instrument by which the power of *The Times* was at last reduced. Nearly a century and a half previously the system of the Newspaper Stamp Tax had been introduced as a means of preventing the rise of an independent, popular and powerful press. Now it was seen that it was behind the shield of this very tax that *The Times* held its power and that this power could not be reduced unless the tax itself were abolished.

The newspaper stamp had already been reduced from 4*d*. to 1*d*. and it may seem strange that this small remaining tax, which was also a postal frank, should have so much effect. It did so because the fact that stamped papers were carried free through the post gave *The Times* with its big country sale a tremendous advantage over all others. Because of its strong commercial position and the great demand for its advertising space it was able to produce a much bigger paper than any other: twelve or sixteen pages plus regular advertisement supplements, compared with its rivals' six or eight. But it paid the same Stamp Tax, secured the same free carriage and was sold at the same price of 5*d*. Moreover not only did this position favour *The Times* compared with all other London papers it favoured all London papers compared with provincial ones. Circulating in comparatively small local areas these benefited little from free distribution through the mails but had to pay exactly the same tax as the London papers which did so benefit. As a consequence they had to sell at the same price. On such terms they could not hope to compete successfully; for in the nature of things and with communications as they then were it was impossible for a provincial newspaper to command the same sources of information as a Metropolitan one or to be as up-to-date with foreign news. There were plenty of provincial weeklies. But outside Scotland none of the daily papers launched from time to time, like the *Mercantile Gazette, and Liverpool and Manchester Daily Advertiser* of 1803 and the *Northern Express and Lancashire Daily Post* printed in Stockport in 1821, found it possible to survive for more than a year or two at most.

What the opponents of *The Times* in alliance with those who had long campaigned against 'taxes on knowledge' now proposed was that the compulsory Stamp Tax should be abolished so that those that did not use the mails should not pay it, while for those papers carried by the Post Office the existing 1d. stamp should remain, not as a tax but as a postal charge, and should cover the conveyance of newspapers up to four ounces in weight. Papers weighing more would pay excess.

Such an alteration was bound to have two consequences. It could not help but assist all provincial papers in relation to all London papers, for without a tax or postal charge they would be able to sell locally below the London paper price. And it could not help but favour all other London papers in relation to *The Times*, for *The Times* was the only one that weighed above four ounces— usually five or six and sometimes when there were supplements much more. *The Times* would therefore either have to pay excess and increase its price above other London papers or reduce to their size and lose its special character.

The campaign against the Stamp Tax had a double appeal: it served a great principle, the final removal of the hated taxes on knowledge, and it hit *The Times*. It mixed idealism and sharp commercial practice in a combination well suited to the political conditions of the time (perhaps of any time). To fix the cheap postal rate at a level that excluded *The Times*, although *The Times* accounted for four out of five of all the daily newspapers read in the country, and to claim that this was being done to help the press, as though *The Times* were not the largest part of it, was hypocritical as well as discriminatory on the facts as they then stood. But in a deeper sense the claim was justified and in the long-term view it was correct.

Nor is it an accident that the man to whom a great deal of the credit for the final success of the campaign must go was Richard Cobden.

Barnes had given *The Times* its unique position because of his understanding of the power vested in the middle classes. To these classes he had brought cohesion and self-confidence. But in this campaign it was Cobden who more truly spoke for them than did *The Times*, or at any rate for that ever-growing part of their number who lived, worked and prospered in the growing industrial cities of the North and Midlands, and for the small tradesmen and skilled workers next below them in the social hierarchy. The case for ending the tax was, in fact, twofold. The interests of the expanding business classes in the great commercial and industrial cities outside London could not be represented properly unless they had papers of their own to speak for them. And without cheaper papers the even greater body of public opinion that was not confined to men of property was without adequate information or public voice.

Free trade had triumphed in Britain in the 1840s with the repeal of the Corn Laws. The great popular forces that had won this victory were by their nature no less opposed to the taxes on knowledge that kept food for minds too dear for the poor. Indeed a wider combination of interests than it had ever been possible to bring together against the Corn Laws joined forces to compel first a reduction and then the abolition of the Stamp Tax. Cobden, Bright, T. Milner-Gibson, Hume and Ewart joined with working-class radicals and chartists and with such veteran campaigners of the great battles of reform as Francis Place and Henry Hetherington to organise propaganda against the Stamp Tax by petitions, public meetings, pamphlets and Parliamentary motions.

'So long as the penny [stamp duty] lasts,' said Cobden in 1850, 'there can be no daily press for the middle or working class. Who below the rank of a merchant or a wholesale dealer can afford to take a daily paper at fivepence? Clearly it is far beyond the reach of the mechanic and the shopkeeper.' And he

proclaimed with a truth that all previous experience supported:
'The governing classes will resist the removal of the penny
stamp not on account of the loss of revenue . . . but because they
know the stamp makes the daily papers the instrument and
servant of oligarchy.'

As a free-trader he saw also that not only did the Stamp Tax
keep the price of newspapers artificially high but that it created
conditions of trade that were almost bound to give monopolistic
advantages to the established and hinder free competition. *The
Times*, he repeated over and over again, had become a monopoly
with all the sins of monopoly attending it. And to Delane's
intense indignation he asked how it was possible in such circumstances to regard talk of the freedom of the press as anything but
arrant nonsense.

It is of course true that in so far as *The Times* did enjoy a near-
monopoly it was one that had originally been secured in fair fight
against competitors working under exactly the same conditions.
Nevertheless in the long view of the public interest there is no
doubt that Cobden was right. The grounds of battle had changed,
as change they do from generation to generation. In fighting
The Times Cobden was striking as much of a blow for press
freedom as 'Junius', Wilkes—or Barnes—had done in their day
against very different opponents.

His case against *The Times* was strengthened by the attitude
taken up by Mowbray Morris before the Select Committee
appointed to report on the newspaper taxes. When asked by
Cobden if he did not think it desirable that cheaper papers should
be made available to the general mass of the public Morris replied
that he had 'very little opinion of the sagacity of uneducated
people'. To the question whether he really considered it in the
public interest that the production of newspapers 'should be
limited to a few hands and be in the hands of parties who are
great capitalists', he answered that he did.

As frequently happens in journalism and outside it *The Times*
which at an earlier stage had done more than most to make popular
opinion an effective force in public life had by now come to

identify public opinion and the public interest with that group with which it was itself most closely identified and for which it could most directly speak: the upper middle class. Even the members of this class, however, had grown restive under *The Times* tutelage. They valued its support but did not like its power to ignore them, its independence and its omnipotence. They failed to rally to its defence.

The reformers carried the day and on 2 July 1855 *The Times* for the first time in its history came out priced 4*d.* unstamped and 5½*d.* stamped. The rest of the Metropolitan press was 4*d.* unstamped and 5*d.* stamped. It was not a big difference. But it was enough to set the stage for the modern popular press with all its qualities and all its imperfections.

VII

THE IMPORTANCE OF 1*d*.

IT may seem odd—indeed almost inconceivable—that the mere difference of a penny should bring so vast a change as it did in the situation of the press. Yet so it was.

With the end of the tax—indeed as soon as its ending could be foreseen with some confidence—men began to think of newspapers in a quite new way. For close on thirty-five years all other daily newspapers had lived so completely under its shadow that hardly anyone had been able to imagine a newspaper except in terms of *The Times*. Now with the removal of the tax they suddenly found it possible to do so. It was as though a spell had been broken.

If commercial considerations only had been involved one might have expected to find the relief of a penny reflected in a general reduction in the price of newspapers from 5*d*. to 4*d*. Instead almost overnight new newspapers sprang into being in every part of the country, not at 4*d*. but at 2*d*. and very soon at 1*d*.

They were not comprehensive news journals in the sense that *The Times* was. Writing to his Manchester agent Mowbray Morris commented on them that although there was no reason why a daily paper should not be published for a penny, 'it is impossible to produce a first class paper at that price'. Granted *The Times* standard of 'first class' this was true enough—although less so than Mowbray Morris imagined: within a matter of three years *The Times* was to be challenged on its own ground by a penny morning paper, the *Standard*, of the same size and appealing to the Conservative section of the same public. The real significance of the newspaper revolution that now began did not, however, lie in any direct challenge to *The Times* but in something quite different: the advent of a new class of readers for daily newspapers.

Until then *The Times* had dominated everything: a towering Everest of a newspaper with sales ten times those of any other daily, combining leadership in circulation, in news services—especially of the most confidential and exclusive kind—in advertisement revenue, commercial profit and political influence to an extent no other newspaper anywhere in the world has ever done before or since. But it did not, of course, exist alone. In its gigantic shadow the rest of the press pursued its restless, bustling, querulous and only too frequently short-lived way.

Of the morning papers that were young when *The Times* was young most had burnt themselves out by 1855; the *World*, *Oracle*, *Porcupine*, *True Briton*, *Morning Star*, *Constitutional New Times*, *Gazetteer*, *Courant*, these and many others had gone to their graves. Only five morning papers other than *The Times* were published in London: the *Morning Advertiser*, *Morning Chronicle*, *Morning Herald*, *Morning Post*, *Daily News*. None of them sold more than a few thousand; probably, although completely reliable figures are unobtainable, only the *Morning Advertiser* and the *Daily News* as many as 5,000. There were four evening papers, the *Sun*, *Globe*, *Express*, *Standard*. None of them had a sale of as much as 3,000 a day. And there were still a number of weekly, bi-weekly, and tri-weekly news-sheets of a kind common in the eighteenth century. Their circulation was tiny.

Until 1853, when the *Northern Daily Times* was started in Liverpool, there was not, outside London, a single successful morning or evening paper, in all England, although there were two in Scotland, both published in Glasgow. No city except Manchester and Liverpool had even a bi-weekly; the rest depended on small weeklies made up for the most part of items cut from the London dailies plus a few local news reports gleaned mostly from the courts, several columns of local advertisements and a certain amount of national advertising, mainly of lotteries and patent medicines. Most of these weeklies were printers' papers, although in the bigger cities some few, like the *Manchester Guardian*, had broken away from the general rut. Even in a weekly form these few were powers in their communities. Their leading articles several columns in length discussed political and economic matters on a high intellectual level and did not hesitate on occasion to cross swords with the great *Times* itself.

But by the nature of news it is daily journalism that must carry the main weight of newspaper influence and in this respect provincial Britain until 1855 was a desert. So indeed, practically speaking, was London itself except for the single phenomenon of *The Times*.

The number and circulation of daily newspapers do not of course give the whole story. This was still the age of news-rooms and reading societies, of the paper bought to be read by scores or even hundreds in the public houses, the coffee-shops and the Mechanics' Institutes. The actual readers of the stamped news-papers numbered, therefore, far more than the figures indicate, and their political influence throughout the movement for Parlia-mentary reform was vastly greater. Some ninety-six newspapers and periodicals were taken each week in such a 'Coffee and News-room', for example, as that kept in Manchester by John Doherty, the trade union leader who helped to found the illegal Manchester Cotton Spinners Society and later the Grand General Union of the United Kingdom until, at the age of forty, he abandoned trade union organisation for political education and bookselling. The reading fee was 1d. Those who came—as scores did daily to keep abreast of news and opinion—could have a cup of coffee for 2d., a cup of tea for 2½d. or a boiled egg for a penny as they read their way through the journalism of the time.

It was also the age of the periodical. The opinions of the *Edinburgh Review*, of the *Quarterly* and of *Blackwood* still governed intelligent conversation, although by 1885 all three had softened the arrogance and brutality of their earlier days—the *Edinburgh Review* indeed had become so mellow that Walter Bagehot declared it to be written entirely by Privy Councillors. Weekly reviews were flourishing. The *Spectator*—not Steele and

Addison's but a new one under the old name, the great-great-grandparent of our own—the *Athenaeum*, the *Examiner*, Bagehot's *Economist*, *Punch*, the *Illustrated London News*, *Chambers's Journal* and in 1855 the newly established and very vigorous *Saturday Review*, all these contributed to the intellectual excitement of the time. Dickens's *Household Words*, Cassell's *Popular Education*, Samuel Beeton's *Englishwoman's Domestic Magazine* and a host of others stimulated and catered for the expanding taste of the mass, its passion to be educated, enlightened and amused.

And below, appealing for the most part to cruder, more primitive and, as the history of journalism would seem to suggest, more durable emotions, was what from their eminence in Printing House Square must have seemed to Delane and Mowbray Morris to be the underworld of the Sunday newspapers.

The peculiarly British tradition of the separate Sunday paper had been begun three-quarters of a century earlier in 1781 with the publication of Mrs. Johnson's *British Gazette and Sunday Monitor*, designed to appeal to those who had neither money nor leisure for a daily paper. Within thirty years the number of such papers had grown to eighteen and the Sunday press had entered upon its destiny as the subject of grave disquiet among the respectable—suitable only for 'shop boys and milliners' apprentices', unfit for 'decent houses'.

'No pains are spared to make their distribution as general and as public as possible', reported the Tory pamphleteer John Bowles as early as 1807. 'Besides the gross indecency of announcing them by the blowing of horns, whenever they contain any extra-ordinary news, greengrocers, hairdressers and pastry cooks throughout the metropolis and its vicinity are furnished with signboards intimating that particular papers are to be sold at their respective shops and they are copiously provided with copies.'

The life of most of these newspapers was uncertain, brutish and short, but five established themselves with some permanence: *Bell's Life in London*, *Bell's Weekly Messenger*, the *Sunday Times*, the *Observer*, whose woodcuts of murders were superior to all others, and the *Weekly Dispatch*. This latter struck the authentic Sunday note in its first number by publishing, along with some political and foreign news, close on two and a half columns of police-court reports (thirteen people were sentenced to death at the Old Bailey, thirty-four to transportation); an indignant account of the indecent manner in which persons bathed off the beach at Ramsgate; and a report of the suicide of a young man 'who had abandoned his wife and children and lived with a woman of the town in common with another paramour, and on the fatal morning the other partner in this unhallowed firm went abroad with the dulcinea immediately after breakfast and had not been ten minutes gone when the unfortunate P—— hanged himself from a hook in the chamber with a piece of twine'.

It is, however, to three papers that came into existence in 1836 with the reduction of the stamp tax to a penny that the major share must go of whatever credit is due for laying the true foundations of the mass-circulation Sunday press of today: *Lloyd's Weekly News*, the *News of the World* and *Reynolds News*. These so far outstripped their earlier models that by 1855 two of them, *Lloyd's Weekly News* and the *News of the World*, had achieved the stupendous circulation of more than 100,000 copies a week each, while *Reynolds* had about 50,000. Their success rested on a formula as old as that of the first broadsheets and as up-to-date as that of next Sunday's *People* or *Sunday Pictorial*: crime (especially when violent), sex (suitably shrouded) and sport were their stock-in-trade.

Helped by the Jack the Ripper murders, the installation of the first Hoe rotary printing press in England and the invention of the system of offering papers to newsagents on sale or return, *Lloyd's Weekly*, in fact, exploited this formula so successfully that it later became the first newspaper in the world to reach a sale of a million. It was edited between 1852 and his death in 1857 by the *Punch* contributor Douglas Jerrold who wrote that minor Victorian literary classic, *Mrs. Caudle's Curtain Lectures*, thus establishing a bond between profitable sensationalism on

Sundays and literary good works on weekdays that was to be much cherished by a later chief proprietor of the *News of the World*, Lord Riddell, whose great pride it was to own not only the *News of the World* but also *John o' London's Weekly*. 'I suppose,' said a friend, 'you hope they'll accept it in mitigation of sentence on Judgment Day.'

The *News of the World* did not at first enjoy so unbroken an advance as *Lloyd's Weekly* but its staying power has proved greater. Indeed as a result of the spread of education the formula that attracted a hundred thousand readers in 1855 brought in eight million in 1955.

As was natural in the climate of those times even the sensational Sunday papers found space amidst their murders, rapes, prize-fights and horse races for more political news than is common with their successors. Sometimes they used pens that might make even the *Sunday Pictorial* envious, as when the *Weekly Dispatch*, defending the Duchess of Kent, Queen Victoria's mother, against some Tory criticism in *The Times* ('This sink of literary gall and political prostitution'), asked darkly: 'Would the Tories like to stimulate us to refer to certain scenes at Windsor Castle, St. James's Palace and Carlton House? . . . Ask where was the present King the morning of his brother's funeral? . . . What were his remarks the day he visited the Palace at Pimlico on the eve of his brother's death?' But for the most part they treated politics rather solemnly, as, indeed, the *News of the World* still does. Radical in tone—it was Douglas Jerrold who gave *Punch* much of its reforming flavour—they had a part of some considerable importance in forming popular democratic opinion during the campaign for Parliamentary reform, reserving their talent for sensation for crime and sport. But those who feel that the readers of the mass Sunday papers of today are given too much crime and pornography would have found equal cause for complaint a century ago. The Sabbath of the British newspaper reader has always been bloody and violent.

This then was the press when the last of the stamp taxes were removed. It was vigorous enough in many ways. The intellectual uplands of the quarterlies and the weekly reviews rang with energetic discourse, the mud flats of the Sunday press were noisy with life. But the great middle reaches were strangely silent. In the foreground of the picture where the daily press has its place there was, apart from the extraordinary institution of *The Times*, a great emptiness.

With the end of the Stamp Tax all this was changed. Morning papers at 2*d.* or 1*d.* sprang into existence in every great city in the country. Manchester, Liverpool, Birmingham, Bradford, Leeds, Newcastle, Nottingham, Sheffield, Darlington, Plymouth, and other English towns found themselves within a matter of weeks or even days possessed of strong daily organs of local opinion. Edinburgh and Aberdeen joined Glasgow in the possession of a daily press. So did Belfast. Never in history has there been so sudden and tremendous a flowering of the press. Many of the morning papers thus brought into existence by the repeal of the tax still flourish as powerful leaders of opinion in great communities, custodians of journalistic tradition at its best, untouched by the holocaust that has consumed so much of the provincial press in our own time. Among them are the *Yorkshire Post*, *The Scotsman*, the *Liverpool Post*, the *Glasgow Herald*, the *Birmingham Post* and the *Sheffield Telegraph* and one that has outgrown its regional beginnings to rival and at times surpass *The Times* itself as a national and world influence—the *Manchester Guardian*.

Some of these new morning papers were produced by men new to journalism, others, like the *Manchester Guardian*, were converted into dailies from weeklies or bi-weeklies. The *Guardian's* early experience, the foundation on which it now established itself as a daily, is typical of many of them.

It began as a radical weekly in 1821, started by a group of 'some of the most respectable and moderate persons in Manchester' to provide a vehicle for one of their number, John Edward Taylor, and had at first a circulation of a few hundred copies. Four years of strenuous life brought this to 2,000, and as is pointed out in the commemorative volume *C. P. Scott*

1846–1932: The Making of the Manchester Guardian, even a sale of this size was a formidable undertaking.

One of the significant features of the taxed newspaper was the slowness of its technological advance at a time when the first flood of the Industrial Revolution was bringing to many other industries vast new developments in machinery. The press on which the *Weekly Guardian* was first printed was capable of turning out only 150 copies an hour. The paper sold at 7*d.* and consisted of four solidly printed sheets of leading articles (a feature of the paper from the first), market news, court reports, foreign news culled from the London papers, and a condensed Parliamentary report three days old, although in its third issue the paper with remarkable enterprise presented its readers with a report of the Commons debate on the Peterloo massacre nine and a half columns long.

Progress was slow. The Reform Bill of which the paper was a forceful advocate was passed in 1832. By that time the population of Manchester had risen to more than 180,000. But the circulation of the *Guardian* which in politics became progressively more moderate after the Reform Act remained at not much more than 2,000. Even so it had the third largest circulation of any provincial paper in the country, exceeded only by the *Leeds Mercury* and the *Stamford Mercury*. It also ranked as the third outside London in the volume of the advertising it carried, being exceeded in this respect only by two mainly advertising sheets, one published in Birmingham and the other in Liverpool. Four years later it absorbed the *Manchester Volunteer* and so brought its circulation up to 3,400. A year after that, encouraged by the reduction in the stamp duty to 1*d.* and by the introduction of a new method of feeding paper to the printing press which increased its potential printing capacity to 1,500 pages an hour, it launched out into a Wednesday as well as a Saturday edition, both priced 4*d.*

By the time its founder, John Edward Taylor, died in 1842 it had in twenty-one years of life achieved a Saturday circulation of about 8,000—enough to give it the largest sale of any newspaper outside London—with the Chartist *Northern Star*, the *Leeds*

Mercury, the *Liverpool Mercury* and the *Stamford Mercury* not far behind. By 1855 it had a circulation of probably around 10,000 on Saturdays but a good deal less than this on Wednesdays. Out of its four pages two or three columns were normally given to leading articles, four or five to miscellaneous paragraphs of 'Local and Provincial Intelligence', another three or four to the Salford Sessions and the same or more to tightly packed reports of local public meetings. From the first those whose views were strongly opposed in the leader columns could be as sure of as good a showing as those whom the paper applauded. If 'hard' news were lacking the available space was taken up by a 'Domestic and Miscellaneous' feature, often close upon a page in length, consisting of solidly printed extracts of 'general interest' taken from the more serious of the weekly reviews and periodicals.

To the *Guardian* and to papers like it the removal of the Stamp Tax brought an immediate and remarkable transformation. They rapidly turned themselves into dailies, reduced their price, as the *Guardian* did, to 2d. and then to 1d., began to publish not only their own Parliamentary reports but also dispatches from their own correspondents abroad, and entered thunderously into debate on local, national and international affairs with the assurance of those speaking for communities in command of solid economic and political power.

Barnes had been able to make *The Times* an independent newspaper because he recognised the importance not only of metropolitan but also of provincial opinion and took pains to keep in touch with it through agents stationed in every part of the country. Now for the first time the provinces had their own daily voices growing steadily in authority. If the removal of the Stamp Tax had done no more than this, it would have to be accounted the beginning of a social revolution.

The consequences of the removal of the Stamp Tax were no less significant in London in this year of newspaper destiny.

On 29 June, just twenty-four hours before the formal demise of the Stamp Tax, the *Daily Telegraph and Courier* made its appearance: four pages, price 2*d*., but to be reduced in a few weeks to 1*d*. and shortened in name to the *Daily Telegraph*.

The new provincial dailies springing to life with such energy in every part of the country appealed to local interests but not in the main to popular ones. They were produced for provincial segments of that great middle public that read *The Times* and although for the most part they did not try to emulate its comprehensiveness, for they lacked the resources to do so, they accepted the journalistic principles that governed its conduct, applying them to a narrower field.

The *Daily Telegraph* and two other penny dailies that followed hard on its heels, the radical *Morning Star* and *Evening Star*, represented a break with the past of a much more fundamental character: the beginning of the end, indeed, of an attitude of mind that had governed 'respectable' British journalism from its earliest days. The repeal of the Stamp Tax—and it is in this even more than the financial relief it brought that its real significance lies—marked the defeat of an attitude of mind on the part of Governments which had determined the place of the press in British society for a century and a half and which provides the key to newspaper history throughout that period—the conviction that the lower orders could not be trusted. This conviction, it must be said, was shared by most of those who conducted newspapers as well as by those who taxed them. That is the reason why Cobbett, who spoke, or tried to, for the 'commons of England', hated *The Times* so much and why *The Times* hated his unstamped 'Twopenny Trash'. It explains also why most of the established papers, including not only *The Times* but the *Manchester Guardian* and most other leading provincial weeklies and bi-weeklies, were much less enthusiastic in the campaign for the abolition of the Stamp Tax than were radicals like Cobden, Bright and Milner-Gibson. Like the economist J. R. McCulloch in his *Dictionary of Commerce* published in 1854, they doubted whether 'the circulation of low-priced journals can ever be of advantage'.

This feeling that newspapers were safe only so long as they

were kept out of the hands of the general mass of the people stamped every stage of newspaper development up to the end of the first half of the nineteenth century. Only the new Sunday papers with their radical inclinations challenged it in any serious way and they devoted most of their space to crime, an activity thought less threatening than politics to public morals.

It was the formal official surrender of this position that made the repeal of the Stamp Tax so decisive an event in the history of the press. And it was the recognition that a general daily news-paper not only could but should be produced at a price within the reach of a wide public which made the penny *Daily Telegraph* symbolic of a revolution.

The *Daily News*, the 'Little Benjamin of the Press' as *The Times* derisively called it, had made an attempt to attract this public in 1846. After Charles Dickens's disastrous three weeks as its first editor, Charles Wentworth Dilke took over control as manager, with John Forster as editor, cut the price by half to $2\frac{1}{2}d$. and raised the circulation from 4,000 to 22,000. But at $2\frac{1}{2}d$. the paper was ahead of its time. It could not pay its way. Dilke tried $3d$. That was no good either. He had to go back to $5d$., at which price he lost more than three-quarters of his circulation but escaped bankruptcy, although in its first ten years of life the paper lost four times its original capital of £50,000.

Nine years later the repeal of the Stamp Tax had so altered not only the trading position of newspapers but the whole climate of public demand that whereas the $2\frac{1}{2}d$. *Daily News* had had to double its price to save itself from extinction the $2d$. *Daily Telegraph* had to halve its price to survive. At $2d$. it fell into such debt to its printer, Joseph Moses Levy, that there was nothing for him to do but take it over and see what a reduction in price would do. The effect was magical. Within a few weeks the sales of the $1d$. *Telegraph*, catering as it proudly declared not only for 'the highest classes'—there has rarely been a paper that has not claimed this—but for 'the million', exceeded that of all London papers, other than *The Times*, put together. That was merely a beginning.

Soon even the sales of *The Times* were passed. By its sixth birth-day the *Telegraph* had more than double that great paper's circulation although, after bringing down its price to 3*d.*, *The Times* was selling more than at any previous time in its history—over 65,000 copies a day. By the end of another ten years the *Telegraph's* sales had risen to more than 240,000 and it was able to print on its front page the proud boast: 'The Largest Circulation in the World'.

This triumph was in part achieved by emulating American popular journalism and even today *The Times* seems to find some difficulty in forgiving Levy for turning to American models to topple it from its circulation throne.

'The *Daily Telegraph* which in its maturity was to reach a notably high standard of journalism', stiffly remarks the author of the second volume of *The Times* official history, *The Tradition Established,* 'began that imitation by London newspapers of sensational New York journalism which, as was feared and prophesied in 1825 and 1855, has since gone far to destroy the English type of popular newspaper and periodical.'

In fact Levy's borrowing from American journalism was comparatively slight. He, and still more his son Edward, the first Lord Burnham, learnt something from America of the value of more and larger headlines and of a more human approach to news. They later shared with the *New York Herald* one of the most successful newspaper enterprises of all time, H. M. Stanley's expedition to Africa to find Livingstone. But although it shocked *The Times* and some others the *Telegraph* remained a very English paper.

In turning to American journalism for guidance in this new trade of writing for a large public Levy was moreover, whether consciously or not, paying recognition to the deeper revolution of which the *Daily Telegraph* was a part. British journalism had fought its way into existence under the constant shadow of official disapproval, the almost unremitting antagonism of the most powerful interests in the State. By concentrating within its own single grasp all the latent sources of power that journalism can command *The Times* had for a time turned the tables. But the press as a whole—and especially the new press 'for the million' represented by Levy's *Daily Telegraph*—was still inferior and still suspect. To prevent the development of cheap newspapers had proved impossible: that battle was lost with the removal of the Stamp Tax. But the idea that such newspapers could have any real importance—other than a potentially damaging one—or could play any useful part in public affairs was derisory. 'Could it be maintained', Lord Robert Cecil was to ask with aristocratic contempt when the last of the taxes on the press, the duty on newsprint, was repealed in 1861, 'that a person of any education could learn anything from a penny paper?'

It was far otherwise in America. So far from struggling to a position in which it might, when it behaved itself, aspire to deserve Macaulay's extravagant compliment that it had become the Fourth Estate, the American press occupied as of right from the beginning a position at the very heart of American society. Its power was accepted as paralleling, sometimes, indeed, almost exceeding, that of Government or Congress: a force as de Tocqueville said that 'impels the circulation and political life through all the districts of that vast territory'.

The United States had rejected—rejected indeed with the greatest vehemence as one of the necessities of its being—the influences of Monarchy, Lords and Clergy that had for centuries shaped British society, so colouring its various elements that the influence of the press upon it could at most be no more than marginal. The cement that bound together the non-hierarchical society of this new land, giving its scattered and often radically disparate communities a sense of membership in a common society with common ideas and common habits of life, was none of these ancient powers; it was more than anything else the press. 'Newspapers become more necessary in proportion as men become more equal', said de Tocqueville and within the egalitarian context of American society it was not too much to claim, as he did, that 'to suppose that they only serve to protect freedom would be to diminish their importance: they maintain civilisation'.

From the earliest days of the new republic when Hamilton and Madison put forward their proposals for a federal constitution in the columns of the *Daily Advertiser* and the *Independent Journal*, through all the expanding years of the first half of the nineteenth century, the press marched step by step with those who opened up a new continent. Hard on the heels of the sheriff, if not ahead of him, the newspaper editor set up his printing press in every frontier town; in the still developing legend of American history the great journalists moved with the Indian fighters, the railway pioneers, the cowboys, in a pageant that had to find new figures of heroic myth to replace the princes and prelates of European history. The American press was what kept America together, the ladle that stirred the vast melting pot of a new democracy. It had the confidence natural to its part in the making of a nation.

Nor was the power that belonged to the American press vested simply in the hands of a few great organs of opinion as that of the British press was. It was common to all. The power exercised in Britain by *The Times* was basically an extension of the general system of oligarchic power. It rested on the ability of one such power to bring pressure to bear on another. That exercised by the American press, however, derived wholly from its popular character. It was widely dispersed. And it was essentially democratic. American newspapers were selling at $1\frac{1}{2}d$. when those in Britain were still $7d$. At a time when no English city outside London could support a daily paper there was not a single town of 10,000 inhabitants in the whole of the United States that did not have at least one.

To the controllers of *The Times* and the members of the ruling classes of British society linked in mutual contempt of the masses and common fear of the impact of a popular press upon political opinion the American press could hardly seem other than noisy, vulgar and sensational, as indeed it often was. But to Levy and others of the new men grappling with the first possibility of popular journalism in Britain it must have seemed to possess something of the *élan* and panache, the liberating self-confidence, that inspires the armies of a successful revolution—such *élan* for example as the armies of Napoleon carried with them like a banner in their first march across Europe.

It was natural therefore that Levy should turn to American journalism for a model. It was the pioneer in a field which the British press was only now entering. In the years ahead it was to be shown that in England as in America the popular demand for newspapers could become one of the great social forces of the age and that the demand itself was almost insatiable once the price was reduced to a figure that put them within the reach of all. In 1851 there had been in the whole of the United Kingdom 563 newspapers of all kinds. By 1867 the number had grown to 1,294. By 1895 it was 2,304.

The rise in the circulation of the daily press, both collectively and individually, from that June day in 1855 when the Stamp Tax ended after more than 140 years was no less remarkable than the increase in the number of newspapers. Unlike the increase in numbers it is still continuing; a phenomenon of our times well summarised in one short paragraph by Mr. A. P. Wadsworth, whose death last year robbed modern journalism of one of its greatest figures and the *Manchester Guardian* of one of its most distinguished editors, in a valuable paper on 'Newspaper Circulations, 1800–1954' before the Manchester Statistical Society in March 1955. 'In 1800', he remarked, 'no paper had a daily circulation of more than 5,000. In 1850 no daily had more than 50,000. In 1905 none had more than 750,000. In 1955 there is one with getting on for 5,000,000.'

The day of the 5,000,000 sale for a single newspaper, of the more than 30,000,000 newspapers all told bought each twenty-four hours by the British people, was still distant when the *Daily Telegraph* came down to 1d. on 17 September 1855. But the movement had begun. If the popular press had not yet quite entered it was knocking at the door.

VIII

THE WORLD A FLEET STREET PARISH

THE barriers were down. The press was at last free to make its own way in the world governed only by the ambitions and talents of its several proprietors and editors.

Nor was it only the end of the taxed press that marked this as the beginning of a new period in newspaper history. If the price at which the *Daily Telegraph* was offered to the public symbolised one revolution its name was no less representative of another. The galvanic magnetic telegraph had arrived to transform the speed and scope of newspaper reporting: in some ways, indeed, to alter its nature almost out of all recognition.

Whether written for the serious consideration of statesmen and students of affairs or for the quick information and entertainment of a mass public a newspaper is a messenger from the outside world. Until the telegraph it had perforce been a messenger delayed. To reduce the gap between events and the receipt of news of them *The Times* had spent, by the standards of newspaper income and expenditure of the time, immense sums. On its 'Extraordinary Express' from India alone it paid well over £10,000 a year—far more than any other newspaper could afford. Its arrangements involved the permanent maintenance of a fast cross-channel steamer from Boulogne to Dover and the hiring of a special train from Dover to London. Highly paid agents were posted at Alexandria and Malta to transfer to fast steamers dispatches brought by overland desert route from Suez via Cairo. A special courier service was maintained from Marseilles to Boulogne—by travelling day and night without a pause the couriers did the journey in seventy-four hours. They were paid an annual retainer of £100 and £1 an hour on every trip they made. If by prodigious efforts they succeeded in cutting the seventy-four-hour schedule they were given a bonus of £2 for every hour saved.

The development of the electric telegraph made available an agency faster than the fastest courier or the speediest steamer and special train, infinitely quicker and more reliable than the pigeon post from Paris to Boulogne organised by *The Times* in 1837 (the birds did the journey in four hours as against a courier's fourteen) —and made that agency available to all. In 1825 the mails from Calcutta to Falmouth took nearly four months. Even when an overland route from Suez to Alexandria was opened ten years later the time was still nearly seven weeks. With the invention of the telegraph this was cut to days. Before long it was to be cut to hours, finally, for the most urgent messages, to minutes, until the whole world was shrunk to the size of a Fleet Street parish.

In 1844 is seemed amazing that with the aid of this 'extraordinary power' *The Times* should be able to announce the birth of a second son to Queen Victoria at Windsor a mere four hours after it had taken place: the news was transmitted along the new electric signalling system of the Great Western Railway and moved *The Times* to the unwonted extravagance of two single-column headlines. Six years later, Paris, Brussels and Berlin were all linked by telegraph. The year after that, the year of the Great Exhibition, the first submarine cable was laid between Dover and Calais, England and the Continent. The age of swift communication between nations had begun with all it meant to commerce, to private exchange and to the press. Everywhere now the cable advanced. Overland it went to India via Russia, Constantinople and the Persian Gulf. It moved on under the oceans to Singapore and China; to Japan which had begun its fateful rendezvous with the Western world scarcely twenty years earlier when Commander Perry sailed into Tokyo Bay; to Java and from Java to Port Darwin and the thriving new cities of Australia and New Zealand; across the Atlantic from Ireland to Newfoundland, gateway to the exuberant thrusting life of the United States with its tremendous future—although this took three attempts, one before, two after the Civil War—and from Europe to Brazil and so to the whole of the South American continent.

Wherever the cable went the newsmen followed, in their van the agents of a middle-aged German Jewish owner of a pigeon post between Cologne and Brussels whose name deserves to rank among the very first in the gallery of odd, extravagant, noble and curious characters who have for better or worse made British journalism what we know it today: Paul Julius Reuter.

Reuter was thirty-five when true to the instinct that was to guide him all his days he followed the cable to London in the year of the Great Exhibition. So far the electric telegraph had been his enemy. Its advance had 'relentlessly destroyed' his livelihood. But now, the pigeon post abandoned, he determined to make it his ally. From two rooms in Royal Exchange Buildings in the City he organised a commercial cable service of stock market prices between London and Paris, later extended to Amsterdam, Berlin, Vienna and Athens. But he had wider ambitions. He dreamed of a service of political news collected by his agents on the Continent for distribution to every newspaper in England and later perhaps to the Continent, although, there, Havas of Paris and Wolff of Berlin were ahead of him. It took him seven years to make a start.

The Times, the first object of his ambition, would have none of him. 'They generally found', replied Mowbray Morris, 'that they could do their own business better than anyone else.' He wasted a good deal of time trying to persuade Morris to change his mind but finally came to the sensible conclusion in December 1858—three years after the removal of the Stamp Tax—that if *The Times* would not listen to him he must try to get along without it, and called on James Grant, the editor of the *Morning Advertiser*. To him he offered free for two weeks a service of 'earlier, more ample, more accurate and more important information from the Continent' than the *Advertiser* received from its own correspondents. If the fortnight's free trial proved satisfactory the paper should thereafter take the same service for a fee of £30 a month, £10 a month less than it was paying for Continental telegrams. Reuter explained that he proposed to offer the same service to other newspapers and that he intended to confine himself to facts, leaving descriptions and exposition to individual newspaper correspondents. Speed and accuracy would be his watchwords.

Mr. Grant accepted his offer. So did the *Daily Telegraph*, the *Daily News*, the *Morning Herald*, the *Morning Post*, the *Standard*, the *Morning Chronicle* and the *Morning Star*. So too, indeed, did *The Times*, when the value of the service Mr. Reuter had to offer had been thoroughly demonstrated by other newspapers and the costs of the transatlantic cable were beginning to weigh heavily on its finances. Characteristically it was unwilling for some time to admit the fact in print, preferring to pay Mr. Reuter double for the privilege of not acknowledging the source of his telegrams. By 7 December 1858, however, even *The Times* was ready to give way and use his name as well as his material. One of the most famous names in British—indeed in world—journalism had arrived and an organisation begun that was to play a part of the most profound importance in the future history of the press. Today it has developed under the brilliant leadership of its present general manager, Sir Christopher Chancelor, and its editor, Mr. Walter Cole, into a great world news agency owned by the newspapers of four countries, Britain, Australia, New Zealand and India: the first and so far the only example of what is surely one of the most hopeful developments for the future of journalism, international cooperation in factual news-gathering on a world scale.

The advance of the cable and the complementary expansion of Mr. Reuter's service of basic news—wherever the cable went there his agents followed, soon they were to be found everywhere in the civilised world—was one of the major facts in the popularisation and democratisation of the press throughout the second half of the nineteenth century. The invention of the electric telegraph may well be regarded, indeed, as second only in importance to the invention of printing itself in the history of journalism.

For the first time it now became possible to report great events with an immediacy to excite the interest and stir the imagination of readers to whom the leisurely mailed dispatches of an earlier era, dealing of necessity with happenings already weeks or even months old, had made little appeal. Moreover the high premium placed on brevity and hard facts by the cost of cabling precipitated a revolution in reporting methods that did a great deal to end the prolixity of much previous newspaper writing and replace it by a direct and simple style more likely to appeal to the ordinary reader. By 1869 even Mowbray Morris, who sixteen years before had confessed himself sceptical of the telegraph's usefulness ('I do not much confide in the telegraph and I would it had never been invented', he wrote to *The Times's* Berlin correspondent) and had described the first transatlantic cable as 'a great bore', found it necessary, with whatever inward regrets, to write to T. A. Trollope, brother of the novelist and an occasional *Times* correspondent in Italy, warning him that 'the telegraph has superseded the news letter and has rendered necessary a different style and treatment of public subjects'.

The extension of the telegraph and the gradual development of a system of cheap rates for press messages sent at hours when normal commercial traffic was small stimulated the public appetite for news. With Julius Reuter's aid it also spread this news more widely, offering to all newspapers a foreign news service comparable to that previously possessed by *The Times* alone. As surely as the undermining of its favoured trading position by the removal of the Stamp Tax marked the beginning of the end of that political 'despotism' of which *The Times* had been accused for thirty-five years, so did the swift development of international telecommunications end its former exclusive position in the field of foreign information. A window was opened through which the readers of the penny press could, if they so wished, enjoy a view of the world hardly less comprehensive than that offered by *The Times* itself.

This advantage did not at first extend to the new provincial dailies. Paradoxically the immediate consequence of the arrival of the telegraph so far as they were concerned was not to raise but lower their journalistic standards. The *Manchester Guardian* in its first few years as a morning paper carried not only its own excellent Parliamentary reports but also long mailed dispatches from correspondents in Paris, Berlin, Hamburg, Vienna, Trieste, Danzig, Naples, Brussels, New York and Rio de Janeiro, providing a service of responsible and informed foreign intelligence such as no provincial newspaper audience had ever before been able to enjoy. But with the development of telegraphic communication it fell into a bog of mediocrity, a bog that for a time engulfed the whole of the provincial press.

The reason for this is to be found in the ambition of the British and foreign telegraph companies. Conscious of the immense potentialities of the means of rapid news-transmission that they controlled they sought also to make a corner in the news itself, establishing their own service and endeavouring to force all newspapers to accept it by imposing prohibitive rates for individual press messages, which, indeed, in some cases they refused to accept at all.

This attempt to turn a communications monopoly into a news monopoly Reuters and the London newspapers were for the most part powerful enough to resist: 'We would much rather remain in ignorance of information conveyed in such a manner,' growled Mowbray Morris when a German telegraph company sought to impose such an arrangement. The provincial papers were less fortunate in their dealings with those who controlled the internal telegraph system on which they depended for the relaying of messages from London. They found themselves compelled by the smallness of their individual financial resources to bow to the monopoly power of the telegraphic companies and accept at a fee fixed by them a single ill-written, ill-edited service of foreign and Parliamentary news compiled by telegraph clerks without journalistic experience or sense of public responsibility.

In somewhat similar circumstances the New York newspapers

had earlier taken the bold line of establishing a cooperative organisation of their own—the Associated Press of New York —for the collection and transmission of foreign news. Now, led by John Edward Taylor, owner of the *Manchester Guardian* and son of its founder, the Association of Proprietors of Daily Provincial Newspapers decided to take a similar step. It formed a cooperatively owned Press Association to distribute Parliamentary, foreign and domestic news to its members and called on the Government to end the 'despotic and arbitrary management' of the private telegraphic companies.

The telegraph companies had overreached themselves. The Select Committee appointed to examine the provincial newspapers' complaints recommended that the whole of the internal telegraphic administration should be taken out of the hands of private interests and put under the control of the Post Office which should provide preferential rates for press messages but not itself collect and sell news.

In February 1870 the Press Association sent out its first telegraphed dispatch from London to member newspapers all over the country. Another name that was to become no less famous in British journalism than Reuter's had been written into newspaper history.

But it was not only in the transmission of news that a revolution took place halfway through the century. The whole character of the printing industry was transformed under the stimulation of the new market opened up by the end of the Stamp Tax.

As one looks back on the history of newspaper development the slowness of its technological advance before 1855 seems particularly amazing. The printing presses that produced Bell's *World* and Perry's *Morning Chronicle* and Stuart's *Morning Post* hardly differed in any important respect from that on which the first copies of the *Canterbury Tales* were printed. When John Walter I began publication of his *Daily Universal Register* in 1785 the whole resources of his printing works were sufficient to produce only 500 copies of a four-page paper throughout a whole night. Not until John Walter II, a true man of his time, excited by mechanical discovery and breathing deep of the air of the Industrial Revolution, called in two Saxon engineers, Friedrich Koenig and Andreas Bauer, to experiment in adapting steam power to printing in 1814 was there any break with hand printing. Yet without steam printing it is doubtful whether even the genius of Barnes could have given *The Times* its power and independence. By its means Walter was enabled to print 7,000 copies of an eight-page paper every night and thus secure the revenue from sales and advertisements that freed him from dependence on party funds or private bribes.

But although after 1814 steam did the work of man and did it many times as fast, the technique of printing from type locked in chases on a flat bed which had been employed for more than three centuries remained, despite some improvements, basically unchanged for another four decades. Nor were such improvements as were brought about in the press room by Walter's energy paralleled in the composing room. All type was set by hand almost identically as Johann Gutenberg had done in 1440 when he first composed movable types cast in a mould and after inking transferred their impression to damp sheets of paper in a press modelled on that used for pressing grapes.

The new popular newspaper that became possible with the end of the Stamp Tax was still tied mechanically to the past.

Within two years of the removal of the newspaper Stamp Tax, however, John Walter III was forced to take action by the competition of the new penny press and the complaints of the newsagents about delays in delivery. These complaints *The Times* could no longer brush aside as it had been able to do when it was without serious rival, and it began experiments which were to revolutionise large-scale daily newspaper production.

The limitations inherent in the principle of a flat bed moving slowly backwards and forwards beneath a roller which pressed sheets of paper on to the inked face of the type had been clear for some time to Walter and others. It was slow and it was costly; a major break with the past was essential if the speed of newspaper production was to keep pace with rising demand. But what form could it take? One answer seemed to lie in some method of rotary printing by which paper would be printed from rollers rotating more quickly than a flat bed could move backwards and forwards. But the problem was how to fit straight lines of type to a round surface.

Walter's chief printing engineer, Augustus Applegath, had earlier tried to get over this by using a polygonal cylinder on each face of which a column of type was clamped and which then rotated vertically. This was quicker than flat-bed printing but could print only in columns, not pages.

Moreover there was another obstacle to faster production. Each page or column had to be set separately for each press, whether flat or rotary. If, as was the case in *The Times* office, a number of presses had to be used to carry the printing load the whole of the paper had to be set several times over by hand at great cost. There was also the risk of long delays in the composing room, which had to carry as many as 1,500,000 separate pieces of type to cope with the nightly demand.

Because of the urgent need to increase printing capacity following the removal of the Stamp Tax John Walter invited an eminent printing engineer, James Dellagana, to carry out a series of experiments for him. Two years after the ending of the tax Dellagana hit on a method as simple in conception as such epoch-making discoveries often are which overcame both difficulties at the same time. Using damp *papier-mâché* board, he produced moulds from each page of type into which molten lead could be poured to make as many stereotype plates as were required. This in itself brought an immense saving in cost and time by doing away with the need for resetting. But this was not all. By bending the *papier-mâché* moulds into a half-circle before the casting process curved stereotype plates could be made for clamping on to the vertical cylinders of Applegath's improved press.

Across the Atlantic other experiments in rotary printing were going on. In Philadelphia William Hoe produced for the *Public Ledger* a horizontal cylinder rotary press using fixed type but capable of a much greater speed than Applegath's vertical one. The inventive genius of the Old and the New World met: the curved stereotype plate invented in Printing House Square was, to the benefit of both, married to the horizontal rotary press invented in Philadelphia.

Still John Walter was not satisfied. Great as was the advance made by these new horizontal rotary presses, they shared one limitation with the old flat-bed presses; they printed only on one side of a sheet of paper at a time. He saw that by feeding paper over and under two cylinders both carrying stereotype plates the rotary principle could be perfected to print both sides of a sheet in one operation and the speed of printing doubled. That was the next advance.

Now the paper trade took a hand. Until 1861 when the paper duty ended paper was both expensive and poor in quality. The removal of the duty stimulated enterprise in the paper-making trade no less than the ending of the Stamp Tax had stimulated it in the printing industry. New sources of raw material of which the most important was wood pulp were developed and the strength and quality of paper improved. The paper trade was in a position to assist in the next big development of the printing press. This came when John Walter hit upon the idea of adapting to newspaper publishing the method used by textile printers of printing designs on to a continuous roll of material. Paper strong enough to be wound on and off a roller instead of having to be fed into the press in separate sheets was produced and in 1866 the Walter Press printing on both sides of the paper from a continuous roll came into operation. It was capable of printing 10,500 copies of *The Times* an hour and embodied all the basic principles of rotary letterpress still relied on today. The giant printing presses of modern newspaper production each covering 3,700 square feet or so of floor space and capable of running off 50,000 copies or more of a full-sized newspaper an hour had begun to take shape.

Meanwhile under the stress of this age of competition in Britain and expansion in the United States a comparable revolution was being prepared in the composing room, although here it came even more slowly. Attempts to speed up hand-setting by mechanical aids and later to replace it altogether by the invention of composing machines had been going on since 1822 on both sides of the Atlantic—Mark Twain, at one time a journeyman printer, ruined himself financing one of them. But not until as late as 1872 was the first mechanical composing machine operated by a keyboard introduced into Printing House Square. It doubled the speed of setting. Three years later a method of casting lead type new for each setting instead of using the same type over and over again until it was worn out was devised. And then from America came the Linotype capable of setting and casting complete lines of type as fast as an operator could work a keyboard. The twenty-six soldiers of lead had been transformed into a mechanical army.

But although mechanically the press had been transformed from a trade into an industry editorially it remained a profession.

The young lions of the *Daily Telegraph* had let fresh air into it. They had harnessed the winds of 'sensationalism' from across the Atlantic and adapted American methods, or some of them, to British tastes. G. A. Sala, the *Telegraph's* famous descriptive writer, was verbose and highly coloured but he brought gusto and humanity back to journalism after its long sojourn in the higher realms of politics: he had the popular touch. So had Clement Scott, its dramatic critic, and Le Sage, its correspondent in the Franco-Prussian War and later its editor. As for Dr. Emile Joseph Dillon, its correspondent in Russia and wherever else there were international secrets to be found, with his formidable accomplishments of learning (he could write equally brilliantly in five languages), his mysterious past and his intimate friendship with emperors and ambassadors he was designed by nature to give the public just the romantic picture of a great foreign correspondent it wanted. On the *Daily News*, now down to 1*d*. and selling 150,000 copies a day as a result of the Franco-Prussian War, was Archibald Forbes, a war-correspondent of genius who used the telegraph with a disregard of cost unknown before and who, as a distinguished later editor of his paper, R. J. Cruickshank, has said, 'rarely waited for the end of a battle to report it and sometimes did not even wait for the beginning'. With him was Labouchere, who sent gay dispatches from besieged Paris by balloon, and brought to journalism a similar zest and exuberance.

But although a new and more popular spirit was moving in journalism its purpose remained very much the same. So for that matter did its appearance. These Victorian papers were written to be read—to be read by a wider public than formerly, but still to be read. The era of vast headlines and exciting typographical display, of papers to catch the eye, had not yet arrived. Headings were small and limited in number, even cross-heads to break up the long columns were as yet hardly respectable although they were coming into use—*The Times* stuck out against them until 1890. Whether they were new or old, produced 'for the million' or for solemn men in club chairs, all including the most 'popular' assumed that those who bought them were primarily concerned to be informed about the world and assisted in reaching sound judgments about what was taking place in it.

They were political papers; more political in a partisan sense, indeed, even than those of a few years previously, for the truce in the party struggle that Palmerston's habit of mind and dominating political position had imposed had ended with his death. The party struggle was back, and back with more distinct frontiers than ever before, for these frontiers now represented deep differences of principle and found dramatic expression in the Parliamentary battles of Gladstone and Disraeli, both men to attract to themselves the deepest feelings of admiration or dislike. In such circumstances the freedom from party that Barnes and Delane had thought a necessary part of journalistic independence seemed to men swayed by political passion not merely irrelevant but immoral—and those who owned, edited and wrote for newspapers were all still predominantly men of passion, not of commerce. They took heed of their figures but gave even more thought to their souls, regarding circulation as less important than public respect. So much so, indeed, that they ignored most of the opportunities for greater circulation that opened before them as the century drew to a close. In this matter they were soon to be taught a lesson.

Nor was it only the morning papers that thus held to an old tradition. Although the leading evening papers carried the new techniques of writing and display learned from the other side of the Atlantic farther than did the morning papers and often disturbed them by doing so, they were no less unconcerned about circulation as an end in itself.

Under Frederick Greenwood the *Pall Mall Gazette* brought wit, lightness, urbanity and intellectual polish back into journalism at a time when the morning press had turned staid and dull. But it never reached a circulation of more than 9,000. That of the *Globe*, the *Evening Standard* and *St. James's Gazette*, which Greenwood founded when a change in the proprietorship of the *Pall Mall* led to a change in its politics, was of the same order. Even under W. T. Stead, the most brilliant 'popular' journalist of his day, who introduced the interview into journalism, the *Pall Mall* never reached much more. In the course of his six years of exciting editorship (Lord Milner who worked as his assistant editor for a time called him in a phrase that might provide the recipe for every good popular newspaper editor, 'a compound of Don Quixote and Phineas T. Barnum', adding 'it was such fun to work with him') he stimulated, annoyed, bedazzled and out-raged public opinion, bringing back into journalism a note of thunder that had not been heard since Barnes's day.

But he did not get, nor much concern himself with getting, a large circulation. His crusades against commercialised vice and the exploitation of the poor were genuine and not synthetic. They were not dreamed up to catch readers but arose from a deep social and political passion. He was often accused of sensationalism. But he would have thought the whipping up of sensation for its own sake immoral. When he wrote 'The Maiden Tribute of Modern Babylon' to expose the horrors of a white slave traffic to which polite society preferred to close its eyes, and himself 'procured' a girl of fifteen in order to shock the House of Commons into raising the age of consent (then only thirteen) he was not trying to titivate the senses of his readers under the guise of exposing evil. He was fighting wrong with all the force, courage and rectitude he possessed. When he opened his 'Maiden Tribute' articles with the words 'The report of our secret commission will be read today with a shuddering horror that will thrill throughout the world', he did not do so because he and his circulation manager had decided that was the way to 'get them'. He used those words because he genuinely believed they were true and that it could not be otherwise if the Christian morality to which he so passionately subscribed meant anything at all.

The 'Maiden Tribute' campaign landed him in prison for three months but its effect on the circulation of the *Pall Mall Gazette* was such as to drive the circulation manager of a modern popular paper to drunkenness and despair. It remains indeed, as A. P. Wadsworth has commented in his paper to the Manchester Statistical Society, 'Newspaper Circulations, 1800–1954', one of the oddest things in newspaper history that this magnificent piece of muck-raking containing almost every ingredient of circulation-raising only succeeded in putting up the *Pall Mall Gazette's* sale from 8,360 to 12,250. The *Pall Mall* was not, however, as Stead must have well known, the sort of paper likely in view of its 'polite' readership to benefit much commercially from such a campaign. But the Criminal Law Amendment Bill was passed because of it. It was this, not circulation, that Stead cared about.

The end of the Stamp Tax, the revolution in communications and newspaper production methods, the fall in the price of paper, all these had altered the newspaper pattern enormously. In the case of some morning papers circulation figures had been achieved of an order such as had scarcely been dreamed possible before. Yet despite the immense changes that had taken place in the previous thirty-five years, the total circulation of the morning and evening press in the nineties was still astonishingly small by the standards that were shortly to rule: probably not much more than three-quarters of a million for the whole of the London press together, not a great deal more than a million for the daily press of the entire country.

Now, however, the curtain was about to rise on a very different scene and the comedy—or melodrama—of press and public to take a very different turn.

IX

NORTHCLIFFE MOVES IN

THE makers of the new journalism had done much. But they had failed to notice one thing. Or perhaps for all the *Daily Telegraph's* talk of a paper for 'the million' they were not much interested in it. They had forgotten the Elementary Education Act of 1870.

When this Act was passed and still more by the time it began to produce results they had already grown set in their ways. The new public for which they catered when the end of the Stamp Tax made expansion possible was essentially a middle-class public; the public of the ambitious petit bourgeoisie making its way in the world. Like all such groups in the hierarchical structure of British society it aped its social betters. It could neither afford nor digest *The Times*. The *Morning Post* was too aristocratic and High Tory for its taste: a paper for dukes—or their butlers. What it wanted was a respectable cheap substitute for the daily reading matter of the superior classes looking, as all the best substitutes do, as much like the original as possible but easier on an unsophisticated palate. After its first flirtation with American methods, this the *Daily Telegraph* settled down to become, shedding its original radicalism in the process. The *Morning Standard* which had been Conservative from the start served the same public in a less 'popular' way, while the Liberal middle-class public took the *Daily News*, livelier in tone but equally sedate in appearance. To appeal to Liberal Unionists of the shopkeeper class there was the *Daily Chronicle* recently converted from a London local weekly, the *Clerkenwell News*, and bought by Edward Lloyd of *Lloyd's Weekly News* fame.

Such papers were for men established in their station in society, or on the way to being so; men with morning coats and top hats—at least on Sundays. They were—these journals of the Victorian interlude whose shadow falls so far—heavily political, long-winded, and restricted in interest: much more so in the 'nineties than they had been in the first exuberance of the new journalism of forty years previously, a great deal more so than the journalism of the eighteenth century. They almost entirely ignored the fact that even women could read and they were for the most part by now extremely dull. This quality of dullness had become indeed one of their virtues. It gave those who read them moral confidence.

Below, unseen or ignored by the proprietors and editors of these papers, the new literates of the Board Schools were emerging, a lower middle and working class public, ambitious, eager to educate and amuse itself: the public of the white-collar worker, the shop assistant, the skilled artisan, of the man and a girl on a bicycle on Saturday afternoon; the new public that was to change the face of journalism. Other journalists in earlier times had been aware of the public of the working class. Cobbett had written for it, although it was a different working class then. So had Hetherington with his *Poor Man's Guardian* and Charles Knight with his *Penny Magazine* which sold 200,000 copies a week when it first appeared in 1832 and John Cassell with *Cassell's Magazine* and *Cassell's Illustrated Family Paper*. So even now did the popular Sunday papers. And there were one or two newspaper men in the provinces, among them Edward Hulton of Manchester, who had started developing $\frac{1}{2}d$. evening papers to meet the new popular taste for sport which had come to life with the first Association Football Cup Tie in 1871, the first Australian Test Match in 1878, and the beginning of professional football in 1885. But the major newspaper publishers ignored this public; it is indeed surely one of the oddest things about the Victorian age, so full of good works and so commercially minded, that the commercial potentialities of the vast new market created by good works in the shape of popular education left most of those professionally engaged in journalism uninterested.

The new public pushing its excited way through the door of popular education was left to be discovered not by a journalist but by the thirty-year-old representative of a London fancy-goods firm living in Manchester: George Newnes. He came upon it— it is probably still one of the basic recipes for success in mass journalism—by backing his own taste. In his case the taste was for snippets of information and odd facts about people and things: the same taste, in fact, as inspired the *Athenian Mercury* in 1690 or inspires the *Reader's Digest* today. He was a great snipper of newspapers. 'Now that,' he said to his wife one evening, reading a paragraph from an evening paper, 'is what I call an interesting tit-bit. Why doesn't someone bring out a whole paper made up of tit-bits like that?' 'Why don't you?' she said, being a practical woman.

Newnes had a scrapbook full of cuttings. But he lacked capital. He got it by exploiting another popular taste of the moment; he opened a vegetarian restaurant. The profits gave him the money to start his paper. He called it *Tit-Bits from all the Most Interesting Books, Periodicals and Newspapers of the World* and sold it at a penny. It consisted of sixteen large pages, each of three columns, and everything in it was short. There were no politics. The first number came out on 30 October 1881, and its impact was immediate and lasting. It is not too much to say, indeed, as the *History of The Times*, commenting with due seriousness on its arrival, has remarked, that this penny paper of scraps culled by Newnes from odd sources was 'destined to modify in the most profound degree, the intellectual, social and political tone of the Press as a whole'.

Probably Newnes himself would have been more surprised than anyone if he could have foreseen the effect of his brain-child on the daily press. His own idea of a daily paper remained austere, as he showed eleven years later when he decided to use some of the profits of *Tit-Bits* and its brilliant stable companion the *Strand Magazine* to start an evening paper in the Liberal interest and launched the *Westminster Gazette*. On this he lost between £10,000 and £15,000 a year with unruffled cheerfulness for sixteen years.

The *Daily Courier* which he started as a penny morning paper in 1896 had even less popular success. It lasted only a few months.

Tit-Bits was a different cup of tea. Without realising it Newnes had stuck a vein of untapped gold.

The printer he went to in Manchester refused to handle the first number unless he was paid cash in advance so certain was he that it would fail. Six weeks later he was offering the young man from the fancy-goods firm £16,000 for it. This Newnes sensibly refused. Within three months he moved to London and before any of the established publishers woke to what was going on around them had a sale of 900,000—three times as much as the circulation of the *Daily Telegraph*.

He gave the public of the newly educated exactly what it wanted: potted, easily assimilated information. He brought it to their notice with a series of exciting sales-promotion campaigns like the burying of bags of golden sovereigns for discovery by those clever enough to spot the clues hidden in a serial story. At first his tit-bits were taken from books, magazines and newspapers but later, following the same pattern as the *Reader's Digest* in our own day, he included original material also. Everything was short, everything was written simply and clearly: a predigested literary breakfast food for all the family.

What was even more important was that for the first time the new paper offered advertisers a channel direct to the heart of the vast new mass-market of the ambitious lower middle class eager to raise itself in the world by buying the branded goods and cheap products that industry was now capable of turning out at an ever-expanding rate. The sales of *Tit-Bits* made Newnes wealthy, its advertising revenue gave him a great fortune.

The lesson passed the established newspaper proprietors and journalists by. The contempt and distrust of the lower orders that had for so long governed the attitude of all Governments to the press had transferred itself to them also. It was fifteen years before Newnes's discovery found expression in a morning newspaper and even then the lesson was applied, not by one of the established newspaper publishers nor, for that matter, by Newnes himself, but by a young man who was a schoolboy of sixteen when *Tit-Bits* was started and who became one of its earliest contributors: Alfred Charles William Harmsworth, later Lord Northcliffe.

Although the solid phalanx of the serious—and for the most part very dull—morning press remained unbroken the possibility that the readers discovered by *Tit-Bits* might like a newspaper of their own did not, however, go altogether unnoticed. Six years after *Tit-Bits* appeared a brilliant Irish journalist, T. P. O'Connor who had worked on the *Daily Telegraph* and in the London office of the *New York Herald* and found English newspapers stuffy and obsolete, persuaded a group of rich Liberals that the way to make Liberalism successful was to make democracy attractive. He proposed to do it through an evening paper that should be 'animated, readable and stirring'.

The *Star*, the first of the modern evening papers, was the result. When it appeared on 17 January 1888, it was unlike anything seen on the London streets before. Its headlines clamoured for attention in a size and variety never previously known outside America. Everything about it was bright, brisk, and human. Its longest article was only half a column—and there was only one of that length. It was as crisp, cheerful, humorous and common-sensical as a Cockney bus conductor—it still is—and its first number sold 142,000 copies at $\frac{1}{2}d.$, half the price of the lordly *Pall Mall*, *Standard*, *Globe* and *St. James's*.

The *Star* was not the first $\frac{1}{2}d.$ evening paper. *The Echo*, owned by a philanthropic businessman, Passmore Edwards, already sold at that price. But Passmore Edwards felt he had a mission to uplift, not merely to amuse, his readers and refused to publish racing tips. The *Star's* 'Captain Coe' on the other hand was a great hand at picking winners. There was also the $\frac{1}{2}d.$ *Evening News*. This started life as a Liberal evening paper in 1881 but lost so much money that its backers were glad to sell it to the other side. It now combined a doctrinaire support for Con-servatism with the strong conviction that all the halfpenny paper public really cared for was crime.

But although there were other $\frac{1}{2}d.$ papers there was nothing else like the *Star* with its bold headlines, its impudent contents bills ('The Pope: No News' it shouted at the street corners one dull day and sold thousands to those who believed that this strictly truthful statement must mean something very different), its interviews, signed articles and human touch. It was the first newspaper wholeheartedly to acknowledge the fact of a new public. It did not make the mistake of talking down to it. Bernard Shaw wrote about music in its pages, A. B. Walkley about plays, Richard Le Gallienne about books, W. T. Hewart, later Lord Chief Justice, was its leader writer. Not only was it the first genuine expression of the new journalism, it was its school and university. It bred editors. No less than eight first learned their trade on its staff: there was a time, in fact, when you could hardly open an editorial door in Fleet Street without finding a *Star* man sitting behind the desk—Robert Donald, H. W. Massingham, Thomas Marlowe, James Douglas, Ernest Parke, W. T. Evans, Clement K. Shorter all acquired by its twinkling light the skills they later took to such diverse papers as the *Daily Chronicle*, the *Nation*, the *Daily Mail*, the *Sunday Express*, the *Morning Leader*, the *Evening News* and the *Sphere*.

But although the *Star* attracted readers it did not attract money. T. P. O'Connor was a remarkable journalist but he was no business-man. He lacked a John Walter II. The paper's backers were politicians, not business-men. They wanted a sound, disciplined party paper and although T. P. O'Connor gave them much he did not give them this. After two years of brilliant although sometimes spasmodic editorship he was induced to sell his personal interest in the paper for £17,000. When the term of his undertaking not to start a rival expired he tried his hand with a new venture, the ½d. *Sun*. But although it shone brightly it lacked financial resources and did not last.

On the *Star* H. W. Massingham moved to the editor's chair. But only for six months. At the end of that time he too was judged unsatisfactory by the paper's political owners. They considered him 'socialistic' and asked him to resign. In his place Professor James Stuart, M.P., a close friend of Mr. Gladstone assumed editorial responsibility, with a working journalist, Ernest Parke, as managing editor. The first attempt to provide a popular newspaper for the masses had been put on political ice, although Ernest Parke continued to do his best to turn the ice into ice cream—with flavouring.

The new public had to wait another six years for journalism to catch up with it, although two ½d. morning papers were started during this period, one of them, the *Leader*, as a companion to the *Star*, the other, *Morning*, as a Conservative rival. Both, however, were strongly political, as much captives of the party organisations as any of their penny rivals or as the eighteenth-century press before Barnes. Although the *Leader* survived for twenty years until it was finally absorbed in the *Daily News* neither it nor *Morning* made any real impact on the new, eager but largely non-party political public of the lower middle classes.

This then was the position when the future Lord Northcliffe moved on to the newspaper stage—bringing with his coming a violent shift in the action of the play, indeed one might almost say the beginning of a new one of a different kind.

Northcliffe was five years old when the Education Bill was passed. As his father was a barrister, although an unsuccessful one, he came of a social class that would have preferred bankruptcy to sending its children to a Board School. Since his parents could not afford a public school he went, naturally, to a private one— rather a good one as it happened, owned by A. A. Milne's father, who earlier had H. G. Wells as one of his ushers. This he left when he was sixteen.

But although he did not belong by birth or schooling to the lower middle class he was almost an adoptive member of it. When he left school he sold articles to *Tit-Bits* and then landed a job on the staff of a cycling paper called *Wheel Life* published by William Iliffe. In its interests he pedalled furiously about the countryside attired, according to his brother Cecil, in a uniform like that of a skating master. Cycling was in its beginning as a great popular pastime. It was more than a form of exercise, much

more than a means of transport. It was a way of life: an enrich-
ment and escape for thousands of Mr. Pollys and Mr. Kipps's, a
means to wider horizons and the promise of opportunity. There
could have been no better apprenticeship for one who was to
make a fortune out of reading matter for the newly educated
masses than the club rallies and club dinners at which the youthful
Harmsworth was so regular and popular a guest as the representative of *Wheel Life* and later as the editor (commencing
salary £2 10s. a week) of *Bicycling News*.

By the time he was thirty-one and ready to launch into morning
journalism Northcliffe had probably a livelier appreciation of the
tastes, ambitions, potentialities and limitations of the immense
new reading public created by the Act of 1870 than most men in
Britain. To think as it did, but at a level infinitely more charged
with energy and imagination, had become second nature to him.

This flair for knowing what the public wanted and giving it to
them he had first demonstrated in *Answers*, a weekly penny paper
designed on the same lines as *Tit-Bits* ('a weekly storehouse of
interesting information' said the first advertisement) which he
launched when he was twenty-one with a capital of £1,000, most
of it from his own savings. *Answers* was followed by a host
of other cheap periodicals aimed—and always aimed successfully
—at the same market: *Answers* for the family, *Comic Cuts* for
the children, *Chips* for the errand boy, *Forget-me-Not* for the
factory girl, *Home Chat* for the housewife—the list grew longer
and longer. *Home Sweet Home*, the *Funny Wonder*, *Union Jack*,
Halfpenny Marvel, *Sunday Companion*, *Boys' Friend*, *Pluck
Library*—there was not one of them that did not make money.
All came into existence within seven years of the starting of
Answers and within thirteen of Newnes's discovery of the lower
middle class.

Newnes, after his first success with *Tit-Bits*, went after a
higher readership taste with the *Review of Reviews* and the *Strand
Magazine*. Northcliffe stuck to the original paying lode. And to
an even greater degree than Newnes or than Arthur Pearson
(the third of those who built great publishing businesses on the

foundation laid by the 1870 Education Act and of somewhat higher social and educational class than the other two, a Wykehamist—like the present chairman of the *Daily Mirror*) Northcliffe understood the importance of advertising and the value of stunts in attracting readers. *Answers* began slowly. It soared to success when Northcliffe offered a prize of £1 a week for life for the best guess of the amount of money in the Bank of England on a certain day—the prize was won by a sapper in the Ordnance Survey Department whose guess came to within £2 of the correct total. More than 700,000 people went in for the competition and as each competitor was required to send the signatures of five witnesses to his identity *Answers* became known to millions. A competition for a house followed and then one for £2 a week for life. (There is incidentally an interesting piece of social research still to be done on the kind of newspaper prizes that attract people at various stages in the social ethos: £1 a week for life in the closing decades of the nineteenth century; an invitation for two to the wedding of Miss Grace Kelly and the Prince of Monaco plus a private yacht anchored in the bay for a week and £1,000 to spend in the middle of the twentieth in the judgment of the *Daily Express*, a country pub in that of the *Daily Sketch*.) After that the law stepped in. Such guessing competitions were declared illegal. But Northcliffe had discovered the secret of success. Produce reading matter for a mass public and then sell it in the same way as any other article of commerce. Advertise it. Make it talked about. What you say about your product is just as important as the product itself. What other people can be made to say about it is even more so. It was the magic formula of the new age of journalism.

Within four years of the offer of £1 a week for life *Answers* was floated as a public company with a capital of £275,000. Three years later it and all the other periodicals in the Harmsworth Group were turned into a public company, Harmsworth Brothers Limited, with a capital of £1,000,000.

It was with this success in periodical publishing to stand on that Northcliffe ventured into the morning newspaper field in May

1896. Two years previously an opportunity to apply to an evening paper the lessons learnt from *Answers, Comic Cuts, Home Chat* and the rest had come his way. Kennedy Jones, a journalist trained first on the *Birmingham Daily Mail* and' then under T. P. O'Connor on the *Sun*, of which he was chief sub-editor, sought him out and offered to sell him an option to buy the *Evening News* for £25,000. This had come Jones's way through a friend of his, a reporter on the *Sun* named Louis Tracy, who had friends among the Conservative backers of the *Evening News*. They had sunk £200,000 in the property and had decided it was time to stop. Jones and Tracy had the option but no money. They offered it to Harmsworth for a 7½% interest each in the business and jobs on the staff. He took it, met the *Evening News* proprietors, persuaded them to sell for £23,000 instead of £25,000 (£5,000 was in cash the rest in shares) and launched into daily journalism.

The venture quickly proved—as T. P. O'Connor's *Star* had earlier done—that the principles of the cheap periodical press could be applied with equally startling results to newspapers. In its previous fourteen years of existence the *Evening News* had never made a profit. In Harmsworth's first year it made £25,000: £2,000 more than he had paid in cash and shares for the whole of the property including machinery. Thereafter it moved forward with unchecked momentum to the largest circulation of any evening paper in the world.

T. P. O'Connor's journalistic talent had foundered on party political control and lack of an efficient commercial partner. Northcliffe was free of the one and had the other. The previous owners of the *Evening News* were in no position to dictate political terms when they sold it and he had his own John Walter II in the family in the person of his brother Harold, later the first Lord Rothermere (not since Napoleon has any man enriched the nobility with so many of his relations as Northcliffe did; by the time he was done he and Harold were viscounts, another brother was a baron and the two youngest were baronets).

Although Harold had his brother's liking for personal power he

had little of his journalistic flair or instinct for popular feeling:
the *Mail* became progressively more reactionary when it fell into
his sole control after Northcliffe's death until he was in some
danger of finishing it off altogether when he turned it pro-fascist
and anti-Jewish in the 1930s. But he was a business-man and
financier of genius. From the day that his mother—the real head
of the family, a woman of great force of character—made him
throw up his £4 a week job as a twenty-year-old clerk in the
Mercantile Marine Department of the Board of Trade to help her
elder son Alfred out of the business tangle he had got into with
Answers he gave to the Harmsworth publications what John
Walter II had given to *The Times*: a firm commercial foundation
for expansion. He was an unattractive character, narrow, egotistical
and boorish, although like many such rich men given in latter
years to large-scale public benevolence. But without him the
mercurial and infinitely more attractive Northcliffe could not
have made the impact he did on the history of journalism. The
other brothers were brought in to benefit from Alfred's
prosperity; Harold made that prosperity secure.

With impressive profits from his periodicals to support him
and the success of the *Evening News* to prove that the Harmsworth
touch was just as effective in news as in cheap magazines. Northcliffe was ready for the next step. The moment had arrived for
the birth of the *Daily Mail*.

In retrospect that newspaper, marking as it did from its first
number so decisive a watershed in the relations of press and public,
has often seemed to symbolise the triumph of the sensational in
daily journalism, the first true example of the 'yellow press'.
Yet in fact the *Daily Mail* that appeared on 4 May 1896 was far
from being sensational in appearance or style and was much less
'yellow' than a great deal that had preceded or was to succeed
it. It was a halfpenny paper of eight pages, standard size, with
advertisements on the front page, the Royal Arms in the middle
of the title and a slogan at each side: 'A Penny Newspaper for
One Halfpenny' and 'The Busy Man's Daily Journal'.

Its news pages were conservative in make-up. Although it

employed more headlines and cross-heads than its penny competitors they were all modest in size. All its news stories, domestic and foreign, were short. So were its articles. It carried the first instalment of a serial story (all his life Northcliffe had great faith in serial stories as a means of holding readers), a column of political gossip, another of society news, Stock Exchange prices for City readers, a page of sporting news, and a number of informative features for women.

The first of its four short leading articles proclaimed its purpose: to give all the news for half the price. But although it cost only a halfpenny, this, it was explained, was not what really mattered: 'The note of the *Daily Mail* is not so much economy of price as conciseness and compactness: it is essentially the busy man's paper.'

The first number sold 397,215 copies, more than had ever been sold by any newspaper in one day before. Within two years it was selling an average of around half a million copies and making profits not equalled by *The Times* in its greatest days. Within four years it was printing in Manchester as well as London and selling nearly a million. Although this circulation fell slightly after the Boer War ended it remained round 800,000. For more than three decades the *Mail* dominated newspaper circulations almost as completely as had *The Times* in the greatest days of its 'monopoly' half a century before.

Moreover on the foundation of the *Daily Mail* and the profits of his periodicals Northcliffe built a newspaper empire vaster than any existing before or since. He acquired the *Weekly Dispatch* for £25,000—like the *Evening News* it was nearly bankrupt when he bought it—and made it the most successful Sunday paper of the time, outstripping *Lloyd's Weekly* in the circulation race, with the *News of the World* still, at that stage, far behind. He established the *Daily Mirror* and after a false start as a paper 'written by gentlewomen for gentlewomen' turned it into the first popular picture paper, rivalling, and indeed at times during the First World War excelling, even the *Daily Mail* in sales. Turning from the popular field he saved the *Observer* from extinction and under J. L. Garvin's editorship set it on its way to becoming the great quality Sunday paper it now is. And in 1908 when *The Times* with its financial resources dangerously depleted and its circulation down to only 38,000 was in grave peril of extinction, or at the least of fundamental change in character, he became its principal proprietor, injected new life into it and saved it as a great British institution.

The Times, the *Observer*, the *Daily Mail*, the *Evening News*, the *Weekly Dispatch*, the *Daily Mirror*, the *Continental Daily Mail*, two provincial newspapers—the *Glasgow Daily Record* and the *Southern Daily Mail*—*Answers*, *Home Chat*, *Comic Cuts*, *Union Jack*, *Forget-Me-Not*, *Sunday Companion*, *Funny Wonder*, *Half-penny Marvel* and a host of others—there has never been a newspaper empire like it; never in the history of journalism a career quite like his.

How did this career affect journalism and the relationship between press and public?

The answer and more especially that part of it that is still relevant in considering the social influence of newspapers and the nature of their power, little concerns his association with either the *Observer* or *The Times*. He rendered great service to these papers and especially to *The Times*—his association with the *Observer* was shorter and slighter and although he set it on its feet financially he was never deeply involved in it; it was Garvin, not he, who impressed his personality on it. But even his ownership of *The Times* was in a sense an interlude—although an important one—in his career.

He brought it financial support at a time when it was crippled by losses and torn by internal dissensions among minority shareholders with an out-of-date eighteenth-century constitution wholly inappropriate to the conditions of the twentieth century. He shook it out of the editorial lethargy of the late nineteenth century and made it conscious of the modern world, capable of stepping across the crevasse between its past and its future instead of falling into it as it seemed likely to do. To him, as is gratefully acknowledged in its official history, *The Times* 'owes its transformation from a bankrupt nineteenth-century relic into a flourishing twentieth-century property'.

This was a great service and one to be remembered whatever else may be said for and against him. But in the fourteen years during which he was its chief proprietor *The Times* never became in any true sense his paper as these others were and as the *Daily Mail* especially was. The ghosts were too strong for him. The paper's traditions were theirs, not his, and were more powerful than he, who liked to make his own traditions.

In a sense and despite the great material services he rendered it *The Times* was his one great failure, at any rate in personal terms. Indeed it might well have proved manifestly and openly so if he had lived longer. By 1922 when he died, its circulation, after rising to 318,000 under the stimulation of a reduction in price to 1*d.* during the First World War, was again falling. Its financial position had become dangerously unstable and Northcliffe was engaged more and more on personal interventions in editorial policy which, if continued, could hardly have done other than fatally damage its then already waning prestige; for *The Times* could not be turned into the personal instrument of one Press Lord and remain *The Times.* This final conclusion was fortunately avoided. Northcliffe's contribution to *The Times* remains a great one. But its ownership was an episode only in his career, not part of the main stream. The real significance of that career lies elsewhere. For that one must return to the *Mail.*

X

THE GREAT DICHOTOMY

THE *Daily Mail* was a success because it continued the revolution the *Daily Telegraph* left unfinished.

It did not appeal to the largest public of all, the public of the mass working class then making its protest in such struggles as the London dock strike of 1889 and beginning to demonstrate its strength in the new Trade Unionism. Although Northcliffe can hardly have been unaware of the ferment from below that coincided with the starting of the *Daily Mail* the cultivation of this, the last and numerically greatest of all mass newspaper publics, had to await a later phase in national and newspaper development—indeed it is only with the modern *Daily Mirror* that it has begun to be fully exploited. The conditions that make newspapers possible are economic as well as literate and in 1896 the working class lacked, as yet, the buying power to attract large advertisers.

It was to the class just above this that Northcliffe appealed: the white-collared lower-middle class expanding rapidly in numbers under the stimulus of commercial development. It was an ignorant public but an eager and inquisitive one, keen to better itself and looking for the knowledge that would enable it to do so. Ill-informed on public affairs and not deeply interested in politics, particularly of a party kind, it was conscious, sometimes dangerously so, of Britain's world power and of its share in the white man's burden; a public acquisitive, proud, imperialistic and boastful as befitted Englishmen at the turn of the nineteenth century.

'Could it be maintained that a person of any education could learn anything from a penny paper?' Lord Robert Cecil had asked thirty-five years before. Now with true aristocratic aptitude for the proper comment on the changing social scene he contemptuously called this new halfpenny paper 'a newspaper for office boys written by office boys'. But although the public Northcliffe was after might consist of office boys (and their girl friends) they were office boys who intended to be something better tomorrow. Tom Clarke who was for many years day editor of the *Mail* and one of Northcliffe's favourites describes in *Northcliffe in History* how Northcliffe used to tell the young men on his staff that the readers of the *Daily Mail* were people with £1,000 a year and when this was daringly challenged by one of them amended it to: 'Well, they like to imagine themselves £1,000 a year people and they certainly prefer reading the news and doings of £1,000 a year people.' He defined the man-in-the-street for whom *Mail* reporters must write as 'tomorrow's £1,000 a year man, so he hopes and thinks'. He added, 'He likes reading news about people who have succeeded. He sees himself as one of them eventually and he's flattered.'

'We don't', he said, 'direct the ordinary man's opinion. We reflect it', and went on to declare that what flattered a reader most was to see his own opinions and prejudices echoed in, and thus given authority by, his newspaper.

Northcliffe once remarked with a good deal of truth that before the *Mail* practically everything that was a subject of conversation was kept out of the papers. He altered all that. He printed the sort of news people like talking about when it happens to someone they know and like to read about when it happens to other people, particularly people well known. In politics he went after personalities rather than principles and developed political and society gossip features. He exploited the trivial but he insisted on facts. He wanted news, and news he described as 'anything out of the ordinary'; anything that would make people talk in buses and trains and in the office. But although he drove his staff to search ceaselessly after news and especially exclusive news as any good editor must he also revived an interest well known to

Addison and Steele, Bell and Perry and Stuart but forgotten by most daily newspaper men since the eighteenth century, the interest in features and above all in features that women would like to read and like to talk about. One page of the new paper was devoted each day to 'The Daily Magazine', a page of topical articles. There were articles for women on clothes, food, furniture, gardens, health, children; a serial story and a children's feature. The leader page soon included many signed articles. And always he insisted upon the importance of women readers: every page had to have at least one news story that would appeal specifically to them. 'Women', he said, 'are nearer to the fundamentals of life than men—nearer to children, the home, health, pictures, art and music.'

Northcliffe brought to the *Daily Mail* all the knowledge of popular reading tastes acquired through *Answers*, *Home Chat* and the rest of the Harmsworth publications together with some he had learned from a careful study of the history of journalism—a subject not much favoured, unfortunately for them, by his rivals. To this he added a passion for news and a flair, without equal in his time, for knowing what would excite interest and create controversy. He brought newspapers out from the study and the political meeting into the common world where ordinary men and women live. His reward was great.

In seeking and interesting a new public Northcliffe was of course only doing on a wider scale what many others had done before him. He was following a track long since beaten by Defoe's *Review*, Steele and Addison's *Spectator*, Bell's *World*, Perry's *Morning Chronicle*, Stuart's *Morning Post*, Barnes and Delane's *Times*, Levy's *Daily Telegraph*, O'Connor's *Star*.

It is for other reasons than this that the *Daily Mail* marks so decisive a watershed in the history of newspapers. After 1896 the world of journalism was never to be quite the same. Previously despite the differences between individual newspapers the press, or at any rate the daily press, had been one organism, governed by an aim essentially the same for all. Now there was to develop within it a dichotomy that has become more characteristic of the journalism of Britain than of any other country even including the United States: a division into two presses, the serious and the popular, so contradictory in purpose that sometimes they seem hardly to belong to the same species.

This may in any event have been inevitable, deriving from social causes to which the press of the twentieth century could not fail to respond. But its beginning is marked most surely by the success of Northcliffe's *Daily Mail* and by the methods employed to achieve this success.

Until the arrival of the *Daily Mail* all newspapers had been private or family properties valued, to quote the report of the Royal Commission on the Press in 1949, 'for the prestige and the political and social influence their possession conferred rather than as a source of dividends'. The first publishing venture of any kind to offer shares to the general public was the company formed by Newnes in 1891 to acquire *Tit-Bits* and his other magazines. The first daily newspaper in the history of journalism to become a public company inviting investment in its shares as a straight commercial proposition was the *Daily Mail*. It thus began the commercial development of the press that has since transformed the newspaper trade into a major industry. In so doing it was, of course, simply following the trend of the times: it is inconceivable that even if Northcliffe had never lived the development of the joint stock principle would not very soon have affected the newspaper business like all others.

But the commercialisation initiated by the two Harmsworth brothers carried with it consequences far exceeding those that were bound in any event to flow from the development of the joint stock system.

It was clear that if the new mass market uncovered by *Tit-Bits*, *Answers* and the rest was to be exploited by a daily newspaper that paper must not cost more than $\frac{1}{2}d$. But at this figure a national morning paper could not possibly cover production costs by sales alone. It must have a large income from advertisements. This was not a new problem. A century before it had confronted Perry in a different form. The 4,000 circulation he had achieved for the *Morning Chronicle* was not, he declared, enough to pay half his production costs and without advertisements its price would have to be raised from $6\frac{1}{2}d$. to $1s$. The strong position of *The Times* had depended not only on sales but on advertisements. The whole development of an independent press had, in fact, rested as much on advertisement revenue as on sales.

But whereas in the past advertisement revenue had been a valuable prop to newspaper sales it became in the Harmsworth brothers' conception of newspaper development one of the key-stones of the whole newspaper structure. Their experience with *Answers* had shown them, as it had previously shown Newnes with *Tit-Bits*, that in the conditions created by a rapidly developing mass market for consumer goods the greatest profits were to be found in selling space to advertisers, particularly large commercial advertisers who would go on taking space day after day, week after week, year after year. In the past the newspaper had been important as a vehicle for ideas or as a source of political influence. Its new importance lay in its ability to put advertisers in touch with the mass of consumers.

To tap this fortune in advertising revenue it was first necessary, however, to prove not only that it paid to advertise in the *Daily Mail* but that it paid better to advertise there than anywhere else.

The means to do this had already been devised by the Harmsworth brothers in *Answers*. Harold had there hit upon the idea of a net sales figure certified by Chartered Accountants and widely advertised. This idea translated into daily newspaper terms became the basis of the *Daily Mail's* huge commercial success. It was one ideally suited to the new journalism. Not only did it offer the way to commercial prosperity, it provided a means whereby the standard of value by which a newspaper was to be judged could be moved from the intangible world of political influence and public esteem to the tangible reality of guaranteed circulation figures.

The *Mail* was committed by the nature of the new market to a popular circulation: the fact that it appealed to those whom older newspapers ignored was its journalistic justification. But the central position occupied by the net sales certificate in the Harmsworth plans gave circulation as such a more dominating importance that it had ever previously possessed on any newspaper.

Circulation had, of course, been a large factor in the influence exercised by *The Times* under Barnes and Delane. But although Delane's own salary actually rose or fell with the number of copies sold the effect on circulation had never been allowed to occupy more than a secondary place in considering the paper's composition. It had not had even that place in decisions on policy except in so far as Barnes used circulation figures as a guide to public feeling. Indeed although *The Times* could probably, as Mowbray Morris claimed, have doubled its circulation without difficulty in 1850 no attempt to do so was made because larger sales might involve some alteration, however slight, in the character of the paper. The *Daily Telegraph* paid more attention to circulation and made a great effort, eventually successful, to obtain 'the largest circulation in the world'. But this effort was mainly editorial. Circulation flowed from the fact that the paper was, in its day, a new kind of paper of a type to appeal to a new public.

For the *Daily Mail* as conceived by its creators circulation was, however, important as an end in itself—or rather as a means to an end not itself journalistic: the selling of more and more space at higher and higher prices to more and more advertisers. To achieve circulation and also to convince advertisers of his own faith in advertisements Northcliffe advertised the *Daily Mail* itself on a lavish scale. In those halcyon days when newspaper publishing, if not quite a profession, was not yet an industry £15,000 put up by himself, his brother Harold, and Kennedy Jones had been enough to start the paper. But it was not sufficient to promote it on the scale the two Harmsworths had in mind. For this larger capital sums were required. They were drawn in the first place from the money secured by the flotation of Harmsworth Brothers Ltd., but as soon as the *Daily Mail* itself was in a position to produce an attractive prospectus a public issue of shares in The Daily Mail Limited was made. A new element was thus introduced into the daily press: the outsider shareholder interested in newspapers as a financial investment and not as a public service or a means of political influence.

In so far as it lessened the dependence of newspapers on political parties or rich patrons this marked another welcome stage in their progress towards independence. But in the context of the Northcliffe revolution it sharpened the break between the old idea of newspapers and the new, and emphasised the cleavage between papers of opinion and papers of circulation that was henceforth to become one of the most striking features of the British press.

In the thirties of the twentieth century the chase after circulation for its own sake and the domination of the net sales certificate inaugurated by Northcliffe and Rothermere were to turn newspapers to the most fantastic courses and introduce into journalism promotion methods which Northcliffe himself— always primarily a journalist, although of a new school—would have deplored. And he would most certainly have deplored the attempt to win circulation by the exploitation of sexy serials that has at times characterised the *Sunday Dispatch*—but neither the *Daily Mail* nor the *Evening News*—in recent years. These consequences of the search for the lowest common denominator of mass taste were still in the future. But they were inherent in the concentration upon net sales which was at the heart of the *Daily Mail* promotion campaign.

Because circulation was so important to the Northcliffe enterprises there had to be stunt after stunt to attract mass readership and make the paper talked about. Some were good, like the large aviation prizes Northcliffe offered and his encouragement of radio development. Some were harmless, like the campaign for *Daily Mail* Standard Bread, and the big money prizes given for improved sweet peas, roses and such things. Some were ridiculous, like the campaign for the *Daily Mail* hat. And some, when the technique was carried into the political field, were pernicious. But the real charge against Northcliffe is that despite his personal pride in accurate news reporting the promotion methods he adopted could not do other than debase the whole relationship between newspapers and their readers.

He turned newspapers into super-hoardings for the display of advertisements to the largest possible number of people—carefully counted by a Chartered Accountant. Because he did so, and because on this premiss what was important was the number of people who could be corralled into buying a newspaper by whatever means, it became natural to him to adopt the same techniques in the editorial columns. To inform the interested and persuade the intelligent had previously been regarded as the true aim of journalism. Now what was important became the power given by a large circulation to sway the mass, to 'telegraph a message to millions with damnable reiteration', as Northcliffe himself put it. In this new conception of journalism power was seen as deriving from mass suggestion, from the slogan repeated over and over again until it produced an instinctive reaction, from the translation of a highly complicated situation into an emotional challenge capable of being expressed in short phrases that could be beaten home day after day after day by every technique of propaganda.

Like the public he catered for, Northcliffe was without intellectual discipline or much settled intellectual purpose but he had immense intellectual facility, a never-ending curiosity about almost everything and a remarkable magpie gift for jumping from subject to subject and carrying away from each some glittering bauble of a 'verbal vignette', as he liked to call the slogans and headlines that came constantly tumbling into his mind.

In the end the methods he adopted not only corrupted the whole relationship between newspapers and their readers, they also distorted his own personality. He helped to create a new type of journalist more aware of the ordinary man than his predecessors and he raised the wages and professional standing of the ordinary reporter and sub-editor almost out of recognition. But there is something more than a little nauseating about his relations with many of his chief associates; one wonders how they could stomach the humiliations he imposed and retain their self-respect.

When one remembers S. J. Prior and Thomas Marlowe, both appointed editor of the *Mail* by Northcliffe at the same time, racing for the office each morning to be first in the scramble for the editor's chair in the hope that the symbol would bring the substance with it; or the manner in which he kept men who had served him responsibly for years 'on the jump' by warnings that they were 'on trial' and subject at any moment to the sack; or the daily telegrams of complaint (often shown privately to the man's subordinates) to a victim selected for 'treatment'; the list, constantly revised, of those to whom he would and would not speak on the telephone, which provided an office guide to who was in favour and who was out; or the anonymous 'spotters', 'ferrets' and 'eyes' who, unknown even to each other, were required to report daily to him on the doings of the *Mail* staff; the sudden grandiose rewards—the trips to the Villa Roquebrune on the Riviera or half round the world with instructions to spend money like water at the office expense and so on—for those who were lifted into favour, the equally incalculable insults and demotions for those from whom favour was withdrawn; the brusque orders and counter-orders; the strain of petty spite shown, for instance, in such incidents as the instructions to his staff—obeyed it would seem without journalistic protest—to find the most unpleasing photograph of Asquith and print only that, or to give Marshall Hall's name in law reports as M. Hall—all these bring irresistibly to mind the atmosphere at the court of an Eastern despot or a modern dictator.

The great editors of the past had usually been autocrats— great newspapers do not grow under divided authority—but they had been autocrats with respect for those who worked with them. They listened, discussed and were prepared to argue. They recognised that the voice of a newspaper was more than one man's voice. They ruled as the first among equals. Not so Northcliffe. There were some on his staff who stood up to him and whose independence he respected. There were some such as the present editor of the *Yorkshire Post* who learnt a good deal about popular journalism from him without divesting themselves of their professional principles. But in general his staff were his creatures. The financial rewards he offered were great; the loss in human dignity often greater. It is not a good thing when men concerned in an occupation directly touching the public interest are ready to regard themselves as no longer members of a profession—subject to its responsibilities and obligations and supported by its rules of personal and public conduct—but as the hireling creatures of a single employer to whose tune they will dance however arbitrary its personal or public consequences.

Along with a good deal of credit for humanising news and bringing it to a wider public Northcliffe must take a large part of the blame, not so much for the commercialisation of the press for that was inevitable, as for the form commercialisation took and its consequences on the relationship between newspapers and their readers and on the professional status of journalists. But he does not stand alone. When one considers the results of the immense widening of newspaper readership at the end of the nineteenth century and asks whether it was inevitable that these should be what they were most of the greatest journalists of that time, such men as J. A. Spender, E. T. Cook, Frederick Greenwood, John Morley, Alfred Milner and even W. T. Stead must stand alongside him. His sins, if such they were, were of commission, theirs of omission. But their responsibility is hardly smaller.

To the challenge of this new popular readership which he so gladly and so vigorously accepted these others had nothing to say. They gathered their skirts around them and fled to ivory towers. They cannot but have been aware of the immense opportunity and responsibility presented to journalism by this new reading public. It was their professional business to understand it. But they did nothing about it.

The growth of a press with circulation as its major and sometimes its only standard of value and with the 'damnable reiteration' of slogans as a substitute for argument was likely enough in the circumstances of that time. So was the dichotomy of the press that springs from it. But it was not mandatory. Popular journalism as conceived by Northcliffe and his successors remains in many of its manifestations largely a British phenomenon, at least so far as Europe is concerned. And although across the Atlantic industrialisation and the battles for circulation between Hearst and Pulitzer produced some of the same results, even there the division between the 'serious' and the 'popular' press is scarcely so wide as it is here. Nor despite the popular British myth to the contrary can American journalism rival British journalism in the exploitation of the sensational and the frivolous.

Northcliffe harnessed, he did not create, the social forces that made him. Spender, Greenwood, Morley and these others refused to have anything to do with them.

In his Life of Spender, Mr. Wilson Harris described him with much justice as 'the very mould and pattern of the highest type of journalist, alike in competence and in character, a man to whom, for the example he set and the standards he maintained, the whole profession owed incalculably much'. This was the most testing period in British journalism when much of its future was in hazard and an immense new field was opening out before it. One would have thought it of a nature to excite the energy and promote the social conscience of such a man, indeed of any journalist who took his profession seriously and who shared that sense of public mission that had survived and eventually triumphed through more than three centuries of struggle against the strongest forces in the State. Yet at such a period Spender and his peers in Victorian and Edwardian journalism chose to stand aloof from most of the new forces that surely demanded their interest and fidelity. Instead of seeking to engage the broad mass of public support that might have been theirs if they had been prepared to serve and guide it they devoted themselves to the provision of reading matter for a small diminishing group, withdrawing almost contemptuously from the main stream of history to a punt on a backwater.

There have been few more curious interludes in journalism than the reign of the group of influential London evening papers over which they presided: the *Pall Mall Gazette*, the *Westminster Gazette*, the *St. James's Gazette* and the *Globe*. Cultured, erudite and brilliantly written these newspapers were for all their editorial integrity faithless to both the past and the future of journalism. For close on three centuries the whole struggle of the press had been for political independence. The cumulative experience of the greatest figures in daily journalism from Perry and Stuart to Barnes and Delane had combined to show that this independence could only rest in economic strength rooted in popular support. This historical lesson these great journalists of the turn of the century completely disregarded, just as they disregarded the opportunities that Northcliffe vigorously seized for a press based on a wider social and economic power than was previously possible. In contradiction both to the lessons of the past and the social and political climate of their own time they deliberately chose to tie themselves to the purse-strings of the political parties or turn for sustenance to the favours of some rich man prepared, as a gesture of political loyalty or social ambition, to subsidise the newspapers they edited to the extent of several thousands a year. Not only did none of these papers of theirs pay their way and stand on their own feet, they were excluded almost deliberately from so doing by their very character. All four were designed and written for a cultivated West End–Whitehall–Club public that was scarcely sufficient to support one.

Within its small field of readership this politically tied and subsidised press exercised great influence. Edited and written by journalists of large intellectual power who moved as their equals among the greatest political leaders these papers sometimes seem in retrospect to represent the finest flowering of journalism, an Athenian Age in which civility was King. So in a sense they did.

There was of course always present the danger that a paper might, as several did, change sides overnight as one rich man grew tired of footing the bill and another of different political complexion took his place. In such circumstances the editor and his chief associates resigned and went in search of a new patron. But so long as he remained in the chair the editor of such a paper enjoyed a remarkable eminence and independence. When Sir Alfred Mond who succeeded Newnes as chairman of the *West-minster Gazette* Board and its chief financial patron sent signed letters to that paper for publication on two successive days Spender rounded on him like an angry schoolmaster. Such action, said he, was embarrassing and likely to have an adverse effect upon the newspaper's reputation. 'It is', he wrote magisterially to the unlucky Mond, 'almost an absolute rule among proprietors of newspapers not to write over their own names in their own newspapers. Experience shows that it does the proprietor no good, for the public invariably discounts what he writes, and does the paper harm, since this curious British public seems to have a rooted objection to any newspaper influence which it conceives as personal.'

This it may be noted was written in August 1909, thirteen years after the foundation of the *Daily Mail* and at a time when the most significant development in British journalism and the one that was to have the most far-reaching effects on its character was Northcliffe's discovery of the personal power that the owning of newspapers could give.

Yet although Spender regarded it as a breach of journalistic principle for the chief proprietor of a newspaper to presume to write a letter for publication in it he appears to have been conscious of no discomfort that his own position rested entirely on the readiness of a rich man to spend his money on supporting a luxury newspaper instead of a racing stable or a mistress. Along with practically all his immediate contemporaries in the leadership of the metropolitan journalism of that time he seems to have had no inkling of that truth an understanding of which had been the cause of the initial success of *The Times* that the only lasting foundation on which a great paper can build is economic independence.

Even Stead who had more awareness of the movement of

public taste and opinion and more understanding of the need for a change in journalistic method than Spender or any of the rest of his contemporaries in serious journalism was either unable or unwilling to understand that the ability to survive and succeed as an independent press power depends not only on the quality of editing and writing in a newspaper but on its trading position.

With great skill and courage Stead introduced into journalism during his editorship of the *Pall Mall* a new spirit of bold campaigning and a popular style well suited to the changing times. But he did it in the wrong newspaper, never seeming to realise that what he did was foredoomed to failure because it appealed to the wrong public in the wrong medium. It is possible that if Stead had had the good fortune to meet with a new John Walter II he, not Northcliffe, might have been the parent of the new journalism. So might T. P. O'Connor. That good fortune was not theirs. In its absence and in the refusal of Spender and his fellows to concern themselves with the challenge presented by the new public the field was left to Northcliffe.

In his *Study of History* Professor Toynbee accuses the popular press which Northcliffe created of polluting 'the pure river of enlightenment' that might otherwise have flowed from popular education. The charge has weight. But it has to be said in fairness that those who should have been the powerful wardens of the river preferred to occupy themselves with other things.

The newspaper writing of the *Westminster*, the *St. James's*, the *Pall Mall* and the *Globe*—so elegant and so influential—has the bloom of a perfect flowering of journalism. But it was the bloom of a hot-house plant. The real tragedy of that time—if tragedy indeed it was—lies not in the Northcliffe revolution but in the *trahison des clercs* that allowed it so easy and so complete a victory.

XI

A FRIEND TO WITHSTAND YOU

THERE appears to be a compulsive element of conformity in British newspaper reading habits that gives the most popular newspaper in any age a power of attraction so great that no other paper can even approach it in circulation.

It was so in succession with *The Times*, the *Telegraph* and the *Mail*, each of which progressed through a curiously similar time-schedule of advance, consolidation and regression, holding the lead in each case for a period of some forty years. *The Times* had held first place in circulation for almost exactly four decades, when it lost it in 1856 to the *Daily Telegraph*, which held on to it from 1856 to 1896, forty years exactly, only then to lose it to the *Daily Mail*, which similarly retained circulation supremacy for approximately forty years: from 1896 to the middle thirties of the new century.

Although several others, notably Pearson with the *Daily Express* which he founded in 1900 and which was the first British paper to print news on its front page, tried hard to capture the new daily newspaper reading public none of them succeeded as Northcliffe did. Right up to the end of the First World War the *Mail* and its stable companions remained not merely the chief but almost the only beneficiaries of the revolution Northcliffe had begun. No part of the daily press was unaffected by this revolution. Those who tried to stand out against it, maintaining the dignity of the penny press against the halfpenny interloper, suffered most. The *Telegraph* which had a circulation of more than 300,000 when the *Mail* arrived lost between 50,000 and 60,000 of it almost immediately and continued to go on losing

year by year. The *Standard* which before Northcliffe's inter-
vention had been next to the *Telegraph* in public popularity
suffered even more. Like a bird shot on the wing the curve of its
flight turned dramatically down. By 1904 it had lost two-thirds
of its former circulation and although Pearson—determined to
show himself as great a newspaper magnate as his rival—then
bought it along with the *Evening Standard* neither his money nor
his energy could save it. It went on falling until it died in 1917.
The *Morning Post* with its higher Toryism fared little better.
The *Daily News* and the *Daily Chronicle* both came down to ½d.
to meet the *Mail's* challenge. The reduction in price helped their
circulations but left them far behind in the race. The *Tribune*,
founded at the height of the Liberal Party's triumph in 1906 to
restore penny dignity to Liberal morning journalism, survived
less than two years: 'It was', as Sir Philip Gibbs who wrote *The
Street of Adventure* around its fortunes remarked, 'too good and
there was too much of its goodness.'

As for the 3d. *Times*, which the challenge of a halfpenny press
might have been expected to leave wholly untouched, its circulation had fallen to only 38,000 when Northcliffe stepped in to save
it in 1908. Nor were the provincial dailies much less affected.
Almost all of them except those like the *Glasgow Herald* which
were outside the *Mail's* immediate circulation range suffered both
in circulation and in what was even more serious, advertising
revenue. From the beginning of the century to the First World
War Northcliffe's were the only daily papers to make satisfactory
profits. Most others made losses. Several found it impossible to
continue.

Northcliffe liked to believe, and was supported in this belief by
many sycophants and much uninformed opinion, that his financial
and circulation success was balanced by an equal power to
influence public and political opinion. There is little evidence that
this is true. He voiced, and not infrequently exaggerated, the
political prejudices of the readers of his popular papers. He played
on their fears and hopes and sometimes stampeded them into
hysteria. The noise he made in doing so often scared weak or

opportunist politicians into courting his favours. But although he affected the climate of mass opinion at times, the direct influence he exercised on the course of politics between 1896 and 1914 was small: it is difficult to find any major or even minor act of policy during those years of great policy-making on which one can put a finger and say: 'This happened because of Northcliffe'; or: 'This did not happen because of him.'

He performed an important public service by his exposure of the shell-shortage in the early days of the First World War, but his attacks on Kitchener which so infuriated ignorant but patriotic stockbrokers that they publicly burnt *The Times* and *Mail* on the Stock Exchange probably delayed rather than accelerated changes on which the Cabinet had already decided. In so far as he did exercise public influence on these occasions it derived much less from the mass circulation of the *Daily Mail* than from the traditional authority of *The Times* in whose columns Colonel Repington, its military correspondent, first published the facts about the shell-shortage from evidence given to him privately by the Commander-in-Chief, Sir John French. Although Northcliffe believed himself to be largely responsible for forcing Asquith to widen his administration and make Lloyd George Minister of Munitions he was unable to exercise any influence over the composition of the new administration. When this Government was replaced in its turn by the Lloyd George administration he was, despite the allegedly immense power exercised by his press, neither consulted by any of the chief architects of Asquith's dismissal, Lloyd George, Bonar Law and Sir Edward Carson, nor even informed of what was afoot. His future rival and successor as Press-Lord-in-Chief, Lord Beaverbrook, had a much bigger hand in that affair—but not as a newspaper proprietor. Northcliffe sounded the trumpets. The walls fell because they had been mined from the inside by much shrewder politicians than he.

In this, as in several other matters, he believed himself to be using Lloyd George. The truth is that he was adroitly used by Lloyd George for his own purposes. When those purposes were served and Northcliffe seemed likely to become a nuisance he was at once persuaded to go to the United States as Head of a British Mission. There he did work of great national value. Later he was to do work of equal value at Crewe House as head of propaganda to the Germans. But neither job put him near the real centre of political power. From that he was carefully excluded.

His final quarrel with Lloyd George in 1918 demonstrates even more clearly how nugatory was his true political power. He demanded a voice in the composition of the new Government in return for the support of his papers at the forthcoming General Election—a demand somewhat similar to that presented to Mr. Baldwin some twelve years later by Lords Rothermere and Beaverbrook who received an even dustier answer and one that finally pricked the bubble of their political reputations. His proposal was met with contemptuous derision. This appears to have surprised him. It can hardly have surprised anyone who knew how politics work for it had long been obvious that although Lloyd George was very ready to pay for Northcliffe's support in honours and flattery he had no intention of paying for it in real power. Nor did the break with Northcliffe have any perceptible effect on the result of the subsequent election.

Even at the height of his newspaper success Northcliffe's political power was, in fact, so small that not all his importunities could procure for him what he most wanted, an official place at the Peace Conference at Versailles. Of all statesmen Lloyd George showed most surface deference to the idea that Northcliffe was a great political force. But as events repeatedly showed it was a surface deference only. Their relationship, indeed, presents a picture of curious naivety on Northcliffe's part from their first meeting in 1907 when Lloyd George was Chancellor of the Exchequer. On that occasion, as Northcliffe's brother Cecil, who was there, later related to Mr. Tom Clarke, Lloyd George concluded an exhibition of Welsh charm lasting nearly an hour by presenting Northcliffe with a draft of the Development of Roads Bill to use as he pleased in the columns of next morning's *Daily Mail*—a gesture of 'splendid imprudence', according to Cecil

Harmsworth, that delighted Northcliffe and 'laid the foundation of the admiring relations between the two men that continued with intermissions until the Peace Conference'. One has only to imagine the response of those earlier masters of political press power, Barnes and Delane, to so obvious—and insignificant— a bribe. One may recall Delane's chilling comment to the bearer of a confidential Ministerial document that he was not interested in such official favours for the information was bound to reach him from one source or another without any condition of reserve, in order to recognise how childlike was Northcliffe's grasp of the real processes of press influence compared with theirs.

What is most remarkable about the Northcliffe revolution, in fact, is not that it brought with it a dangerous increase in, and concentration of, political power comparable to the increase in, and concentration of, circulation, but that it did not. In so far as the mantle of Barnes and Delane passed to anyone during the period of the *Mail's* greatest journalistic triumphs it passed not to Northcliffe but to a man wholly different from him in character and ambition and with not one-twentieth of the newspaper circulation he commanded—C. P. Scott of the *Manchester Guardian*.

A comparison between the progress of Scott's *Guardian* and Northcliffe's *Mail* is revealing. It demonstrates in the most pointed way the dichotomy between papers of influence and papers of circulation brought about by the Northcliffe revolution and the extent to which the old relationship between circulation and influence was ended.

When Scott joined the *Manchester Guardian*, then owned by his cousin John Edward Taylor, the son of its founder, in February 1871 to become its editor a year later at the age of twenty-five it was a soundly established and locally respected provincial morning paper, but no more. It remained so during the first eight years of his editorship, widening its interest in cultural affairs under his direction but showing no particular evidence of future greatness. Its position was comparable to that of several other admirable provincial dailies such as the *Yorkshire Post*, which then exceeded it in circulation, the *Birmingham Post*, which had approximately the same, and the *Liverpool Post*. Like theirs its sale and influence were primarily regional. There was no reason why they should ever be otherwise—except Scott.

In the year 1880, however, the contest over Home Rule for Ireland fired all Scott's imagination and moral fervour. It was a contest, odd though it may seem to a younger generation, that, as J. L. Hammond has truly said, 'absorbed all the attention and excited the deepest emotions of the British people'. The *Guardian* became the most accomplished newspaper voice in the country on the side of Home Rule and as such a political force to be reckoned with in London as well as the North. Having thus begun Scott went on to make the *Guardian* into something unique in British journalism: a provincial paper which came to be accepted not only in Britain but in every part of the civilised world as the supreme expression of the liberal spirit. He edited it for fifty-seven years, from 1872 to 1929, and was sole proprietor as well as editor from 1907 to 1913 in which year he voluntarily divested himself of exclusive financial control in order to safeguard the continuity of the paper, dividing the ordinary shares equally between himself, his two sons, Edward and John, and his son-in-law, C. E. Montague, under an agreement whereby the shares of any one of the four who died or left the paper must be offered to the others.

Although his editorial reign began nearly a quarter of a century before the Northcliffe revolution it thus extended throughout the whole of it, covering a period during which the newspaper face of Britain—like the social, economic and political faces which it reflected—changed almost out of all recognition. Throughout these years the tide of newspaper development ran steadily in favour of the concentration of newspaper power in the hands of great commercial groups centred in London and of success measured in terms of circulation. Yet while *The Times*, so long the epitome of the serious journalism of opinion which Scott himself so signally represented, was able to survive only with assistance from the creator of the new commercialised press, and the future of journalism as a whole began to seem increasingly dependent on flattering a mass public, Scott managed to turn a newspaper published outside London with a circulation wholly derisory by Northcliffe's standards into an instrument of journalistic authority scarcely inferior in influence to that of *The Times* under Barnes and Delane. In doing so he endowed it with a political power at home and abroad such as Northcliffe with his huge press empire never remotely attained and would have given almost anything to possess. He did this, moreover, in conditions very different from those that had made *The Times* the leading journal of a compact, tightly knit, oligarchic political society and without the aid of either the predominant circulation or the unique trading position it enjoyed. And he did it by methods the exact antithesis of those suggested by Northcliffe's success as the only certain means to press power in a mass society.

He lacked both Northcliffe's flair for the popular and Delane's nose for news. He rarely if ever brought his newspaper the exclusive and confidential information that had been so much the basis of Delane's power. Indeed when such news was given to him on one of his visits to London, as it often was for there were many Ministers anxious to do themselves the favour of giving him their confidences, it never occurred to him to print it. If Lloyd George had handed to him the draft of the Development of Roads Bill that so excited Northcliffe he would almost certainly have put it in his pocket and forgotten about it. He would frequently enrage members of his staff when other newspapers came out with exclusive details of some important Government decision by announcing blandly that so-and-so had given him all the documents days before—pulling them out of his pocket with a beaming smile. Delane made *The Times* admired and feared by the extent and quality of his private information. Scott kept his paper and his private information distinct.

Although for the encouragement of colleagues he sometimes tried to pretend otherwise he was in fact not much interested in news. Even on ceremonial occasions when it was a matter of courtesy to make all the editorial department feel members of a joint team he found it difficult, according to W. P. Crozier, to conceal his view of the gulf that separated the leader writer, the creator of opinion, from the reporter, the purveyor of news. News never excited him like an idea. For that form of it on which Northcliffe was building his empire, news that resounds without significance, he had nothing but contempt.

The attitude of the journalist of opinion to the reporter, which he so much epitomised, is not one in general to be commended. In other and lesser hands it has perhaps done as much harm to British journalism as almost anything one can think of. By denigrating the status of the reporter it has helped to reduce the quality and independence of a good deal of essential news-gathering, sometimes leading persons in authority in public affairs to the dangerous assumption that although it may be wise and proper to be polite to leader writers it is all right to be rude to reporters, and leading reporters to the still more dangerous assumption that they ought not to consider themselves the equals of the public men they interview and should feel flattered when courteously given nothing.

This is a mistake that has never been made by the American press where the greatest journalists are proud to think of themselves as, and describe themselves by, the honourable title of reporter and where the single-minded belief that it is a journalist's primary job to get at the facts irrespective of the social or political eminence of those who may have to be cross-examined in the process has contributed immeasurably to the quality of the best American political and international reporting. In the British press those reporters who have got on in the world and made themselves specialists in some subject tend to think of themselves not as reporters any longer but as 'correspondents': 'political correspondents', 'diplomatic correspondents', 'industrial correspondents'—the list is endless. They sometimes demonstrate their increase in status by mixing their own opinions and interpretations with the facts to a degree that would be regarded as highly tendentious in the best American and Continental journalism, where reporters make reputations by getting the facts that others do not have, not by interpreting those that are common knowledge.

But although Scott regarded the man who interpreted the facts as a more important individual than the man who reported them, over-stressing perhaps the difficulty of the one function and under-stressing that of the other, he never, as the owners and editors of more popular papers have often tended to do, regarded facts as things to be adapted to a policy line.

When he considered the proper business of a newspaper he was in no doubt that, as he wrote in a famous leading article on the *Guardian's* Centenary in May 1921, 'Its primary office is the gathering of news. At the peril of its soul it must see that the supply is not tainted. Neither in what it gives, nor in what it does not give, nor in the mode of presentation must the unclouded face of truth suffer wrong. Comment is free, but facts are sacred.'

The general news-service of the *Guardian* under Scott was not better than others, in fact it was often inferior. Yet because when there was important news to report he chose able and brilliant men to cover it and gave them their heads, not asking them to trim their sails to any wind whether from Cross Street, Manchester, or anywhere else, he made the *Guardian* into a remarkable *news*-paper in a special sense. It was not, however, news but opinion that made it into a great one. Or rather what made it great was the conception of journalism that governed everything he did and that found its most complete expression in that section of the paper to which he himself gave the greatest importance, for which indeed more than for any other single purpose he believed it to exist, the leader columns and especially the first leader: 'The Long', the primary instrument of policy, the voice of the paper.

It is instructive in the light of the political and public influence of the highest kind that came Scott's way while so constantly eluding Northcliffe—as it has eluded the most brilliant of his successors, Lord Beaverbrook—to compare their approaches to journalism.

Northcliffe ordered his staff to remember that they were there 'not to direct the ordinary man's opinion, but to reflect it'. What flattered a reader, he told them, was to see his own opinions and prejudices echoed in, and thus given authority by, his newspaper.

To Scott, as C. E. Montague wrote, 'to exploit popular ignorance, to play up to the vices or weaknesses of half-formed characters and half-filled minds would have seemed a policy no more worth considering than a policy of living on the profits of disorderly houses. With eyes perfectly open to the formidableness of the new forces at work in journalism, he determined to maintain his previous course and endeavour only the more resolutely to give the public, not what it was currently rumoured to desire, but what he believed to be true.'

Northcliffe believed that influence came from the great instrument of mass suggestion that control of a vast circulation put in his hands. Scott sought to persuade. To describe an article as 'persuasive' was the highest compliment he could pay. He demanded of those who wrote for him reasonableness and moderation. 'The voice of opponents no less than of friends has a right to be heard', he wrote in that famous definition of the kind of journalism he believed in, contained in his leading article on the *Manchester Guardian* Centenary. 'Comment is justly subject to a self-imposed restraint. It is well to be frank; it is even better to be fair.'

His was a quieter voice than Northcliffe's. But it carried farther and it influenced more of those who themselves shaped or influenced national policy.

That it should do so is as much a matter of significance in considering the relationship between press and public in the first half of the twentieth century as the circulation figures of the *Daily Mail*.

Scott was not, of course, alone in holding such principles. They were held equally by Spender, Cook and the rest of that brilliant band of London evening paper editors to whom I have already referred. Where Scott differed from them, however, was in his practical appreciation of the commercial and trading foundations on which independent journalism must rest.

He conducted his paper as a public service and not for profit: from the time he acquired it in 1907 until his death in 1932 he at no time drew a salary of more than £2,500 a year from it. Its profits, and they were never large, all went to strengthening and improving it. But although he was not interested in profit, as such, he never made the mistake, as Spender and those others did, of ignoring the trading position of his paper. He did not deceive himself, as they did, that a great independent journal can exist permanently on the charity of a rich man or the favour of a political party. If it came to the point he was perfectly ready to sacrifice the commercial success of his newspaper to its journalistic integrity. That risk John Edward Taylor and he had taken without a quiver during the Boer War and he was ready to take it again at any time—better extinction than a failure of principle. But he never forgot that, to use his own words, 'a newspaper has two sides to it' and that one of them is that 'it is a business like any other business, carried on for profit and depending on profit for prosperity or existence'.

The *Guardian* did not always make a profit, indeed at the time of his death it had run into a period of substantial losses. But the organisation of which it was the most important part did. Careful accumulation of reserves during prosperous years had made possible the purchase between 1923 and 1930 of the *Manchester Evening News* and this extremely prosperous paper brilliantly run by William Haley, later director-general of the B.B.C. and now editor of *The Times*, was well able to meet the *Guardian's* deficits.

Scott was a careful and thrifty man of business in all matters that affected his paper. At a time when the full flood of journalistic enterprise and popular taste seemed to be running against him he was able to make it a great paper because he was so.

Nor did he ever despise the ordinary public as some of his contemporaries among the opinion-forming journalists of the metropolis seemed at times to do. He had Defoe's passion for plain muscular English and insisted that everything that appeared in the *Guardian* should be understandable by ordinary men and women. Nor did he consider concern for circulation lowering in an editor. He was prepared to lose it for a principle but he was ready to consider any modernisation not contrary to the character of the paper that would help to increase it and did in fact carry through a good deal of modernisation in the course of the years. 'He desired more readers', as W. P. Crozier said, 'in order that his ideas might be, if not accepted, intelligently discussed; he sought the circulation that brought the advertisements that provided the revenue that improved the paper as an engine for the moving of opinion.'

He was fortunate, of course, in being some distance from the centre of the struggle for circulation and in having a newspaper with roots in a strong local and commercial community. 'There are', he said on his eightieth birthday, referring to the growth of newspaper syndicates and the buying up of provincial newspapers by the Rothermere and Kemsley groups, 'papers which will never be sold—which would rather suffer extinction. And it is well that it should be so. The public has its rights. The paper which has grown up in a great community, nourished by its resources, reflecting in a thousand ways its spirit and its interests, in a real sense belongs to it. How else except in the permanence of that association can it fulfil its duty or repay the benefits and the confidence it has received?'

But although he was conscious both of his debt and his responsibility to the Manchester community he made no concessions to it where principle intervened. 'In a Lancashire gradually moving from the Left Centre to the Right Centre', as C. E. Montague noted, 'Scott moved almost continuously from the centre towards the left, converting a Whig journal into an organ of advanced Liberalism, while a large proportion of its readers, sons and grandsons of the followers of Cobden and Bright, were pretty obviously destined to pass through the ante-chamber of Liberal Unionism into the Conservative household.'

He stood like a rock against the general tide of journalism in his time, and like a rock he refused to bow to most of the popular prejudices and mass passions that assailed him. Yet against all the omens he gave his paper a position of authority and influence totally beyond the reach of those who counted circulation, not in thousands as he did, but in hundreds of thousands and were soon to count it in millions.

How did he do it? He was, of course, served by a remarkably able staff of his own choosing. He did not pay them well by Northcliffe reckoning; indeed on the whole he paid them poorly by most of the standards that were then coming to rule in modern journalism. Nor, although the brilliance of many of them was such that it broke through all veils and made their names ones to conjure with wherever good journalism and fine style were honoured, did he offer them personal fame. The tradition of journalistic anonymity was strong in him. Yet if they had neither the money nor the publicity that Northcliffe and his successors offered they had what Northcliffe too often took away, a sense of freedom and independence and the moral power that comes from self-respect in a great profession. They stayed with the *Guardian* because they were proud to serve it.

But although others contributed, and contributed vastly and variously, to the *Guardian*'s progress there is no question that Scott was the chief architect of its greatness. His secret is to be found in his conception of journalism—and in his pleasure in it. 'What a work it is!' he wrote. 'How multiform, how responsive to every need and every incident of life! What illimitable possibilities of achievement and of excellence!' And writing of the demand it makes on its practitioners: 'Upon this earth there can be no much greater responsibility than that involved in the control of a great newspaper. All a man's days and all his powers, all the conscience that is in him, and all the application he can give are surely not too much fitly to discharge so great a task.'

The authority he brought to the *Guardian* came from sources not much thought of as contributors to success in the battleground of commercial journalism that swirled around him throughout all the latter and most influential half of his career. They are often not much regarded on the same battlefields now. But they have their significance in any consideration of the relations between

press and public. This significance has been perfectly expressed by
C. E. Montague.

'That Scott's long editorship should, after many vicissitudes,'
he wrote, 'have raised his paper to the enjoyment of the highest
prestige and prosperity attained in its whole history tells us
something alike about this most English of Englishmen (in spite
of his Border name) and about the English men and women to
whom he addressed himself. Without any glamour of beauty or
wit in writing or speech, without any skill in the study of his
readers' prejudices, with unfashionable politics and a cold side
for the strongest emotions of crowds, he pursued his own slowly
chosen and frankly declared line in total indifference to what
people might say about it or him. And yet the further he went the
more influence did he gain over those to whom he made so few
concessions, so strong is the instinctive feeling of many plain and
sane minds—in England at any rate—that the friend who, in all
friendliness and for no worldly motive, will withstand you to
your face must be worth listening to anyhow.'

This is a reading of the English character that helps to explain
the *Manchester Guardian*. It was not one that played any large
part in the fantastic chapter in British newspaper history to
which we must now move.

XII

THE PRESS IS BIG BUSINESS

ADVERTISING had made it possible for newspapers to free themselves from political subservience in the eighteenth century and had given Northcliffe the key to popular journalism on a great commercial scale at the end of the nineteenth. A quarter way through the twentieth a new advertising development brought hardly less extensive consequences, marking, if one may take the word of so first-hand an authority as Lord Beaverbrook, a turning point in the history of the press. The large London department-stores took to display advertising on a scale hitherto unknown.

This may seem a small matter to set against the great landmarks of earlier newspaper history, Milton's *Areopagitica*, the struggle for freedom by 'Junius' and Wilkes, Barnes's bold insistence that *The Times* should be governed not by party but by popular opinion, Delane's arrogant declaration of independence in reply to the strictures of Lord Derby, the abolition of the Stamp Tax, the advance of the telegraph and the development of the rotary press. But other times, other manners. By 1924 the commercialisation of the press had reached a stage where the decision of the department-stores was an event of the first importance. It opened up immense new fields of revenue for the successful newspaper. To a larger degree even than before it defined success in terms of circulation.

The appeal of classified advertisements is to groups, the appeal of display advertisements is to a wide general public. With the immense development of general advertising that came on the heels of the department-store campaigns mass circulation took on an importance far exceeding even that given to it by Northcliffe.

Less than three-quarters of a century earlier a circulation of 10,000 a day had been enough to command success: with a circulation of 50,000 *The Times* had dominated the world of journalism and advertising like an eighth wonder of the world. Even half a century previously a national penny paper with a circulation of 150,000 could get along comfortably: with 300,000 the *Daily Telegraph* was a giant indeed. Northcliffe with his halfpenny *Daily Mail* made 300,000 look small, but right up to the First World War a circulation of half-a-million was still comfortable enough: with over 800,000 the *Daily Mail* had the world of advertising at its feet. By the time Northcliffe died in 1922 such figures had ceased to have significance. The *Mail* had a circulation of 1,750,000 and within two decades the judgments brought by display advertising were to make even this figure seem small.

Once it had been possible for a group of public-spirited people or even one moderately rich man to establish an independent paper for other than commercial reasons without much regard for cost. Now newspaper-owning became big business, offering on the one hand the reward of fantastic profits, on the other the penalty of fantastic losses.

This change not only brought profound alterations in the character of the national press, it tore apart the whole structure of the provincial press whose emergence as a great force in public life had been one of the happiest consequences of the ending of the taxes on knowledge in the middle of the nineteenth century.

The journals then established by men representative of the political and commercial interests of their community were deeply rooted in their localities. Vigorously expressive of conflicting political views and interests they played a part of the greatest importance in the lives of the areas they served, giving powerful voice to new forces of public opinion.

This pattern was now to be ruthlessly broken in many areas. Newspapers that had come into existence in response to local needs and that had built up a relationship of peculiar intimacy with the communities they served found themselves turned into mere units in great financial deals, bought and sold like so much merchandise. Some were forced out of existence by the rising cost of newspaper production, others by the competition of national popular dailies printing in Manchester as well as London. Still others were forced into amalgamation with former rivals, often of different political views, or became members of chains controlled by great newspaper trusts centred in London. Most of those that managed to maintain independent existence did so in a gravely weakened condition.

Three years after the end of the First World War forty-one morning papers served great and varied communities throughout the provinces. Only nineteen now survive. In 1921 thirteen cities outside London had more than one morning newspaper and local public opinion could draw vitality from the clash of opinion and the rivalry in local reporting between them. To-day only two, Glasgow and Manchester, have, and since the death of the *Daily Dispatch* even Manchester only clings to the distinction because it is the publishing centre for the northern editions of the national dailies. Birmingham, Liverpool, Edinburgh, Cardiff, Leeds are great and popular cities. Not one of them can now support two morning papers. Although evening papers are less exposed to the competition of the metropolitan press than are morning ones even the number of towns in which there is a choice between evening papers has been reduced to eight.

This does not necessarily mean that the forty-six towns in Britain which now depend exclusively for local news and the press scrutiny of local public issues upon one newspaper—often owned by a London combine with no local roots—are badly served with general news. From the professional newspaper standpoint many are better served than they were—or could be now—by competing independent local journals with inadequate resources. Nor does it invariably mean that they must expect political bias. Although they frequently have to take it into

account a local newspaper necessarily in close and continuous relationship with readers of differing opinions cannot for
commercial reasons alone risk too strong a charge of partiality.
What it does mean is that much of the colour and vigour and
most of the diversity that the ending of the Stamp Tax brought
to provincial journalism has now gone for ever.

Democracy operates best where the strong clash of divergent
opinions compels the lively examination of great issues. It was
through the stimulation of debate that the provincial press best
served the nation in the great flowering of journalism that
followed the abolition of the taxes on knowledge. It is not the
one-sidedness of the monopoly newspaper that contains the
greatest threat to local democracy now but its circumspect
neutrality in many matters where the clash of opinion is desirable.

The process of trustification had already gone a good way
when Northcliffe died in 1922. It was carried immensely farther
by his brother Lord Rothermere—to whom, to a degree never
true of Northcliffe, newspapers had always been mainly important
as a source of wealth and commercial power. Fortunately for
itself and the nation Rothermere lost *The Times*. But under his
brother's will he was able to acquire the rest of Northcliffe's
newspaper and magazine interests for the comparatively modest
sum of £1,600,000. Of this he recovered £1,440,000 by a public
issue of debentures, keeping the equity, and with it control, for a
mere £160,000. Added to his own personal newspaper interests
this transaction made him master of the *Daily Mail*, the *Evening
News*, the *Daily Mirror*, the *Weekly Dispatch* and the *Sunday
Pictorial* in London, the *Daily Record*, the *Evening News*
and the *Sunday Mail* in Glasgow and more than a hundred
periodicals.

Such concentration of press power was sufficient to arouse
some public disquiet. But it was only a foretaste of what was to
come. The age of big business in newspapers had arrived.

At this stage Lord Rothermere was approached with an
interesting proposition by a man who had already shown himself,

in business and in the wider field of politics, well versed in the intricacies of negotiation and in the subtle playing off of one set of interests against another: Lord Beaverbrook. Lord Beaverbrook had acquired control of the *Daily Express* during the war and had later founded the *Sunday Express*. He was now anxious to obtain control of a London evening paper and had his eyes on the politically influential *Evening Standard* belonging to Sir Edward Hulton, who also owned the *Daily Sketch*, the *Manchester Daily Dispatch*, the *Manchester Evening Chronicle* and three Sunday newspapers.

Hulton was ill and was known to be thinking of disposing of his interests. Beaverbrook's proposition was that he should privately act as Rothermere's agent in negotiating for them on the promise that if he were successful Rothermere would pass over to him a 51% controlling interest in the *Evening Standard* in return for a minority interest of 49% per cent in the *Daily Express* and the *Sunday Express*.

There were other prospective purchasers in the field but Beaverbrook, adroit in the nice timing of large deals, out-manœuvred them and persuaded Hulton to sell to him for a flat £5,000,000. This done, the agreed transfer of control of the *Evening Standard* to Beaverbrook and of the minority interest in the *Daily* and *Sunday Express* to Rothermere was completed according to arrangement (Lord Beaverbrook bought back the Rothermere holding in the *Daily* and *Sunday Express* in 1933, acquiring at the same time the balance of the *Evening Standard* shares: since then he has been the principal proprietor of all three) and Rothermere took over the rest of the Hulton papers. At this stage he controlled three national daily papers, two provincial morning papers, three evening papers and five Sunday papers apart from his periodicals and his interest in the *Daily* and *Sunday Express* and the *Evening Standard*.

Fortunately perhaps his main interest in the Hulton papers was financial. Whatever journalism might have meant to Barnes or Delane or might still mean to C. P. Scott, to the first Viscount Rothermere it meant money—money and, of course, the illusion of personal power on which his vanity fed until it became so fat and gross as to be both ridiculous and horrifying. This illusion had even less to do with reality than Northcliffe's—or Beaverbrook's—as the utter failure of all his maladroit efforts to blackmail Conservative leaders into doing his will would surely have convinced a man less insensitive.

Now he looked around for a quick profit. Beaverbrook was not the only new power in the newspaper world. There were also the Berry brothers, Sir William Berry (later Lord Camrose) and Sir Gomer Berry (later Lord Kemsley). These two had begun their newspaper careers some twenty years previously with the ownership of the *Advertising World* and had subsequently acquired for a song the then derelict *Sunday Times* which they had transformed into a highly valuable property. In association with Sir Edward Iliffe, owner of the *Midland Daily Telegraph*, they were now possessed of the *Sunday Times*, the *Financial Times* and the *Daily Graphic* and had been among those after the Hulton properties when Beaverbrook intervened.

Rothermere now offered them the Manchester interests only of the Hulton group for £5,500,000, a figure substantially in excess of the price for which they had originally expected to buy the whole group and that Beaverbrook had paid for it. But if they wanted to expand they had to buy. They paid Rothermere's price.

As Lord Iliffe and the Berry brothers subsequently resold what they had bought from him to a new public company established under their control for £7,900,000 there is no reason to shed any tears for them. And indeed the mounting profits from newspaper publication at this period provided ample commercial justification for such profitable buying and selling—if commercial justification were the only test.

Having thus made a profitable beginning in newspaper trustification the Berry brothers turned their attention to the provincial evening paper field which, consisting for the most part as it did of small independent newspapers with no very highly developed commercial sense, seemed ripe for exploitation. They rapidly acquired a string of such papers. Their operations whetted Lord Rothermere's appetite. He concluded a second deal with them, this time for the Amalgamated Press which they bought from him for £8,000,000. He used the money on a buying spree of provincial evening papers in competition with theirs.

Nor were Rothermere and the Berry brothers the only ones to see a potential goldmine in the provincial press. The Westminster Press controlled by Lord Cowdray, the oil and public works contracting millionaire who had bought the *Westminster Gazette*, also embarked on a programme of provincial expansion. So did a fourth group, the Inveresk Paper Company, headed by an ambitious solicitor, Mr. William Harrison. Mr. Harrison broke into the press field first with the purchase of a group of illustrated papers headed by the *Illustrated London News* and the *Tatler*. He followed this up by buying United Newspapers Ltd., owners of the *Daily Chronicle*, *Sunday News* and a number of provincial papers, and went on to buy others—all, he said, to give 'the Inveresk Company an assured market for a large output of paper'.

By the end of 1929 the Berry brothers had twenty-six daily and Sunday papers under their control in addition to the Amalgamated Press. Lord Rothermere controlled fourteen and had a substantial interest in another three. The Westminster Press owned thirteen. The Inveresk Paper Company nine. Between them these four groups with no fewer than sixty-two daily and Sunday papers in their hands controlled close on half the entire newspaper press of the country. The long struggle for the independence of the press and that further struggle in the middle of the previous century to prevent this independence concentrating too much power in too few hands had taken an ironic twist indeed.

However, trustification had reached its climax. The economic crisis of 1930–31 cut advertising revenue and reduced the ease with which capital could be raised on the Stock Exchange. Checked in full flight the movement never regained the impetus that had carried it so fast and so far in the 'twenties. The greatest of the groups—the Berry group—split up, Lord Camrose taking

the *Daily Telegraph*, the *Financial Times* and Amalgamated Press;
Lord Kemsley the *Sunday Times*, the *Sunday Chronicle*, the
Sunday Graphic, the *Empire News*, the *Daily Sketch* and the
provincial papers owned by the group. Although the number of
provincial morning and evening papers controlled by the major
chains is still considerable—more than 40% of the total—it has
fallen since 1929 and shows little sign of increasing again now.
But it had gone far enough to destroy for all time much of that
pattern of independent local papers serving local interests that
had previously seemed so permanent a part of the national life
since the mid-nineteenth century.

Not all the damage done to independent provincial newspapers
in the hectic ten years that followed the First World War can be
blamed on trustification. Rising costs and loss of circulation and
advertisements to the nationals put many out of business. But at
the height of the struggle between the great trusts independent
provincial papers that got in their way were forced out of
existence without mercy. Others were bought and sold at
fantastically inflated prices.

One such head-on clash between the Berry group and Rothermere's provincial chain, Northcliffe Newspapers, found in 1929 a
sordid if dramatic expression in a fight for dominance in three
cities, Bristol, Newcastle and Derby. In the course of this several
formerly independent local papers were driven to the wall while
the invading giants spent money with wanton recklessness on
trying to force each other out of business. In the end the stakes
became too high even for them: Rothermere spent according to
Lord Camrose more than £1,000,000 in the course of the
Newcastle fight alone. A truce was called. The Berry interests
agreed to withdraw from Bristol and Derby and the Rothermere
interests from Newcastle, their formerly competing newspapers
merging with each other on the stricken fields.

In none of these arrangements, whether of war or of peace, were
the interests of the local communities given any substantial claim
to attention. In Bristol the effect was to leave a city which had
formerly enjoyed the service of four independent morning and

evening newspapers at the mercy of one Rothermere invader, the *Evening World*. In this instance, although unfortunately not in others, readers rebelled against the role of captive audience. A group of local citizens got together and started a second paper of their own, the *Bristol Evening Post*, which, after a struggle costly to both sides, forced Rothermere to come to terms with it. It still flourishes.

Nor although the material pattern of the provincial press suffered most was it only in the provinces that the character of journalism was changed by display advertising.

The extensive exploitation of display advertising gave an altogether new importance to the value a national newspaper could put on its space when calculated in terms of the rate per column inch per thousand readers. Of course the kind as well as the number of readers attracted to a newspaper still mattered to some advertisers and to some proprietors. Although their total circulations were small, quality papers such as *The Times* read by professional and business groups with relatively high incomes could then, as now, command advertisement revenue out of all relation to circulation figures because each unit in their circulation totals represented considerable individual buying power. But mass circulation newspapers were judged primarily by total numbers, as indeed they still are despite refinements in market research. What counted over most of the field of newspaper enterprise was the ability to offer the advertiser a mass market worthwhile in terms of total consuming power even though the individual purchasing power of those comprising it might be small.

The prizes for victory in the circulation race grew year by year. With a circulation of 1,750,000 the *Mail* was able to charge £1,400 a day for its front page and still be certain of a long waiting list of claimants. (It now, so much have advertising rates risen, charges £3,250 for a full page inside the paper: the *Express* has no difficulty in getting more than £5,000.) But as the rewards of success in the circulation race grew in magnitude the penalties of failure increased. Without large circulation it became virtually impossible for any popular paper to attract enough advertising to pay its way. It became necessary to spend more and more to win and hold readers: more on news services, more on features, more on pictures, more on a host of ancillary activities from free insurance to the organising of concerts and the provision of free advice on every topic under the sun, more, infinitely more, on newsprint as papers swelled in size in the attempt to offer something for everybody.

Even before Northcliffe's death it had already become clear that the *Mail* could not expect to hold its leadership much longer without serious challenge, and clear also that the newspaper war ahead would take forms which had little relationship to journalism as it had once been practised. The modest first step in free insurance had been taken by the *Daily News* in the First World War when it offered comfort to its readers by giving them free insurance against the risk of being killed in Zeppelin raids. It now developed into a vast scramble in competitive bribery.

By the 'twenties those who chose their daily reading advisedly could walk through the world armed against practically every blow a malign fate could offer from the collapse of a grandstand at a football match to the birth of twins. The husband and wife prudent enough to be killed in the same railway accident could be sure of leaving at least £10,000 to their heirs. These insurance schemes represented a heavy burden on top of rising editorial and production costs—they cost the *Daily Mail* £1,000,000 up to 1928 and the *Express* not very much less. This was small to what was to come.

Northcliffe was in the middle of plans for this new circulation war when he died. He rightly calculated that the most serious challenge would come from the *Daily Express*. 'Those who under-rate Beaverbrook,' he said to Tom Clarke shortly before his death, 'are fools. He is a young man—far younger than I am. He is an ambitious man. He is a clever man. . . . But do not worry. My plans are all made.'

Whatever those plans were, with Northcliffe's death the fire went out of them. The *Mail* had immense financial resources but the touch of genius was gone. While Rothermere gambled away millions in the provinces it fought increasingly on the defensive in London. To an extent that had not been the case for more than a quarter of a century the battle was now open.

The fortunes awaiting those who succeeded in this battle of the press attracted others besides Beaverbrook. Since newspapers had become big business the big business-men began to move in, usually disastrously. The first to do so was Lord Cowdray, whose activities in provincial journalism have already been noted.

He bought the evening *Westminster Gazette* and finding it easier to think in terms of losing thousands a day than hundreds turned it into a morning paper—one, said Lord Northcliffe in a sardonic pamphlet on 'Newspapers and Their Millionaires' published just before he died, with 'ignorance, provincialism, extravagance, mismanagement and muddle written all over it'. It survived only seven years before being absorbed by the *Daily News*, losing much money and destroying a great reputation in the process. Although newspapers had become big business, much more than big business was required to make them a success—a fact that was soon made plain by experience not only to Lord Cowdray but also to successive owners of the *Daily Chronicle*.

This paper had been acquired in 1918 by Lloyd George, who spent £1,600,000 of the money he had gathered from the sale of honours in buying it from the Lloyd family, owners of *Lloyd's Weekly News*. His brushes with Northcliffe had persuaded him, no doubt, that while the ownership of a newspaper did not automatically bestow on a press peer the political power he liked to assume a politician with his own paper in his pocket might well be in a stronger position to defend himself when knives were out in Fleet Street and Whitehall.

But the day for personal party journals was past. Lloyd George merely succeeded in destroying the reputation of the *Chronicle* for political independence without notably strengthening himself in his battles with his enemies, and when the profits to be made in Fleet Street began to excite the interest of business-men he very sensibly decided to strengthen his Liberal Party chest by cashing in on commercial optimism. He sold the paper to two eminent gentlemen in the city, one of them a merchant prince from India, Sir David Yule, the other Sir Thomas Catto, later Governor of the Bank of England, at a profit of £1,400,000 to his private party funds. These two distinguished leaders of business kept the paper for two years, found they were in danger of losing, not making, a fortune and sold it to Mr. William Harrison and the Inveresk Paper Company for the price they had paid Lloyd George.

Harrison flung the *Daily Chronicle* into the circulation race with extravagant vigour—so much so indeed that although its circulation was close on 1,000,000, second only to that of the *Daily Mail*, its losses within three years reached such a level that its bankers summoned back Sir Thomas Catto and asked him to act as honest broker in disposing of the property before still more was lost. Thus brought to its death not by any failure as a newspaper but solely by the financial operations of successive proprietors the *Chronicle* was sold to the *Daily News*, following the *Westminster Gazette* into a common Liberal grave in the offices of that newspaper which having taken the name of the *Daily News and Westminster Gazette* after its lunch at Lord Cowdray's expense, now changed it to the *News Chronicle* after dinner at Mr. Harrison's (late supper at the Kemsleys' has now made it the *News Chronicle*).

Trustification and high finance combined with rising production costs, changing public tastes and the fierce scramble for circulation to attract advertising revenue had sadly changed the face of London journalism as the 'thirties opened. Of the eight evening papers that had once instructed and entertained the London public only three remained. Three morning papers, the *Daily Chronicle*, the *Westminster Gazette* and the *Daily Graphic* (which the Berry brothers amalgamated with the *Daily Sketch*), had gone, joining the *Tribune* and the *Standard* which had failed earlier. Although *The Times* rescued from Lord Rothermere by Colonel J. J. Astor was safe and the *Daily Telegraph* whose circulation had fallen to less than 84,000 was on the eve of a remarkable rebirth under the control of Lord Camrose, the *Morning Post* despite—or perhaps because of—its fine literary quality and highly idiosyncratic approach to affairs was failing fast and for it there was to be no reprieve. In the race for circulation the *Daily Mail* still had the lead but the *Daily Express* was now hard on its heels, constantly narrowing the gap by superb popular journalism of a more sophisticated flavour than was to be found in the columns of the *Mail* and one more suited to the brittle gaieties and light-hearted extravagances of an age in which publicity had become the social king.

It was at this stage that a new figure, Julius Salter Elias, later Lord Southwood, moved to the centre of the stage, marking with his arrival yet another turn in the commercialisation of the press and one more squalid and fantastic than any that had preceded it. It is not without irony that the methods he introduced had for their purpose the sales promotion of the official socialist newspaper, the *Daily Herald*.

XIII

MR. ELIAS SELLS NEWSPAPERS

LORD SOUTHWOOD can claim no such place in a gallery of press portraits as falls of right to Lord Northcliffe or Lord Beaverbrook by reason of that flavour of genius, bold and original if destructive, which is to be found in their personalities. He was not an eruptive and pervasive force in journalism as Northcliffe pre-eminently was and Beaverbrook is. He was above all else an ordinary little man, a man undistinguished in almost every respect save one: his talent for commercial success. He did not cut a new path for himself through the jungle of the Fourth Estate. He went where the guideposts pointed. It was this, indeed, that made him so portentous a figure, for by following the course of newspaper development in the 'twenties to its logical conclusion he made for himself a career that may not unfairly be said to mark the apogee—or perhaps the *reductio ad absurdum*—of the commercial principle in journalism.

The ambitions that inspire those who own newspapers are commonly varied. 'Purposes', as the Royal Commission on the Press remarked, 'are seldom single and motives seldom unmixed; the desire to make money, the desire to make opinion and the desire to make a good newspaper can and do insensibly blend.' It was not so with Elias. His was the single-track mind in journalism. He was as much unlike the popular idea of a press peer—or for that matter his actual contemporaries on this elevated rung of society, Lords Beaverbrook, Rothermere, Camrose and Kemsley—as any man could well be.

He had no interest in newspapers as instruments of political power or public influence, or even as a means to a large private fortune. Although he longed for a peerage and was overwhelmed with delight when he got one, especially so because the recommendation was made by a Conservative Prime Minister (characteristically his first act on receiving the news was to send for a book on etiquette that would tell him the correct manner to address the Prime Minister in reply), he had no desire to play a part in society. He was a noble benefactor of the Children's Hospital, Great Ormond Street, and raised immense sums—more than £20,000,000 in all—for charity which apart from his business was the one consuming interest in his life, but his private estate when he died was little more than £100,000. Apart from an odd passion for buying clothes—he had a standing order with his tailor for two dozen suits a year, all conservatively cut in blue, grey or brown, and never liked to have less than fifty pairs of shoes in his wardrobe—he had no private extravagances. He went abroad only once in his life, for a day trip to Le Touquet, and invariably spent his annual holiday of four weeks at the same place, the Grand Hotel in Eastbourne. There, he and his wife, to whom he was devoted, listened enraptured each evening to the orchestra in the Palm Court, throwing disapproving glances at fellow guests who chatted or rattled coffee cups: their favourite tune was the Blue Danube Waltz.

He rarely entertained, still more rarely went to a theatre, hardly ever read a book, had no interest in conversation except on business matters, listened to almost nothing on the radio except 'Lift Up Your Hearts'. He knew nothing of art—when he decided, on getting his peerage, that he ought to have a country house he made an offer for one lock, stock and barrel including all the furniture and pictures and when the vendor insisted on taking some of the pictures summoned the Editor of *Ideal Homes* and instructed him to fill the blank spaces on the walls as he thought best.

He was a good employer who wanted everyone around him to be happy, happy and loyal. Apart from charity his whole life was concentrated on the firm of Odhams Press. He had joined it as an office boy, saved it from liquidation by tramping London for cut-price orders, and eventually transformed it from a firm of nearly derelict jobbing printers into one of the largest and most prosperous printing, publishing and bill-posting businesses in the world. He worked day and night, had immense commercial courage, as he showed when Horatio Bottomley's arrest and conviction for fraud threatened to ruin not only *John Bull* but Odhams itself, and was wholly untroubled by doubt as to the purpose of the newspapers and periodicals he controlled. He was concerned only that they should sell and thus keep Odhams' printing presses busy.

His entry into daily journalism in 1929 was dictated solely by this latter need, which was, indeed, the one settled principle of his business life. Odhams already owned an extremely flourishing Sunday paper, the *People*, whose circulation Elias raised from the mere 250,000 at which it stood when Odhams took the paper over in settlement of a printing debt to over 2,000,000 by methods which he was now to introduce into daily journalism.

Years before he had replied to the owners of the Church paper, the *Guardian*, when they expressed dismay that the printers of their respectable journal should also be the printers of Bottomley's scandal-mongering weekly, *John Bull*, that he saw no difference between printing periodicals and selling lamp standards, razor blades or hair restorers, nor any more reason why he should consider the morals and opinions of his customers in the one case than in the other. To the *People* he had applied methods of salesmanship applicable to the sale of such goods, employing hundreds of door-to-door canvassers who persuaded householders to take the paper by promises of a great free insurance scheme—the first ever provided by a Sunday paper—free gifts and competitions.

He did not believe much in news. 'The public gets the news in all the papers,' he said. The *People's* success was based primarily on salesmanship and sensational features, of which the most important was a series of 'Confession Stories'. His first big winner was the confessions of Montague Newton a solicitor who extorted huge sums from an Indian maharajah with eccentric sexual tastes in what came to be known as the 'Mr. A' case. His second was the confessions of the housekeeper of Hayley Morris, the central figure in an even more sordid case of sexual offences against young girls.

Hardly less successful on a more respectable plane were 'intimate revelations' of King Carol of Rumania and Madame Lupescu and—a great social triumph for the *People* for which it paid the large sum of £20,000—Lord Lonsdale's life story told by himself. These confession stories were displayed with solid black headlines of a size never seen in any British newspaper before and were supported by news stories of romance, passion, violence and changing fortune for which the *People's* editor, Mr. Harry Ainsworth, scoured Britain and the Continent. The recipe was enormously successful.

But the very success of Elias, the salesman, soon began to put Elias, the printer, in difficulties. To cope with the *People's* weekly print more and more presses had to be bought—and these presses stood idle most of the week. At first Elias hoped to solve this problem by a long-term contract to print the *Radio Times* for the B.B.C. The enormous demand for this journal would have given his presses enough work to keep them busy for a good part of the week and Odhams' rapidly extending magazine interests could have taken care of the rest: indeed if he had got the contract it is unlikely he would ever have troubled to try his skill in daily journalism. But Sir John Reith, director-general of the B.B.C., had married the daughter of one of the original Odhams' partners and austerely decided that to give the contract to Odhams might savour of nepotism. It went elsewhere and Elias turned his mind to thoughts of a daily paper.

The first to attract his attention was the *Morning Post*, which was widely known to be in financial difficulties. Although he sometimes lent the garden of his house at Highgate for Conservative fêtes he was not a member of the Conservative Party and the *Morning Post* was High Tory. He was a Jew and it was violently anti-semitic. But there was nothing in his philosophy to require that differences of principle should stand in the way of a business transaction. 'Political attitudes', as his official biographer Mr. R. J. Minney remarks, 'did not really concern him. Printing was a job of work; machines were machines—and forty of them, great majestic presses, lay idle for six days of each week for fifty-two weeks of the year.' Negotiations were begun. In the end they broke down not on any issue of principle but simply because Elias came to the conclusion that it would be impossible to popularise so idiosyncratic a paper as the *Morning Post* was without driving away most of its existing readers. He would be paying merely for a name. It was not an attractive enough commercial proposition.

He then turned his mind to the Liberal *Daily Chronicle*. Sir David Yule and Sir Thomas Catto had by now begun to realise how little they knew about newspapers and were known to be on the look-out for a purchaser. The *Chronicle* had a circulation of close on 1,000,000 compared with the mere 80,000 of the *Morning Post* and was in all ways a more attractive proposition. But unfortunately others thought so too and before Elias could make a deal the Inveresk Paper Company acquired an option on it for £2,000,000.

At this moment a casual meeting set his entirely apolitical mind on another track. It so happened that John Dunbar who had joined Odhams some years previously as editor of the *Kinematograph Weekly* (formerly the *Magic Lantern Monthly*) but was now in general editorial charge of all Odhams periodicals had served during the war in the Press Department of the Royal Flying Corps. There he had made the acquaintance of Mr. C. P. Robertson, later chief press officer at the Air Ministry, who before the war had been labour correspondent of the Press Association. As a labour correspondent Robertson had come to know Ernest Bevin, then a young organiser of the Dockers' Union but by now general secretary of the Transport and General Workers' Union, a member of the General Council of the T.U.C. and chairman of the *Daily Herald*. Robertson still occasionally met Bevin over lunch in a restaurant in the Aldwych handy to both their offices. Happening to meet Dunbar after one of these lunch-time meetings, he remarked that Bevin was worried by the drain of the *Daily Herald* on trade union funds and was thinking of approaching the Prudential Insurance Company in the hope of persuading it to put up money to develop the paper along more popular lines. Dunbar, who although not a member of the Labour Party had picked up some socialist sympathies during his youth in Scotland and had been active in trade union organisation among journalists and music-hall artists during his early days in London, carried the news to Elias. Neither of them knew Bevin but Dunbar telephoned Robertson and he agreed to act as an intermediary. A meeting was arranged.

The position of the *Daily Herald* itself when Elias, Dunbar and Bevin met throws a good deal of light on the effect of newspaper commercialisation in the 'twenties. The paper had first come into existence as a strike sheet during a printers' lockout in January 1911 but had later been resurrected as a socialist daily paper. By the time the outbreak of war in 1914 forced it to become a weekly it was almost self-supporting with a circulation of 50,000 a day.

To revive it as a daily when the war ended was not easy. Printing costs had risen sharply and the price of newsprint even more so. The standard of news reporting and of the features, pictures and sports coverage expected by readers had been progressively raised under the stimulation of competition. Free insurance and other services had become almost obligatory if a large circulation was to be secured. But the enthusiasm of George Lansbury, its editor and moving spirit, was contagious. He had a genius for collecting money for good causes and managed to secure promises of a total of £100,000 from a number of trade unions. The miners' unions added another £42,000 on their own account, and the Cooperative Movement £40,000. Various private subscribers contributed a few more thousands and the National Union of Railwaymen agreed to act as a newsprint bank, buying and holding newsprint which the *Herald* paid for as it used it. With these resources it was possible to go forward. On 31 March 1919 the *Daily Herald* reappeared with Lansbury as its editor and

Gerald Gould, then well known as a poet and essayist, as its associate editor.

It was as gay, impudent, passionate, rebellious and unofficial as it had been in pre-war days and soon collected round it a band of contributors such as any newspaper might envy. Osbert Sitwell wrote leading articles for it—two famous ones, sharply barbed for the benefit of Winston Churchill, in free verse. Siegfried Sassoon contributed its literary notes. H. M. Tomlinson, H. W. Nevinson, Havelock Ellis, E. M. Forster, Israel Zangwill, W. J. Turner, Herbert Farjeon, Ivor Brown wrote regularly for it. Walter de la Mare, Edward Garnett, W. H. Davies, Rose Macaulay, Aldous Huxley, Robert Graves, Philip Guedalla and a score of others scarcely less well known were among its frequent contributors and Bernard Shaw wrote a series of articles. M. Phillips Price, who had been *Manchester Guardian* correspondent in Russia during the revolution, went to Berlin for it, H. N. Brailsford was its special correspondent in war-devastated Europe, Vernon Bartlett wrote its Paris Letter, W. N. Ewer was (and still is) its diplomatic correspondent. Will Dyson, the brilliant Australian cartoonist whose mordant genius had brought it fame before the war, rejoined it, producing, when the Treaty of Versailles was signed, a cartoon with the caption 'Curious! I seem to hear a child weeping' whose tragic prevision has rarely been equalled: a drawing of Clemenceau walking with President Wilson and Lloyd George down the steps of the Palace of Versailles while in one corner, half hidden by a pillar, a naked baby sobs, around its head a halo marked 'Class of 1940'.

Seldom can there have been a paper with so diverse and so brilliant a staff. It was, said Northcliffe, as it survived one financial crisis after another 'The Miracle of Fleet Street'. But the time when newspapers could live on miracles was over. The whole of newspaper development was flowing in other directions.

By 1920 the *Herald's* circulation had reached 330,000. A decade or so earlier that would have meant undreamed of prosperity for a Labour paper. In the conditions that now ruled it was not sufficient even for solvency. Readers alone were not enough.

Great advertising revenue was needed to keep a daily paper afloat and this the *Herald* could not get. The post-war industrial depression had begun. Unemployment was growing. Its readers were in the main working-class. They lacked the purchasing power to attract large advertisers even if such advertisers had not, for the most part, been unwilling to spend money on a paper whose politics they disliked. The price of the paper had to be raised from 1*d.*, to which all the popular ½*d.* papers had gone during the war, to 2*d.* in an attempt to meet rising costs. Even at this figure—double that of all its popular rivals—the paper managed to hold on to a circulation of 200,000. It was not sufficient. Only constant appeals to readers for donations and gifts from rich sympathisers touched by Lansbury's importunities kept the paper alive: on one occasion only the eleventh-hour discovery of some old rolls of paper in the cellar enabled it to come out. By 1922 Lansbury knew that the *Herald* could not much longer survive as an independent paper. He had received a number of private offers for its name and goodwill from people who believed that with capital behind it it could be made to pay, but he refused to sell it to a non-socialist. Instead he offered to hand it over to the Labour Party and the T.U.C. to be run as an official Labour paper.

This was done. The trade unions affiliated to the T.U.C. agreed on a special levy to finance it (six years later the T.U.C. took the paper over completely, relieving the Labour Party of all financial responsibility) and a new editor was appointed—Hamilton Fyfe, a distinguished war correspondent on Northcliffe's staff who had joined the Labour Party after the war.

With its loss of independence the *Herald* lost also a good deal of its original gaiety and élan. It became more respectable, but also much duller. Most of the brilliant band who had sharpened their pens in its pages drifted away. But its general news service was extended and its interest for the ordinary reader increased. Its political and industrial news was superior to that of most of its more popular rivals—as were also oddly enough its racing tips. It took its responsibilities seriously and sought to deal intelligently with the problems of the day, stating the Labour point of view with force and candour. But it could not compete with the *Mail*, the *Express*, the *Daily News* and the *Chronicle* in entertainment and general appeal—nor in free insurance. It was smaller in size and it carried nothing like as many features as they did. It acquired a solid core of a quarter of a million readers but could not much increase that number or obtain anything like the amount of advertising modern conditions made necessary.

This was the situation when Elias and Dunbar met Bevin. It was one in which the small figure of the apolitical printer Julius Salter Elias could hardly help but seem a remarkable answer to the T.U.C.'s problems when his interest in taking over the financial burden of the *Daily Herald* was made known. His proposition was hardly less welcome to the political Labour Party. Continental socialist parties had met the problem of a hostile press by themselves establishing powerful social-democratic newspapers with circulations and resources comparable to those of their rivals. The commercialisation of the popular press in Britain had made this impossible.

Whatever their political views those who bought popular newspapers had come to expect something very different from either the Continental socialist dailies or the old *Daily Herald* —less political, much more comprehensive in news and features, vastly more costly to produce, dependent to a much greater extent than the Continental press on large advertisement revenue and therefore requiring a vastly greater circulation to pay its way. A circulation of 250,000 might have sufficed if the *Herald* readers had belonged to the upper and middle classes. But they were, by the nature of the case, mainly working class. Individually their purchasing power was not such as to attract advertisers; numbers were essential.

The proposal now made to the T.U.C. by Elias offered a way round this problem of an unexpected and welcome kind. They found themselves invited to do business with a unique phenomenon—a man who although able to command the resources needed to develop a newspaper with a great circulation was not in the least interested in its political views. But he was perfectly prepared to give any guarantees asked for that it should continue to advocate the policies of the Labour Party so long as he, for his part, was given the right to do whatever was necessary to raise its sales to more than a million.

Eight years previously C. P. Scott, examining the nature of newspapers on the occasion of the *Manchester Guardian's* centenary, had said: 'In all living things there must be a certain unity, a principle of vitality and growth. It is so with a newspaper and the more complete and clear this unity the more vigorous and fruitful the growth. A newspaper has two sides to it. It is a business like any other. . . . But it is much more than a business . . . it has a moral as well as a material existence and its character and influence are determined by the balance of these two forces.' Elias was ready in the interests of the commercial principle to deny with every show of assurance that any such unity need exist; to say that what a paper stood for in public affairs —its moral existence—need be of no particular concern to those in charge of its organisation—its material existence—and to affirm that body and soul were perfectly easily divisible by trust deed.

There were those to whom this could not but seem a dubious journalistic principle, not only when judged by the austere standards of a C. P. Scott but even by the more commercial ones of a Northcliffe or a Beaverbrook. For there could be no question that much of the reason for the rapid advance of the *Express* at this time, as of the *Mail* earlier, lay in the wholeness of its personality and the singleness of its purpose; whether one liked it or not its attitude to life was never in doubt, it was expressed not merely in its leading articles but in every headline and paragraph and choice of type.

Yet whatever the journalistic dubiety of Elias's doctrine it could hardly do other than strike the trade union directors, struggling with their apparently insoluble problem, as a political principle of the most welcome kind. They accepted Elias's offer and in so doing precipitated a newspaper war of the most savage intensity that was to have remarkable results on the total circulation of the popular press.

A new company (Daily Herald (1929) Limited) was formed, the T.U.C. receiving £49,000 in shares out of a total nominal capital of £100,000 for their property. Odhams received an exclusive printing contract and put up the balance of the nominal share capital in cash, undertaking at the same time to secure all the large additional finance needed to reorganise the paper in a big way. Odhams had four directors on the Board including the chairman, Elias, the T.U.C. four with Bevin as vice-chairman. The entire commercial management of the paper was vested in Odhams but trust deeds ensured that the political policy of the paper should be that of the Labour Party and its industrial policy that of the T.U.C.

Significantly enough neither side considered it necessary to provide safeguards for the editor or even to discuss his position in drawing up the constitution of the new paper, although this might have seemed of some importance to the day-to-day policy and influence of a political newspaper in such a situation. To the T.U.C. an editor was no more than another paid official at the receiving end of a Congress resolution, to Elias, a technician hired to do a production job. In the event two editors were dismissed in five years and when the whole question of the editor's status and area of responsibility was directly raised by the resignation of a third (the present writer) on an issue of general principle in the early days of the war Odhams successfully maintained in face of Labour and trade-union protests at the subsequent Board meeting and elsewhere that the appointment of the editor and the degree of authority allotted to him fell solely within its responsibility as commercial controller of the paper.

Elias originally estimated that the *Herald* could be made to pay with a circulation of 1,000,000. This figure was reached with the first issue of the new paper on 17 March 1930 (the opening day of the flat-racing season) after nine months of preparation in the course of which Ernest Bevin toured the country appealing for the support of Labour and trade-union audiences while Odhams reinforced political enthusiasm with financial advantage by offering a personal reward of £3 15s., plus a contribution of £2 10s. to local party funds, to any Labour Party member who enrolled a hundred registered readers. Those readers willing to buy the paper for at least ten weeks were themselves rewarded with a prize of either a camera or a writing set according to taste—a method of sales promotion never previously tried by a daily paper.

The new 1d. paper was twice the size of the old *Herald*. It had a specially written serial by Edgar Wallace, a series of articles on world affairs by H. G. Wells, a page of women's fashions, four pages of sport, scores of photographs and a message from Mr. Ramsay MacDonald. Its page size was somewhat smaller than that of the *Mail*, the *Express* and the *Daily News* because it had to be the same size as the *People* and its headline type—bought originally to suit the *People's* special needs in sensational display— was blacker and uglier than was then customary in daily journalism. But it was clearly excellent value for money as a popular news paper and had little difficulty in holding on to the million sale even after the first curiosity-demand passed. Indeed its impact on an already over-stretched industry was such that the already financially weak *Daily Chronicle* survived the arrival of this new competitor by less than ten weeks.

Even in 1930 a million circulation was a handsome enough figure by most standards. The *Daily Telegraph* was being nursed back to great prosperity and substantial political influence on much less than that: its circulation after coming down in price from 2d. to 1d. in 1930 was 200,000 and it took nearly another six years of unostentatious steady progress to reach the half million. Yet even with a million sale the *Herald* was heavily in the red.

The reason for this difference lay, of course, in the fact that the *Daily Telegraph* was edited and produced for a Conservative middle-class public with an individual purchasing power high enough to draw advertisers by the attraction of a 'quality' market, whereas the *Herald* was designed as a mass-circulation paper with a predominantly working-class readership. The big advertisers took space in the early first numbers of the new *Herald* but very soon made clear their unwillingness to continue doing so on a large enough scale for profit with a net sales figure of only just over a million.

Elias thus found himself faced with a situation in which a rapid further rise in circulation was plainly essential if the paper were even to cover its costs. He was caught inescapably by the commercial formula that now governed in the newspaper industry and by which he himself had prospered in his other enterprises.

Five years later a much rougher, tougher and more politically radical character than Elias, H. G. Bartholomew, editorial director and later chairman of the *Daily Mirror*, was to meet this problem in a very different way. Using sensational make-up for news and features, bringing strip cartoons to the British public for the first time, daily exploiting sex and crime in news, features and pictures to an even greater extent than the *People* on Sundays he managed to combine all this with a vigorous, muck-raking policy in social affairs and a hard-hitting, alarm-bell-ringing radicalism in political affairs and thus created a new kind of popular daily journalism that for the first time successfully tapped the great reservoir of working-class readership which all daily newspapers had previously ignored. As a result the *Mirror* was able without any adventitious commercial aids to build up a circulation so vast that it could command what advertisements it needed while getting along with far fewer than most others required because of its large income from sales.

Elias was precluded from seeking circulation by such iconoclastic, swashbuckling, loud-mouthed and radical means both by his obligations as the publisher of the official organ of a serious political party—most of whose leading members had already begun to complain bitterly that the *Herald* was growing sensational and devoted too little space to the serious examination of political, economic and international problems—and by his own character. A shy and modest man, he had no objection to sex and crime if they sold papers but he disliked noise, hated what he considered rudeness—almost the only interest he ever showed in the *Herald's* leading articles was to complain of the adjectives of opprobrium employed in dealing with Mr. Chamberlain and his policy during the period of appeasement—could not bear to be thought politically unrespectable, and longed to be liked by everyone. Nor could he ever bring himself to believe that ordinary people could be excited by politics.

Both the road taken by the *Daily Telegraph* and that to be taken by the *Daily Mirror* were closed to him. So also—although he hankered after it constantly—was that cut for itself by the *Daily Express*, which was advancing rapidly in circulation and advertising favour. This it was doing by making suburbia feel that it belonged to the smart set and that every day was a happy day however ominous the clouds on the national and inter-national horizon might be. But both these objectives were closed to the *Herald* by its political nature. Moreover the *Express* had the advantage of a proprietor who although capricious and mischievous in his political hates and loves was able and ready to plough back the profits he made into the business in order to develop world-wide news services of an exclusive character. Elias could not afford to wait for the long-term results of a long-term editorial policy. Nor had he any real interest in news: he could not help feeling that money spent on foreign correspondence was a wilful extravagance—how much nicer the world would have been if it had ended at Eastbourne.

When a periodical did not pay it had been his habit to cut his losses without further dissipation of energy: he was interested only in success. He did this a little later with the most famous socialist weekly there has ever been, Blatchford's *Clarion*, which he bought in 1933 in the belief that it might be retailored to attract a large public under the editorship of Robert Fraser, now director-general of the Independent Television Authority, only to close it down after six weeks when he found that it was selling no more than 80,000 copies. Too much capital had been sunk in the *Herald* for such a drastic remedy. To finance its expansion and set up a printing-plant in Manchester as well as

London Elias had borrowed heavily on Odhams' assets by means of debentures issued through a finance company, the Investment Registry, with which he had close associations. He could not afford to turn back. But he had plenty of commercial courage and if he did not understand daily newspapers very much nor politics at all he understood a great deal about the selling of goods to an apathetic public.

He dismissed the *Herald's* editor, William Mellor, who had been with the paper since the days of Lansbury's miracle, and appointed another; found him no more satisfactory and dismissed him (in both cases with generous compensation, for he was a kindly man) and appointed a third—a younger one, who, although the circulation rose, turned out a disappointment to him for other reasons and, finally, as mentioned earlier, resigned. The rise in circulation although substantial was not enough.

To increase it the paper must, he decided, be made brighter, less political, less serious, more entertaining—altogether more likely to catch the roving eye of the stray buyer at the railway bookstalls. Each morning he spread all the popular morning papers on the floor of his office—it was rarely his habit actually to read them—and walked among them brooding. He ordered the use of more and more pictures, producing from a disgruntled wit the comment that the only way to get any socialism into the official Labour paper was to write it on the back of a bathing beauty. He did not try to turn it from Labour politics. He had undertaken that it should remain a Labour paper and he held faithfully to his word: all he wished was that its politics could be made less noticeable. Yet despite everything he did the circulation continued to remain below the level that the iron laws of advertising, calculated on net-sales and readers'-income levels, demanded.

It was in these circumstances that Elias decided to go out and buy readers. A million circulation among people who took the paper because they wanted to read it was no good. Even a million and a half would probably prove insufficient. Very well then, the circulation must be raised to two million—the largest in the world. That would make advertisers sit up. Whether those who bought the paper read it was immaterial. All that mattered was that they should become registered readers, units in a net-sales certificate.

The circulation war that this decision precipitated marks the logical climax of the commercial principle introduced into journalism by Northcliffe.

As a consequence of the Northcliffe revolution the intimate relationship that had formerly existed between newspapers and their readers based on mutuality of interest and confidence in the independence, integrity and good judgment of those responsible for editorial policy had become progressively less important. Now not merely whether people bought a newspaper because they trusted it but even whether once bought they actually bothered to read it was of little significance. All that mattered was that they should buy it.

After seven months of fighting existence the new *Daily Herald* had a circulation of 1,082,000, close on four times what it had been when Elias and Bevin made their bargain. Ahead of it were the *News Chronicle* with a circulation of 1,400,000 (the combined circulation of the *Daily News* and the *Daily Chronicle* when they joined forces was 1,600,000 but some of this had been lost), the *Daily Express* with 1,693,000, and the *Daily Mail* with 1,845,000. All these three had now to be passed if Elias was to achieve his aim.

He turned to the methods that came naturally to him. Vast numbers of canvassers were engaged, many of them naval officers axed in the economy wave and glad to earn £3 or so a week touting from door to door. The other newspapers had to do likewise to defend their positions. Soon an army of more than 50,000 canvassers was knocking at doors all over the country, pleading with householders to take this newspaper or that. Included in the bait offered were insurance schemes more grandiose than ever before and a galaxy of 'easy to win competitions' with prizes of up to £5,000.

None of this proved sufficient. Elias was forced to increase the pace. His canvassers were armed with bribes of astonishing variety: cameras, fountain pens, silk stockings, tea-kettles, cutlery; they were the bagmen of the modern world seeking payment not in currency but in a signature on a piece of paper, a promise to become a registered reader for ten weeks. The *Express* replied vigorously, so on a slightly lesser scale did the *Mail* and the *News Chronicle*. The shower of free gifts became a torrent: the cost to the newspapers appalling. New readers were being gained, it is true. But the cost was high: for the *Herald* it worked out at £1 a head for a promise to take for ten weeks a paper costing 1d. a day.

Briefly, sanity returned. At a special meeting of the Newspaper Proprietors' Association which met under the shadow of growing national economic and financial crises the others warned Elias that if he continued in his course they would throw every resource they could command into the struggle and outbid him on every free-gift offer he made. An agreement was reached that although newspaper canvassing should continue, the bait offered to new readers should be restricted to competitions and free insurance, there should be no free gift schemes and nothing should be offered to readers below cost.

The agreement did not, however, last long. Elias was in no position to depend on the same free insurance and competition schemes as the others. His problem was different from theirs. They could rub along comfortably on the circulations they already had. He could not. So long as it could hold its position against attack and look to editorial enterprise to bring a due reward in time his main rival, the *Daily Express*, had no objection to shedding some of the artificial gains which had, from its standpoint, become absurd to the point of fantasy; how absurd was demonstrated when it suddenly called off intensive canvassing and dropped 250,000 in circulation almost overnight.

Elias dared not risk such a gesture. Not only was the *Herald* forced by its need for advertising revenue to hold what it had won at almost any cost, it had to continue to expand or die. Unless it could flourish a net sales certificate of the order of 2,000,000 in front of advertisers it could not hope to pay its way on the level at which it had been forced to establish itself to get into the race at all.

The *Express* continued to spend more and more on news services in all parts of the world. On the *Herald* editorial costs—except for big names that had advertising value—were vigorously cut back. The saving was a mere drop in the ocean. And then pacing his room Elias found—or thought he found—an ace up his sleeve.

Some time before this Odhams had branched out into the popular book-publishing business in a large way. A new process of bookbinding at reduced cost had been developed. With its aid Elias perceived he might find a way to get round the no-free-gifts bargain while holding to the letter of his agreement. He could replace the bait of free gifts to registered readers by the offer of books at prices which although advertised as 'far below real value' would in fact be sufficient to cover costs. No one could accuse him of having gone back on his word. He would not be giving anybody anything—he would be asking them to pay.

Vast editions of the *Home Doctor*, the *Handyman* and a popular dictionary were printed and the canvassing teams increased. The scheme proved even more successful than he had hoped and he moved on to a bolder plan: the offer of a complete set of the works of Charles Dickens in sixteen volumes handsomely bound in cloth or imitation leather—something for every mother to buy for her children and every newly married couple to display in the front room as an evidence of culture. To Elias the man of commerce this was simply a shrewd stroke of business. When complaints thundered from all over Fleet Street he was amazed. No one, he protested, could accuse him of breaking his agreement, he had merely found a way round it. He ought to be congratulated for his shrewdness, not reviled for business dishonesty. Other newspaper proprietors thought differently. A meeting of the controllers of the four papers most heavily involved in the circulation war, the *Express*, the *Mail*, the *News Chronicle* and the *Herald*, was called on neutral ground in a private room in the Savoy. In a minority of one, he offered to compromise. He was shaken by the storm that raged around him and conscious of how heavily he was already leaning on Odhams' other properties to sustain the *Herald* and how much greater might be the financial drain if Beaverbrook, with the *Sunday Express* and the *Evening Standard* as well as the *Daily Express* to rely on, threw all his resources into the attack. Perhaps, he said, some agreement could be reached to limit book offers—innocent though they were. But Beaverbrook demanded total retreat. Nothing less than the complete withdrawal of the Dickens offer would satisfy him as the price of peace. Elias refused and with a dramatic gesture, Beaverbrook, ever the actor, walked over to him. 'Elias,' he said, ' this is war—war to the death. I shall fight you to the bitter end', and drawing an imaginary sword he ran him through the body.

On this note the meeting ended. Elias returned to his office to tell his waiting colleagues what had taken place. Lords Beaverbrook and Rothermere and Sir Walter Layton returned to theirs. The war, as Beaverbrook had declared, was on. Sets of Dickens were hurriedly ordered by the *Express*, *Mail* and *News Chronicle* and flung at the heads of readers increasingly bemused by this concern for their literary education—those offered by the *Express* which lacked the advantage given to Odhams by its book-publishing business cost 14s. 4d. to produce and were sold at 10s., involving the paper in a loss of over £26,000 on the 124,000 sets disposed of.

But as is well known not everyone wants more than one good book. With the original free gift agreement torn to shreds the battle was once more open. Into it the warring newspapers now threw everything they could lay their hands on, hardly excluding the kitchen sink. Cameras, fountain pens, silk stockings, cutlery had been offered before: the canvassers at the doors now offered kettles, tea-sets, fruit services, mincing machines, mangles, overcoats, flannel trousers, mackintoshes, boots and shoes, gold wristlet watches and ladies' underwear. In South Wales, which was a particular target for canvassers because the total readership of daily newspapers there had previously been small, it was estimated that by skilfully timed switches from the *Herald* to the *Express*, the *Express* to the *Mail* and the *Mail* back to the *Herald* a miner's family could be clothed from head to foot at the cost of a few shillings. Neighbours who took different papers found it easy to equip their kitchens at no cost to themselves by ordering each other's paper and swopping over the garden fence. Journalism had reached its zenith as a public service. One had only to be a 'new reader' to get the moon.

The struggle proceeded. First the *Herald* passed the *News Chronicle*. Then the *Express* passed the *Mail*, ending its close on forty years' supremacy. Then the *Herald* passed the *Mail* also and came up hard on the heels of the *Express*. The two of them shot neck and neck down the straight with the *Mail* and the *News Chronicle* racing for third place. Between them the four were now spending close on £60,000 a week, or at the rate of £3,000,000 a year, on clothing and equipping hundreds and thousands of people all over Britain. The *Herald* made a last sprint. It beat the *Express* by a cutlery set and became—although by a matter of days only—the first newspaper in the world to announce a circulation of 2,000,000 copies a day. It was a remarkable achievement and one which Elias felt justified everything. He had increased the *Herald's* circulation eightfold and brought it from nowhere to first place in net-sales rating.

It would be pleasant to report that his troubles were ended. But this proved to be far from the case. The *Herald* found it impossible to hold its lead. Benefiting now from its policy of spending money on news services as well as on silk stockings and flannel trousers, the *Express* first reached and then passed the *Herald*. By 1937 its circulation had climbed to 2,329,000 while the *Herald* still struggled to keep its 2,000,000. The *Mail* was down to 1,580,000 (it had been 1,845,000 at the start of the circulation war in 1930) and the *News Chronicle* to 1,324,000.

Elias had to abandon all hope of being first. Instead his efforts were now concentrated on holding at any cost to the

2,000,000, that magical if by now somewhat blown-on figure that provided the only passport to the sort of advertising revenue he needed. Even to do this did not prove easy. Readers bought in a hurry tended to leave in a hurry. To hold them proved almost as costly as to get them. Although it could boast of a 'more than 2,000,000' circulation the *Herald* losses reached £5,000 a week. Before long they were £10,000 a week. They might have gone higher and become too heavy to carry despite the success of the rest of the Odhams properties if the war had not come along to end all canvassing, prizes, insurance and free gifts by agreement, create a seller's market in advertising space, cut newspaper costs by restricting sizes, and inflate all newspaper sales, as wars always do.

Elias had forced the commercial principle in journalism to the fullest limit it would go and the fruits proved strangely bitter. That he should have twisted the permanent values of journalism as he did, turning the relationship between newspaper and reader so largely into a mere matter of barter, was not solely his fault. He was the victim of a situation from which he could see no other escape. Others might perhaps have sought it in the slow building of circulation on editorial appeal. But in fact that avenue was closed to him when he decided after the deal with Bevin that an immediately spectacular leap forward was the only way by which the old *Herald* could break through the resistance of advertisers and be made into a paying commercial proposition. Having once begun along that road there was no turning back. It may indeed be, as he always insisted, that no other road was open from the first. It was a squalid road and one on which no one, certainly no journalist, can look back with pride or pleasure. But it was one that not Elias but the whole inter-war development of the newspaper industry had marked on the map.

Yet what remains of lasting significance is that despite all its excesses the newspaper war of the 'thirties did succeed to a remarkable extent in permanently increasing newspaper readership. A surprising number of the bought readers stuck. The average daily readership of national morning papers in 1930 was

8,929,000. By the end of 1939 it had risen to over ten and a half millions and all over the country people who had never read newspapers before were doing so. They were to go on reading them in increasing numbers.

XIV

NEW READING PUBLIC

JUST on a hundred and seventy years ago Thomas Jefferson writing to Edward Carrington expressed what he believed to be a fundamental truth of the democratic principle: 'The basis of our government, being the opinion of the people', he wrote, 'the very first object should be to keep that right; and were it left to me to decide whether we should have a government without newspapers or newspapers without government I should not hesitate a moment to prefer the latter.'

We are or should be a wise and happy people. We have more newspapers circulating each day to keep opinion right than any nation in the whole of history. The newspaper campaigns of the 'thirties were dubious in method and extravagant in execution. They hit some newspapers hard. But for good or ill they spread the habit of reading newspapers so wide that mass circulation began to take on a new meaning. By the time they ended a million and a half more national morning newspapers were being bought each day than when they began (much more than that if one dates the start of the battle from the taking over of the *Herald* by Odhams rather than from the beginning of the free-gift campaigns) and the combined circulation of all daily papers in the country—national, provincial, morning and evening—had risen to close on nineteen and a half millions and that of Sunday papers alone to getting on for sixteen millions.

By any standards known before these were tremendous figures. They were soon to be far surpassed by those of the war and post-war years.

The war altered the whole economic complexion of the

newspaper industry. The costly weapons of the struggle for circulation were abandoned and the size of newspapers cut to a quarter of what it had been by newsprint rationing. Advertisers became the wooers instead of the wooed and as the available space declined rates soared. They have continued to do so. So has the total national bill for advertising.

In 1937 some £85,000,000 a year was spent on all forms of advertising according to estimates made by the *Economist* at that time. Of this about £35,000,000 a year went to the press. In 1954 according to estimates published in the *Financial Times* the total national bill for advertising was at least £280,000,000 of which the press got some £160,000,000; 24% of it going to the national morning newspapers, 38% to the whole of the rest of the daily and weekly newspapers and the balance to periodicals. In 1956 according to provisional estimates as much as £210,000,000 out of a total advertising bill of around £350,000,000 was probably spent on press advertising—the estimated expenditure on television advertising was between £10,000,000 and £20,000,000 which may rise to between £30,000,000 and £35,000,000 over the next three or four years if results are good.

The mass-production, mass-consumption, mass-communication, mass-advertising age marches on and the press seems likely in the future, as in the past, to be its chief beneficiary—at any rate in a material sense if not perhaps so noticeably in any other.

It is, however, in the rise of total newspaper readership and particularly in that of national morning and Sunday newspapers that the real nature of the newspaper revolution over the past decade and a half or so is to be seen. In the last sixteen years the population of the United Kingdom has increased by 7%. The sale of national morning newspapers has risen nine times as fast. It now totals more than 16,000,000 a day. Over the same period the sale of Sunday papers has nearly doubled from 15,200,000 to more than 30,000,000. This rise, however, is far from being evenly spread; indeed during this period of phenomenal expansion in newspaper reading the sale of the more serious of the popular newspapers has actually fallen.

All newspapers have their own personalities and serve their own particular publics. There is inevitably therefore something artificial about trying to impress them into particular groups. Nevertheless three main divisions in the national press are broadly recognisable.

The Times, the *Manchester Guardian* and the *Telegraph* with a circulation range of from 160,000 a day for the *Guardian* to just over a million for the *Telegraph* fall naturally enough into one group: that of the so-called quality press carrying out those functions traditionally belonging to a serious newspaper. At the other end of the scale come the two great mass-circulation newspapers of our times, the *Daily Mirror* and the *Daily Express*, the one with a circulation of close on 4,700,000, the other with one just over 4,000,000. In between these two there lies a middle group of medium-circulation popular newspapers of a somewhat more serious character, the *News Chronicle*, *Daily Herald* and *Daily Mail*, with a circulation range of between one and a half and two million. (I have omitted two papers: the *Daily Worker* because it cannot be regarded as a daily newspaper in any sense common to the others, the *Daily Sketch* because although it has been gaining rapidly in circulation since its new proprietors, Lord Rothermere and the *News of the World*, threw the suburban gentility of its former owner Lord Kemsley out the window and turned it into a right-wing imitation of the *Daily Mirror*, its fortunes over the two previous decades were too erratic for generalisation, depending so much on individual idiosyncrasies that its wavering course could not be regarded as significant of anything but Lord Kemsley's changes of mind.)

In terms of numbers the 'quality newspapers' with a combined circulation under a million and a half account for only a very small part of the whole—and even of this the *Telegraph*, which, excellent general newspaper though it is, is the least intellectually demanding of the three (and also the cheapest), accounts for more than two-thirds. Yet although the total circulation of the quality newspapers is small when compared with that of the mass-circulation press it has now been rising steadily for more than a quarter of a century not only in actual numbers but as a percentage of total newspaper readership. Even taking into account the since defunct *Morning Post* the circulation of the so-called 'class' papers twenty-five years ago amounted to only some 6% of the total readership of all national newspapers. Now it is nearly 9%. Contrary to much popular belief sales of the serious quality newspapers have in fact gone up much more rapidly than those of national newspapers as a whole. They have risen by 177% since 1930 and by 80% since 1937 compared with a 91% increase in total national newspaper circulations since 1930 and one of 65% since 1937. In the last quarter of a century the *Daily Telegraph* has attracted new readers at a greater rate than any other newspaper in the country even including the *Daily Mirror*. The *Manchester Guardian* has more than trebled its circulation in the last fifteen years.

Actually and relatively the serious press has thus gained ground to an extent that must seem astonishing to those who deplore a general decline in reading taste. The number of its readers is, of course, small. It always has been. Even in what are sometimes nostalgically regarded as the great days of serious journalism at the end of the nineteenth century no more than 1% of the population bought serious daily journals. The number is now nearly 3%. When the remarkable increase in the sale of both the *Observer* and the *Sunday Times*, which together now serve a serious Sunday newspaper-reading public some 140% greater than just before the war and getting on for three and a half times as much as a quarter of a century ago, is also taken into account the optimism of those who believed that secondary education would eventually produce an increased demand for serious journalism does not seem altogether absurd although it may have been pitched too high. Moreover, despite price increases the serious weekly reviews led by the *New Statesman* and the *Spectator* have held on to much of their big wartime gains, the *Listener* has nearly three times as many readers as it had before the war and the *Economist* five times as many. All-in-all more people are reading serious intelligent journalism today than ever before and they represent a larger—although of course still small—proportion of the public.

The position is far otherwise when one turns to the middle group of medium-circulation papers which seek to combine entertainment with some serious purpose. Despite the great gains made by the *Daily Herald* under the stimulus of free gift schemes in the 'thirties the total sale of the three newspapers in the group of which it is one has increased by no more than 15% over the last quarter of a century and by no more than 3% since 1937, failing even to keep pace with the rise in population.

So far indeed from gaining, or even holding, ground during the last fifteen years of phenomenally expanding newspaper readership the *Daily Herald* itself has lost ground heavily and is now back to where it was twenty years or so ago. So too has the *News Chronicle*. Until the purchase of the title and goodwill of the *Daily Dispatch* gave it a chance to introduce itself to a considerable block of new readers it had fallen steadily in circulation during the post-war years to a level lower than for a quarter of a century.

Like all others these two newspapers benefited from wartime demand. But apart from *The Times* which artificially restricted sales in favour of size during newsprint rationing they are the only ones to fall continuously in circulation from the moment the wartime restrictions on freedom of sale—and thus of readers' choice—were removed in 1947. Since the middle of that year the *Daily Herald* has lost more than 480,000 paying readers and the *News Chronicle* more than 440,000. The *Daily Mail* was at first more fortunate in continuing to attract new readers for some time after 1947. Since the rise in newspaper prices in 1951 it has, however, lost close on 200,000.

During this decade and a half the most significant political development has been the increase in the size of the Labour vote to a level at which it represents practically half the electorate. It seems especially odd therefore that it is the two left-wing newspapers of the more serious popular press that should lose readers at such a rate.

It may be that the *Herald* is now suffering a delayed reaction from the shock treatment given it by Elias in the 'thirties. It was forced to grow too fast. If it could have been allowed to develop more slowly, putting its faith in editorial enterprise rather than in the extravagances of commercial salesmanship and adapting itself step by step to the developing taste of its readers, it might have benefited more than it has from the very large increase in the Labour electorate in the last quarter of a century. It might even have done what it has of recent years signally failed to do, developed a distinctive personality with some power to excite and stimulate readers. As it is it has failed either to extend its hold among the vast working-class public that supports the *Mirror* or attract any of the middle classes who have voted Labour since the war. It would perhaps do better—and also be more useful to the Labour party—if it were possible for it to become an independent socialist paper in somewhat the same relationship to the Labour Party as the *Daily Telegraph* is to the Conservative Party. Instead it has remained that most insipid of anachronisms, a tied party paper subject to the additional disability of dependence upon a commercial organisation unwilling to spend much money on something that is not its sole possession and always falling with a bump between two stools.

The post-war history of the *News Chronicle* is even more puzzling. A Liberal paper in an age of the massive confrontation of vast Conservative and Labour blocs, it has what ought to be the immense journalistic advantage of combining a progressive approach to public affairs with a politically independent standpoint on many of the great issues of our time. It does not, as the *Herald* does, suffer from the fact that its mind is made up for it by a political party: it retains the priceless journalistic gift of surprise. It has a distinguished writing staff of columnists and special correspondents and is cultured, lively and diversified, with more to hold the attention of an intelligent reader than many of its more popular rivals. One would have expected it to gain more than most from the social and educational advances of recent years instead of declining steadily in popular appeal over most of the time.

That it has not done so is no doubt partly due to a lack of clarity on its own part. It seems to suffer from a chronic inability to make up its mind what public it is after and communicates its indecision to its readers. Moreover it has always tended to put its faith too much in special writers and too little in hard news, suffering excessively from a defect to which British journalism with intellectual pretensions is prone: contempt for the hard fact that a good newspaper is made by good reporters and good sub-editors. 'God is for leader writers, I am a reporter', says the newspaperman in Graham Greene's *The Quiet American*. The *News Chronicle* suffers from a superfluity of the God-like, determined to write news in their own image.

It suffers too from an odd refusal to recognise one of the cardinal facts of journalistic life, that although foreign news is important a good home story is always, except on the greatest occasions, more interesting to the general run of readers than a good foreign story. There have been many occasions when its choice of a lead story compared with that of almost the whole of the rest of the press, serious and popular alike, has seemed almost deliberately designed to provide a lesson on how not to win readers and influence people. Yet it has at times great quality. Everyone who cares for good journalism will wish it the courage of its traditions and hope that the shot in the arm it got for itself by securing with the *Daily Dispatch* title some 270,000 of the 465,000 *Dispatch* readers will continue to put its fortunes on the mend. It has lately shown a welcome improvement.

What emerges most clearly, however, from an examination of newspaper circulations over the past quarter of a century and particularly over the past decade and a half or so is the extent to which these years have seen the development of a wholly new market for national daily newspapers as important to the future of journalism as the new newspaper reading publics discovered by *The Times* in the first half of the nineteenth century, by the *Telegraph* and its penny contemporaries in the second half, and by Northcliffe at the beginning of the twentieth.

After taking into account the increase in the number of newspaper readers to be expected during a period of rising population it would appear that out of a total increase of some six and a quarter millions in the combined circulation of national morning newspapers since 1937 at least five and three-quarter millions is due to the development of a new and previously neglected market. What is even more striking is that more than 90% of this market has gone to two newspapers, the *Daily Mirror* and the *Daily Express*, and no less than 57% of it to one of them alone, the *Daily Mirror*.

Each day these two together now sell nearly one and a quarter million more copies than the whole of the rest of the national morning press put together. Their total family readership is probably not far short of half the total population and may well be more. Alone among popular newspapers they have been able to develop a journalism capable of appealing to those who rarely bought a daily newspaper before the war.

The rise in the circulation of the *Daily Telegraph* and the *Manchester Guardian* can be accounted for in the main by the transfer to them from other newspapers of readers who have developed a taste for a more serious treatment of public affairs. The rise in the joint circulation of the *Mirror* and *Express* from a little over three and a quarter millions to around eight and three-quarter millions in fifteen years, and more especially the increase in the sales of the *Mirror* from what was by modern mass-circulation standards a mere 1,328,000 in 1937 to over 4,700,000, cannot be explained in this way.

It is in the exceptional ability of these two newspapers to give the new reading public what it wants that the secret of their immense success lies. If one wishes to understand the nature of this new public it is to them that one must look.

XV

BEAVERBROOK AND BARTHOLOMEW

THE qualities that have enabled the *Daily Mirror* and the *Daily Express* to satisfy so completely between them the needs of the new reading public are clearly not identical. The *Mirror* has succeeded by becoming over the past twenty years the first tabloid in Britain, an entirely new and different paper from what it formerly was; the *Express* by doing more and more expertly what it first set out to do when Lord Beaverbrook assumed command of its fortunes nearly forty years ago.

When the Royal Commission on the Press asked Lord Beaverbrook his main interest as a newspaper proprietor, he replied: 'I run my paper purely for the purpose of making propaganda and with no other motive.' (I remember, but great men must be allowed their inconsistencies, an occasion in his study at Cherkeley when he told me the exact opposite. 'Oh, how I hate propaganda,' he said then.) He explained to the Commission, however, that 'No paper is any good at all for propaganda unless it has a thoroughly good financial position. So we worked very hard,' he said, 'to build up a commercial position of that kind.'

In his career as a newspaper proprietor Lord Beaverbrook has achieved everything except his main purpose. He has made the *Daily Express* the most successful newspaper of its kind in the world and the most imitated: rich, popular and solidly buttressed against future hazards by large reserves. The chains on the Crusader at its masthead are golden. But they are chains nevertheless.

Beaverbrook's interest is power; financial power, social power, personal power, but above all, because that is the most difficult and the most pervasive, political power. Without at least the similitude of it he cannot be happy. He has an artist's interest in it, in its use and transfer, the means by which men can be bent to its purpose, the subtle courses by which it can be directed in this way or that. Such power as this he exercised and exercised in remarkable measure when he first came to this country as 'a little upstart Canadian adventurer', to become the friend of Bonar Law and the intimate of Carson, F. E. Smith and Lloyd George; the back-bench M.P. who was above all the great 'go-between', shrewd in knowledge of men, subtle in persuasion, tireless in intrigue; the private negotiator and *éminence grise*. He has never exercised it in comparable degree since. When he came into the open he lost the touch for it. Since then he has had to make do with excitement—which perhaps most of the time satisfies him nearly as much. If he has missed getting his hand on the real levers of power he has always been in a position to see the wheels go round—and sometimes to throw a shrewdly aimed spanner into the middle of them. He has never failed to be in the know, which is after all one of the supreme journalistic pleasures. He has had a happy life and has enjoyed himself enormously. He still does. Few of his policies have come to much but he has set a lot of cats among a lot of pigeons and he has had, in an impish sort of way, a great deal of fun.

As a newspaper proprietor he has campaigned for many causes —and especially Empire Free Trade. The Conservative Party he supports has ignored them all—especially Empire Free Trade. Not since Bonar Law have any of its leaders taken account of his advice on anything, although he has freely offered it on everything. Only those politicians he has attacked have prospered: his praise has proved lethal. Merely by accusing him and his temporary ally, Rothermere, of seeking 'the prerogative of the harlot throughout the ages, power without responsibility' Baldwin secured an immense popularity, as much one suspects among readers of the *Daily Express* as any other section of the community.

None of these political failures has damaged the circulation of his newspapers. No political campaign run by the *Express*, good or bad, has affected its sales.

For months in 1939 the *Daily*—although not the *Sunday*—*Express* amused its readers with the antics of a comic military character, 'Major Crisis'. It poured derision in large capital letters on anyone who suggested that war might be near. 'There Will Be No War This Year or Next Year Either' it proclaimed on its front page, using the largest and clearest type in its exhaustive battery of type-faces for the purpose. It was not only one of the most contemptibly irresponsible campaigns in journalistic history but was soon to be proved wrong in a more tragic and absolute fashion than normally befalls even Lord Beaverbrook. So total a demonstration of political incapacity might be expected to discredit the paper among some, at least, of its readers. There is no evidence that it did so. As war broke the paper's circulation and popularity advanced by leaps and bounds.

Such an outcome would appear on the face of it discouraging—discouraging, I mean, to the paper's controllers, not to its critics who are past discouragement. It suggests that those who accuse the *Express* of misleading its readers pay it too high a compliment, that in fact those who read it take its political utterances no more seriously than they would those of a music-hall entertainer who interrupted a balancing act to say a few uncalled-for words about the international economic situation. But this is probably to see things too simply. Although the direct political influence of the *Daily Express* is small—smaller even than that of Northcliffe's *Daily Mail*—its indirect influence over the political—and even more surely the social—attitudes of many of its readers may well be profound: it probably, for example, had a great deal to do with creating the mood of irritation against post-war shortages and controls that led to the defeat of the Labour Government in 1951. It can sometimes succeed in destruction when the public mood is on its side. In the direct attempt to influence public affairs in a positive way it has always failed. This failure one suspects is due

to almost identically the same causes as have made it so successful
as a popular daily newspaper.

Both as a human being and as a newspaper proprietor Lord
Beaverbrook is temperamentally several times larger than life.
He is the captive of his own success story. It is a dramatic and
romantic story: the penniless boy from the Presbyterian manse
in New Brunswick who was a millionaire before he was thirty,
an intimate and maker of Prime Ministers before he was forty,
the darling and scourge of social London or at any rate that part
of it avid for excitement, the imp with the poltergeist touch, his
feet in Vanity Fair, his heart—or so he constantly tells us—with
the pilgrims, his head wherever there are secrets to be heard;
the most sensationally successful, hated and sought-after newspaper proprietor of his day.

He sees life through coloured binoculars and has made sure
that even the humblest reporter on his staff shall have the same
romantic vision of the world. As a propagandist this is his weakness. The romantic vision is unsuited to the pace of British
politics: it has prevented him from understanding the power of
understatement. The sword he ran through Elias in the private
room in the Savoy is never out of his hand; all battles are for him
wars to the death, every political campaign a Charge of the Life
Brigade. As a politician and a propagandist he is a prophet on a
mountain top. His friends and his foes are both bigger than life.
He summons the thunder and lightning to his service and hurls
his bolts screaming across the sky; death and destruction surround
him, the infidels are given no quarter—not even that of admitting
that they also are human and capable, sometimes, of being right
as well as wrong. But when the storm subsides those whom he has
obliterated brush the film of volcanic dust off their clothes,
murmur brightly, 'I see the Beaver's up to his tricks again', and
turn to other matters; the spectators, remarking to each other
that it has been a wonderful show, go home to tea.

In every political campaign he has set his hand to he has
failed to recognise the tactical advantage of fair play. The
personal uses to which he puts his papers are too blatant; the

vendettas too many and too obvious. The smears that trail their unpleasing way through the diary columns of his various newspapers are too crude, the attacks and innuendos too capricious, the misrepresentations and half-truths too unconcealed, the contempt for the intelligence of readers presumed capable of being misled by such amateurish skulduggery too manifest. Everything is too smart by half. This is Teddy Boy politics.

He who was so subtle in private, whose fortune was built on the devious weighing of advantage and the skilful balancing of men and interests, seems when he takes to public print to lose all sense of subtlety. Wielding absolute power inside his own newspaper organisation he has lost his touch for those infinitely more delicate transactions of authority in which men must be influenced, not commanded. His original artist's instinct for the manipulation of power has been debased and coarsened by excess until it has become no more than a parody of itself.

The failure in comprehension, the inability not to lay it on too thick, that makes Beaverbrook so poor a political propagandist makes him, however, a superb popular newspaper impresario. He has created a newspaper in which it is impossible, outside politics, for him to overplay his hand, for it is the very fact that everything in the *Express* is larger and more exciting than life that gives it its appeal.

The *Daily Express* was seventeen years old and nearly bankrupt when R. D. Blumenfeld, its editor, persuaded Beaverbrook to come to its rescue and buy control by holding out to him the prospect of a permanent platform for Bonar Law. Its impact on journalism is entirely due to his personality. In the early days of his proprietorship he was to all practical purposes its editor as well as its owner; it was his character that stamped itself on every page. From No. 8 Shoe Lane, where now the huge streamlined palace of today's *Daily Express* towers to the sky, in a flat at the top of the building with a great window looking on the cities of the plain below but with the gold cross of St. Paul's in the heavens above to remind him of what he so easily forgets, that Mammon is not all, in a room furnished and decorated like a film set he toiled—full length on a couch, at the end of a battery of telephones, pacing up and down the carpet, shouting, gesticulating, cooing, flattering, threatening, making his paper as exciting and unpredictable as himself.

R. D. Blumenfeld who had come with the paper taught him the techniques of the trade. But the fire, the energy, the consuming interest in the moment, in persons rather than principles, in money and scandal and activity—almost any kind of activity—the restless, contagious curiosity, these came from him. It was through his eyes, those eyes that see everything so much larger, so much more exciting, so much more colourful, so much more urgent than ordinary men do, that his paper mirrored the world: it was his egotism, iconoclastic, swashbuckling, all-embracing, that infected his staff, giving them the conviction that they were men apart, the best in the bag, servants of ordained success—hallelujah here we come!

The *Express* has won its great public because it has given to millions a passport to a world in which anything can happen; the world of Walter Mitty and a young girl's dreams, of the advertisements, the films, and the give-away programmes, of success, success, success; a world in which when anything happens there is an *Express* man on the spot, if it is exclusive the *Express* has got it. It is a world in which Mr. Robinson of Acacia Avenue knows just what it is like to stay at the best hotels, Mrs. Robinson shares the beauty secrets of a film princess and both of them are entirely at home in that international café society which is so much more amusing on paper than in reality. The *Express* has brought sophistication to the suburbs, but it also brings romance into thousands of rather dull lives. It is the paper of escape, but of escape not into an invented world but into the real one miraculously turned brighter than reality, a world in which everything happens at a greater speed and a higher tension than common experience and all the drab moments are left out.

Beaverbrook is the true creator of the *Express*. His personality is the one constant power that shapes its doings wherever he may be in the world. But he has been blessed with lieutenants superbly suited to its purpose; chief among them E. J. Robertson, who has contributed to it in the way of business skill and decision as much as Mowbray Morris gave to *The Times*, and Arthur Christiansen, who twenty-four years ago bounded exuberantly into its editorial chair as a young man of thirty after a wonderful pyrotechnical display at its Manchester office and has remained there ever since, stamping his personality on it only a shade less indelibly than Beaverbrook himself.

Day by day Christiansen produces a bulletin on the day's *Express*—and its rivals—for the guidance, encouragement, stimulation and chiding of his staff. In these bulletins are to be found the philosophy of the *Express*. If there is any answer to the question why alone among non-tabloid newspapers it has won for itself so large a part of the new reading public that has emerged since the beginning of the war it is to be found here. When he showed me these bulletins I told Christiansen that he ought to republish them as a text book of modern journalism. I hope some day he will, for whether one likes the *Express* or not it is a remarkable paper—one of the most remarkable that British journalism, or the journalism of any country for that matter, has ever known. Meanwhile, here is a short selection of the observations of the editor of the *Daily Express* on his craft:

There is no subject, no abstract thing, that cannot be translated into terms of people.

Our feature pages should be sprinkled with star dust or whatever it is that women wear that catches the light at first nights.

All my journalistic thinking is based on making the news so inviting to people that they read involuntarily news which normally would not interest them. That is why I rejoice when headlines such as 'Four Mr. Europes woo Miss Britain' are written on a story from the Strasbourg Conference. It is the hope that such novel presentations will at least open the door.

Avoid words of Latin or French derivation and try to find the Anglo-Saxon word which does the job.

The *Mail* runs a story about a woman in black being missing in the North of England. The projection of colour is a most important factor in promoting reader interest.

A brilliant, brilliant, brilliant paper today.

I believe that my friends in the back streets of Derby are not aware of the story of Cassius and Brutus. When will the *Daily Express* pay some attention to these good people?

The last paragraph of a story should be as punchy as the first.

Here is a good maxim for the *Daily Express*: one good home story is worth two good foreign stories.

Whenever possible print a woman's age.

This job (a story headed: 'Epstein's New Work is Unveiled') has the old *Express* weakness of being scamped and uninformed. Why was Mr. Butler unveiling Epstein's work in Cavendish Square? What is a Palladian building, my clever ducks? How much did it cost? Was it built by the Government for the Government? What was Epstein paid? What was the sculpture like from an artistic point of view? In writing about Palladian buildings we should always remember that most people know more about the Palladium building.

Always in every story, even stories of high international significance, the warm human element will attract attention.

I journeyed from Rhyl to Prestatyn on Sunday past lines of boarding houses, caravans, wooden huts, shacks, tents and heaven knows what else. In every one of them there were newspaper readers. Happy citizens, worthy, fine people but not in

22222222 DANGEROUS ESTATE

the least like the reader Fleet Street seems to be writing for. These people are not interested in Glyndbourne or vintage claret or opera or the Sitwells or dry-as-dust economics or tough politics. It is our job to interest them in everything. It requires the highest degree of skill and ingenuity.

Always, always, tell the news through people.

You cannot just put things into the *Daily Express*. By and large they must be projected. We have got to tackle the news emphatically with boldness and confidence.

Contrast is the heart and soul of a newspaper. Even the *Manchester Guardian* on a day pregnant with heavy news found space on its front page to say that goats are to be replaced by sheep on the Malayan rubber estates.

Good stories flow like honey. Bad stories stick in the craw. What is a bad story? It is a story that cannot be absorbed on the first time of reading. It is a story that leaves questions unanswered. It is a story that has to be read two or three times to be comprehended. And a good story can be turned into a bad story by just one obscure sentence.

There is often a lot of news to be got out of shop windows.

Never cry down the pleasures of the people.

News, news, news—that is what we want. You can describe things with the pen of Shakespeare himself, but you cannot beat news in a newspaper.

You cannot beat news in a newspaper. A sound maxim. Yet to judge by results it would appear that for 57% of the new newspaper-reading public of the last fifteen or sixteen years it scarcely applies at all. Whatever it is that has made so large a proportion of these new readers prefer the *Daily Mirror* to all other papers it is certainly not its superior coverage of general news. On the contrary the *Mirror* has increased its circulation by 255% in the last eighteen years and by 440% over the past quarter of a century by consistently disdaining a large part of the news that every other newspaper regards as important.

The world into which the *Daily Express* conducts its readers with such polished aplomb is a more exciting and highly coloured world than they would find themselves in should they be tempted to stretch their limbs on the mountain slopes of Printing House Square or Cross Street, Manchester. But it is basically the same world. The world to which the *Mirror* opens wide the door is a different world. It is not necessarily less real for that. Indeed for many of the millions who share in it as readers it may well have a much greater reality: there is far less star dust and escapism in the *Mirror* than there is in the *Express*. But it is a world differently drawn: the geographer has left out a great many of the features common to all other maps and put in much that they ignore.

Those who read only the *Daily Mirror*—and newspaper readership surveys such as those made by the Hulton Readership Survey and the Gallup Poll suggest that out of the 90% of the population over sixteen who regularly read some morning paper at least a third rely very largely on it—are given a view of life very different in its major preoccupations from that to which readers of the news carried by more traditional newspapers, 'serious' or 'popular', are accustomed. In the course of a week chosen at random recently *The Times* carried 514 separate news reports of general interest. Only 68 of these were reported in any way in the *Mirror*, many of them exceedingly briefly. In the same period, however, the *Mirror* published no fewer than 139 'human interest stories' of which *Times* readers and, indeed, the readers of most other newspapers, knew nothing. On no single day during the week were the main news stories the same in both *The Times* and the *Mirror* and on five out of the six the *Mirror's* main news—the news with which it led the paper as exceeding every other event in interest and importance—dealt with events of which *The Times* either knew nothing or which it regarded as too insignificant to mention.

The modern *Daily Mirror* is primarily the creation of one man, a rough, tough, erratic and ruthless genius of popular journalism egocentric to a degree notable even in a profession where egomania is an occupational disease: Mr. Harry Guy Bartholomew. Bartholomew, who in repose looks like a church dignitary and in action like a Labour boss on the San Francisco waterfront in the tough days, fought his way up from the bottom, piling up anger, frustration and a cynical contempt for most of the accepted shibboleths of good taste on the way.

Unlike some others who have climbed from nothing to power and position as controllers of great newspaper enterprises he all his professional life remained, as he began, a working journalist, a superb technician in type and pictures, with an unexampled skill in shock tactics, a decisive scorn for all traditional newspaper methods and as intuitive an understanding of the reactions of millions of working-class people as that possessed in a different sphere by Ernest Bevin. He was a tabloid genius: 'The first Englishman' as the *New Statesman* aptly said of him when he abruptly resigned the chairmanship of the *Daily Mirror* and *Sunday Pictorial* companies in 1951 after some more than usually turbulent clashes of personality, 'who really understood pictures and strips and realised that no one reads more than a few hundred words on any subject.'

Bartholomew joined the picture department of the *Daily Mirror* as a young man in January 1904 from the engraving department of Northcliffe's *Illustrated Mail*. He was paid 30s. a week. The paper was only a few months old but was already—or so it seemed—due for burial. It had been founded by Northcliffe to be 'The First Daily Newspaper For Gentlewomen', one of the few really calamitous ideas on newspaper production to enter Northcliffe's fertile brain. It was written not only for gentlewomen but by gentlewomen. In less than three months they reduced its circulation to a mere 25,000 compared with the more than 265,000 with which it began after the most extensive advance advertising campaign in newspaper history. At this stage Hamilton Fyfe, later editor of the *Daily Herald* but at this time one of the brightest of Northcliffe's young men, was sent in to reorganise it. 'I have learnt two things,' Northcliffe told him, 'women can't write and don't want to read.' To Fyfe fell the task of dismissing the staff of gentlewomen. 'It was like drowning kittens,' he said later.

But the massacre was successful. In January 1904 the paper for gentlewomen became the *Daily Illustrated Mirror*, 'a paper for men and women' and the first halfpenny illustrated daily newspaper in the history of journalism, printing photographs on the high-speed rotary presses by means of a new method invented by a technician on the staff of one of Northcliffe's minor publications, a Mr. Arkas Sapt. Mr. Hannen Swaffer was art editor, the youthful Bartholomew assisted him. Within a month the new picture paper had achieved a circulation of 140,000, within a year 290,000. By the eve of the First World War its circulation rivalled that of the *Mail* and Bartholomew had progressed to art editor and, in 1913 at the age of twenty-eight, to a directorship. He was progressing: but he did not command power. His personality showed itself on the picture pages but was not allowed to make its impact on the paper as a whole. He was still, and how it irked him, a man in harness.

He was one of those who stayed when the paper passed from Northcliffe to Rothermere in 1914. He was there as it fell in circulation and influence under the ineffable touch of that great financier. He was still there in the 1930s when Rothermere, hard pressed by the financial crisis, sold both his own and the Daily Mail Trust's holdings in the *Mirror* and its Sunday companion, the *Pictorial*, on the Stock Exchange, spreading ownership widely for the first time among many shareholders. In 1934—thirty years after he had first joined the *Mirror*—Bartholomew's chance came. The circulation was down to 720,000; the paper was dying on its feet—ruined by Rothermere's humourless persistency in ramming every half-baked reactionary dogma that caught his fancy down its readers' throats, his gloomy denunciations of 'squandermania' in all departments of public life, his supreme capacity for being wrong on every great issue of his time. Neither the chairman, John Cowley, whom the Harmsworths had long ago inherited with the *Evening News*, nor any of the other directors knew what to do with it. Bartholomew did. He got himself made editorial director to do it. He had to wait another ten years before becoming chairman. But the first step was enough for a revolution.

He was fifty-one. As he stepped into editorial control of the *Mirror* he had, if that is possible, fewer of the normal interests of an educated man even than Elias, who had just started to buy his way to the 2,000,000. He practically never read a book, knew nothing of art, literature or music and cared less, had no knowledge of the world of public affairs and was himself almost incapable of writing anything any paper—even the *Daily Mirror* —would want to publish. By the standards of the great journalists of the past he was a vulgar semi-illiterate, cantankerous, suspicious, and jealous of any who withstood his authority, a man with a passion for crude practical jokes, a ruthless determination to trample on anyone who got in his way and an occasional odd flash of genial charm.

But he was also a daemoniac fury and a ball of fire. If he was ruthless he was also courageous; nothing could stop him from printing what he thought. If he was tough and vulgar he had the merit of a freezing contempt for hypocrisy and all mealy-mouthed pretence. He was uncultured, but so were the readers he wanted to reach. If the function of popular journalism is the education of the masses in public affairs by those better informed, more widely experienced and intellectually superior to themselves, and if the standards by which it ought to be judged are those of objectivity and judicial capacity, then no more dangerous and unsuitable man ever acquired control of a widely circulating newspaper. But if the function of popular journalism is to speak with the voice of the crowd, its standard of measurement intuitive understanding of the feelings of millions of common people, and its responsibility not to be objective but to harry complacency and stimulate

controversy, then Bartholemew was the natural creator of a
journalism properly called vulgar because more widely popular
than any known before.

The formula that he adopted was simple in essentials although
requiring great skill to carry out—almost, indeed, a new race
of journalists with none of the inhibitions ruling in other newspaper offices. What he produced was in some ways more like a
daily poster than a newspaper, indeed it was to advertising agents
not journalists that he turned for advice on putting over his new
idea. It depended for its effectiveness on sledge-hammer headlines
of a size, blackness and stridency never seen in any British daily
newspaper before—although not very remote from those employed by Elias to sell the *People* on Sundays—a frenzied gusto
in dredging the news for sensational stories of sex and crime
and a complete lack of reticence in dealing with them. To this
he added radical muck-raking crusading (one of the most
important of his intuitions was that, unlike the middle classes,
the majority of the British working class are still essentially
radical in their political emotions whatever way they may vote
at elections), and an appreciation of the fact that millions of
people are completely uninterested in almost 80% of the news
most serious papers consider it obligatory to publish. He combined these with a shrewd understanding of the further fact
that although masses of people in this country, as in every
other, find considerable intellectual difficulty in reading anything that calls for more than a few seconds' concentration,
they can be thrilled and excited by large headlines, statements in
black type, personal invective, 'live letters' that give them a sense
of participation in a warm communal life, and strip cartoons with
characters with whom they can identify themselves. When he
launched the *Mail* Northcliffe remarked that until it appeared
no newspaper printed the sort of things people talked about.
Bartholomew set himself to publish not what people talked about
at suburban tea-parties or in railway carriages on city trains but
in working-class kitchens, four-ale bars, works canteens, shopping
queues, fish-and-chip saloons, dance halls and jug and bottle

departments. The result on circulation was immediate although
not until the war did the full effect of the Bartholomew revolution
become clear. The paper became the chief, and in many instances
the sole, reading matter of millions in the war factories and the
forces. Speaking an idiom they could understand it identified
itself with the lives of this new newspaper-reading public as no
other paper succeeded in doing; it provided the daily talk and
perhaps the daily thinking of millions who had never read a
daily paper before.

The men Bartholomew gathered around him for his purpose
invaded privacy shamelessly. They embraced every stunt however
contemptible in terms of normal human dignity the public could
be got to swallow and set practically no limits on what was
permissible in print other than those imposed by the niggardliness
of the Law—failing even in this desirable restraint at a later date
when the editor was sent to prison for a contempt of court of
which the Lord Chief Justice declared in measured terms: 'In
the long history of the present class of case there has never been
one of such gravity as this, or one of such scandalous and wicked
character. . . . In the opinion of the Court what has been done
was not the result of an error of judgment but was done as a
matter of policy in pandering to sensationalism for the purpose of
increasing the circulation of the newspaper.'

Sensational, scandalous, corrupting of public taste: there are
few such charges that have not been flung at the *Mirror* of
Bartholomew's creation. Few of them have not at one time and
another been richly deserved. Yet it is not less relevant to note
that out of this journalistic dogfight for circulation, this determination to speak in the voice of the mass and exploit a level of
readership not previously reached by any daily newspaper, there
has developed, whether by accident or design, a social conscience
by no means inferior to that of many more respectable and highly
regarded journals.

What is remarkable, indeed, is not that the *Mirror* has built
up an immense circulation by translating into contemporary
terms and into the idiom of a tabloid daily the kind of themes

whose appeal for a great 'submerged' newspaper public was first demonstrated nearly a century ago by the success of the first popular Sunday newspapers. It is that in the course of so doing it has again and again shown both the will and the means to use its great resources of mass communication to educate its readers in the realities of complex economic and social problems to a degree that puts many more 'serious' papers to shame.

It is often frivolous. It dramatises much that to a sophisticated reader must seem basically empty. Acres of its material are incredibly boring to any person of mature interests. But it has an almost unerring instinct for the things that move the emotions of millions of ordinary men and women: it was almost alone among newspapers, for example, in fully understanding and assessing the movement of popular feeling that gave the Labour Party its sweeping electoral victory at the end of the war. And although it has made many errors of judgment it has rarely been wrong on any of the really big issues of our time. Its record on Hitler stands out, for instance, in glaring contrast to that of many of those whose judgment by all the normal standards of objectivity, impartiality and trained assessment of public affairs should have been vastly superior to its own: *The Times* among them.

By comparison with others who have placed their imprint on modern journalism—Northcliffe, Rothermere, Beaverbrook, Camrose, Kemsley, Southwood—Bartholomew's reign was short, just over sixteen years in editorial control of the *Mirror* and *Pictorial*, less than seven in supreme charge as chairman. Yet for good or ill his influence on the standards of journalism and the reading tastes of many millions of people has been greater than that of any of them except Northcliffe and possibly Beaverbrook.

Working on an American model (as Levy had done with the *Telegraph* three-quarters of a century before) he created a new type of tabloid daily to which the term newspaper hardly applies in the real sense, for an important part of his discovery was that with the mass readership he was after a little news goes a long way and that sensational features, human stories, sport pictures and strip cartoons have the biggest pull. Before him all daily newspapers, even the most 'popular', had made at any rate a pretence of covering all the important news of the day. They might angle it, personalise it, compress it to a few lines, or exaggerate it out of all proportion to its real importance, but at least they did not ignore it. Bartholomew did. He found out what interested his readers by the most careful analysis of the thousands of letters that came daily to the *Mirror* office and having found it he printed it—even if it meant leaving off the first page or throwing out of the paper altogether news that any other paper in the country would regard as obligatory. He was not, unless a campaign could be made out of it, interested in what a newspaper ought to report, only in what would make its readers talk.

His successor as presiding genius of the *Mirror–Pictorial* group is a very different kind of person—an odd one indeed on most counts to find as the chief beneficiary and administrator of a tabloid revolution. Aloof, reserved, quiet-spoken, notably correct in manner and calm in judgment, Cecil Harmsworth King is the son of a distinguished administrator in the Indian Civil Service who later became Professor of Oriental Languages at Trinity College, Dublin, the son-in-law of the Regius Professor of Greek at Oxford, a Wykehamist, an honours graduate in Constitutional History of Christ Church and a collector of china: none of them qualifications leading naturally, it would seem, to the vulgar exuberances of the *Mirror* and *Pictorial*. But—and it is the but that is important in this matter—he is also a nephew of Lord Northcliffe and the first Lord Rothermere.

That he has some of the financial talent of his Uncle Rothermere who first sent him to the *Mirror*—and perhaps his hankering after a newspaper empire—is already clear. How much of the Northcliffe flair he has inherited is not yet so certain. But although in the end he was one of the instruments of Bartholomew's departure from the scenes of his triumphs, he wholeheartedly backed the revolution that Bartholomew instigated in its early dangerous days and has not greatly departed from its main principles now that he has assumed full control. At his right hand as editorial director he has a man hardly inferior to Bartholomew in technical virtuosity, in instinct for popular taste and in 'publish and be damned' exuberance, a man, indeed, whom Bartholomew himself picked and promoted—Hugh Cudlipp, one of three remarkable brothers from Cardiff of whom another is editor of the *News of the World* and the third was until recently editor of the *Daily Herald*.

Cudlipp has not been content merely to inherit the editorial empire created by Bartholomew. He has stamped and is still stamping his own tough and vivid personality on it. Fertile in ideas and ingenious in imagination with a radicalism which if glossed with a surface cynicism is basically less anarchical and more constructive than Bartholomew's, he has developed to a degree which on occasion makes the *Mirror* one of the most remarkable papers in the world the capacity to translate serious political issues into terms that even the politically illiterate can understand. He is one of the shrewdest newspaper executives in Fleet Street and one of its most brilliant technicians. Under him the *Mirror* if it can sometimes be accused of battening on sensation must also be honoured on occasion for some of the most remarkable feats of popular education ever seen in journalism.

So far only one other paper has tried to imitate the *Mirror* technique wholeheartedly—the *Daily Sketch*. Having failed as a 'respectable' tabloid under Lord Kemsley—'clean and clever' was its slogan at that time, but few (except an odd bishop or two) were interested—it has, since coming into the hands of the second Lord Rothermere and the *News of the World*, adopted and cheapened Bartholomew's and Cudlipp's methods.

It uses the same technique of shock, extreme selectivity in news, sensational features, and strip cartoons but goes farther even than the *Mirror* in the exploitation of sex and crime and has so far shown few of the *Mirror's* impressive, if intermittent, displays of social conscience, except in those matters allowing of the most sensational treatment, nor much of its sense of an occasional duty to make hard economic and political facts understood by ordinary people. Although its sales are still not much more than a quarter those of the *Mirror* its circulation has soared since its change in character and it has now become the fastest growing newspaper in the country, demonstrating, as experience of the most eagerly followed programmes on commercial television has also done, that the taste of a large section of the mass public is lower even than the most pessimistic had previously suspected.

The initial huge success (now, it is nice to know, past its peak) of the *Mirror* magazine subsidiaries *Week End Reveille* and *Mid-Week Reveille*, and Lord Rothermere's *Week-End Mail*—all of which exploit a cheapened version of the tabloid technique of sex, cheesecake and sensationalism plus a vulgarised version of the *Tit Bits* and cheap fiction magazine technique without bothering about social or political purpose—shows the same thing; such success indicates how much larger than was previously suspected is the vulgar-postcard-pulp-periodical market of the back streets on which George Orwell turned his inquiring mind in the 'thirties.

Yet although one may deplore the levels to which some confessedly reputable publishers are prepared to go to capture such a market one should not make the mistake of imagining that they created it. What they have done is to bring into the open a submerged demand that reflects one face of our society just as the substantial increase in the readership of the more serious daily and weekly journals reflects another.

To relate newspaper readership too closely to intellectual capacity is, of course, to over-simplify. Not all those who read *The Times* or the *Manchester Guardian* are intellectual giants. Nor are those who read the *Express* or the *Mirror* by any means all less well equipped intellectually than those who buy the *Telegraph*. The *Express* in fact is bought by a remarkably extensive cross-section of society and the *Mirror* which is read even more by women than men and 44% of whose readers are under thirty-five—compared with only 15% of *Times* readers, although 30% of *Manchester Guardian* readers it is interesting to note are also under thirty-five—has a much wider than solely working-class appeal.

The fact that the proportion of the population (2·8%) that reads the serious 'quality' newspapers is very close to that indicated by tests of intellectual capacity now in use in schools as likely to benefit from higher education (2·5%) is, however, surely significant. It may indicate that the top group of serious newspaper readers is unlikely to increase very much further: its growth over the last decade and a half closely parallels social and educational advance.

Democracy does not depend, however, on the fiction that all people have potentially the same intellectual aptitudes, and there is no reason why the reputation of the press should depend on it either. Educationally we now accept the fact that a majority— some 75% of the whole—is more likely to benefit from a practical approach to education of the secondary modern type than from the more theoretical approach of the grammar or even the technical school and that its extra-curricular interests are also likely to be very different. The same is true of newspaper reading which in practice has already sorted itself out into three groups roughly comparable to these.

Reflecting as it does a society in which advances in education and standards of living have released hitherto dormant or only partially satisfied demands the press of today mirrors the totality of our society more clearly than at any earlier time. Only those wholly blind to the nature of this society and to the widely differing levels of intelligence, culture, interest and taste inevitably and, in so far as they are governed by inherent quality, probably permanently characteristic of it, should be surprised to find that many journalistic principles regarded as immutable when the market available to newspapers was much smaller than it now is have no longer any force with a large part of today's newspapers.

Popular Sunday journalism has a much longer history than popular daily journalism but over the last decade and a half its development has followed very much the same pattern with one interesting deviation. There has been a comparable increase in the demand for serious newspaper reading, as the rise in circulation of both the *Sunday Times* and the *Observer*—journals hardly to be bettered as intelligent weekly guides to politics, public affairs, literature and the arts—shows, and there has been the same pressure on the middle group of popular papers. The death of the *Sunday Chronicle* is one example of this pressure, the decline in the circulation of *Reynolds News* another, underlined in this latter instance by the fact that the circulation, which had risen sharply when a policy of sensationalising crime and sex was temporarily adopted, immediately fell when the directors of the paper came to the conclusion that the interests and prestige of the Co-operative Movement which owns the paper could hardly be properly served by such means. Nor has its more recent policy, wholly admirable by any standard of serious journalism, of trying to produce an intelligent paper capable of appealing to a public midway between that of the *Observer* and the mass circulation Sundays brought any compensating reward in sales so far.

In the Sunday newspaper field, also, the Beaverbrook formula of sophisticated escapism and the bright romantic treatment of news without recourse to the exploitation of sex has proved rewarding: like the *Daily Express*, the *Sunday Express*, with its circulation of more than 3,330,000 is a monument to the effectiveness of skilled professionalism in entertaining a huge audience without becoming sordid. There has been, too, a similar but even greater mass success for sensational feature-type journalism based on the exploitation of sex, crime and human interest but not without an occasional salutary attack of social conscience and a capacity for useful crusading of which the *Sunday Pictorial* with sales of more than 5,600,000 and the *People* with around 5,000,000 are the most outstanding examples.

There is, however, one significant exception to the pattern followed in daily-newspaper development. This exception arises from the fact that the 'submerged' demand that the *Mirror* tapped and that the *Daily Sketch* is also now trying to exploit was, for economic and social reasons, able to obtain satisfaction much earlier in Sunday than in daily journalism. The *News of the World* is the last remaining example of this early Sunday journalism. It is the most traditional of all British newspapers. It has scarcely altered in content or even in make-up since the beginning of the century, remaining in essentials, indeed, very much the kind of paper it was when it raced *Lloyd's Sunday News* for the first 100,000 circulation in the 1850s. Yet at over seven millions its circulation, although now falling, is still not only far in excess of that of any of its more modern competitors but is well over double what it was before the war. In the war and immediate postwar years it not only held on to old readers but attracted new ones to a phenomenal extent, reaching an amazing circulation total of over 8,000,000 copies. Although it has been unable to hold the whole of this it is still probably regularly read by close on half the population above the age of fourteen if family readership is taken into account.

This success it has achieved not by altering its methods or changing its selection of news to meet a supposedly new taste in popular reading but by holding rigorously to the same basic formula as served it more than a century ago. Now as then its chief stock-in-trade remains the solid, careful, objective presentation of police-court reports of rape, seduction, violence and marital infidelity in every part of the country.

It thus provides a remarkable example of the durability of popular taste: an evidence to which it is impossible not to give some weight that so far from having changed—and certainly so far from having been debased—the public taste of a very large mass of newspaper readers is almost identically the same as that of its grandfathers, who, indeed, demanded, and got a great many more sordid and sensational details than any Sunday or daily paper provides them with today.

The face of journalism has altered a good deal in the last quarter of a century. What has mainly altered it, however, is not the creation of a new demand but the release of an old one.

XVI

A MONOLITHIC PRESS

C P. SCOTT remarked in that same classic statement on journalism in which he declared that 'comment is free but facts are sacred' that 'One of the virtues, perhaps almost the chief virtue, of a newspaper is its independence. Whatever its position or character, at least it should have a soul of its own.' But what, one finds oneself asking as one looks at the pattern of today's press, does independence mean?

There was in the past no such dubiety. What was then at issue was independence from the State, from the pressures of King and Government and the great vested interests of political power. All this has been won in this country at last. No one today disputes the right of any newspaper in Britain to say what it likes and publish what it pleases so long as it does not transgress the ordinary law of the land. The issue of independence has taken on a different and in some ways a more complicated form.

Control of more than 60% of the nearly thirty million newspapers of all kinds daily sold to British readers now lies in the hands of four major newspaper groups: the *Daily Mirror–Sunday Pictorial* group, Associated Newspapers, of which Viscount Rothermere is chairman, Beaverbrook Newspapers, and Kemsley Newspapers; more than 70% of the circulation of all the national morning newspapers is concentrated in the hands of three of these same four, the *Mirror–Pictorial* group, Beaverbrook Newspapers, and Associated Press. Moreover this tight control of newspaper readership and thus of a large part of the national and international news that reaches the majority of the British public seems likely to increase rather than diminish.

Rising costs, particularly of newsprint but also of wages and distribution, now face all but the most powerful newspaper groups with problems of increasing gravity. The industry is, indeed, in some danger of reaching a position where all but the biggest may soon find it almost impossible to bridge the gap between revenue and expenditure—a consummation which some of the most powerful of the newspaper combines would by no means deplore as a means of crippling their less prosperous competitors and opening the way to additional circulation for themselves.

Newspapers as a whole never 'had it so good' as during the war and immediate post-war years. Costs rose but circulations and advertising revenue outpaced them. Those mellow days are over. The closing down of the *Daily Dispatch* and *Sunday Chronicle* by Kemsley newspapers in November 1955 and the subsequent sale by Kemsley of their three Glasgow papers, the *Daily Record, Glasgow Evening News* and *Sunday Mail,* to the *Mirror–Pictorial* group provided the first dramatic indication of the change of climate. And although the Kemsley–*Mirror* deal involved no more than a transfer of power from one big group to another, giving the *Mirror–Pictorial* group first place among the newspaper giants with control of just over 18% of the newspaper circulation of the entire country, there is no assurance that what has happened to these newspapers may not also happen to others more genuinely independent.

The *Daily Dispatch* did not die because it had failed to find readers. Its circulation was still rising. Indeed the last Audit Bureau of Circulation return published before the decision to close down showed an increase of 14,680 copies a day. At more than 465,000 its sales were the largest of any daily newspaper published outside London, accounting for close on a fifth of the total circulation of provincial morning newspapers as a whole. It had been born with the century and had behind it a life of vigorous and popular activity during the course of which it had established itself as the favourite daily paper of generations of Lancashire and North Country people, many of whom took no other paper.

It died because in the face of rising costs and increasing competition it seemed more profitable to its owners to lease its printing presses to the *Mirror–Pictorial* group on a long contract than to make the effort to keep it alive.

Robert Blatchford's old paper, the *Sunday Chronicle*, with not far short of three-quarters of a century of newspaper history behind it and a current circulation of over 830,000, was silenced at the same time, in the same way, by the same proprietors, for the same reasons. A similar assessment of commercial prospects dictated the sale of the three Glasgow papers. The five newspapers thus killed or disposed of were originally acquired by the Kemsley group in the newspaper deals of the 'twenties. For a time they yielded great profits. They were dealt with as they were in November 1955 because this period of high profitability was coming to an end.

No consideration for their traditions or relationship with their readers weighed in the decision. The three Glasgow papers had been Conservative from their earliest day: they were now required to change their politics with their masters. Certainly none was given to that truth of which C. P. Scott spoke when he said: 'A paper which has grown up in a great community, nourished by its resources, reflecting in a thousand ways its spirit and its interests, in a real sense belongs to it: how else except in the permanence of that association can it fulfil its duty or repay the benefits it has received?' It would have been absurd to expect that any should be. These papers had been bought purely for profit. They were now closed down or disposed of for the same motives. It was a commercial, not a journalistic transaction: its significance that it provided the first clear evidence that the favourable conditions which had ruled in the newspaper industry for more than a decade and a half were over. Since then three more provincial morning papers have died.

Although newspapers are smaller than pre-war the rise in the price of newsprint far outweighs the saving in quantity. It was £11 10s. a ton before the war. It is now £58 and may well go still higher. As paper and ink account on average for between 40 and 46% of the total production costs of a national daily paper the outlook is serious for many. It has become all the more so with the freeing of newsprint for while those with large advertising revenues can afford to foot the bill for bigger papers, even with costs as they are, the rest cannot. Yet if they do not they may fall still farther behind in the circulation race.

Moreover although newsprint production has greatly increased in recent years—it rose from 3,600,000 tons to 6,000,000 tons in Canada alone between 1945 and 1954 and the smaller United States and Scandinavian output has risen in the same degree— world consumption has risen even more rapidly. The gap between them is likely to increase as literacy advances in educationally backward areas. The Commonwealth Press Union was informed at its Canberra Conference in November 1955 that if consumption of newsprint in India alone were to rise to no more than one-tenth of that per head in the United States another 1,000,000 tons of newsprint a year would be required. Even without such new demands the Newsprint and Supplies Committee of the Newspaper Society has estimated that by 1960 world consumption will be well above production despite big increases in productive capacity.

In the United States Du Ponts are at work on the development of a synthetic product, other chemists are exploring the possible use of sugar-cane refuse as a raw material. Failing the large-scale development of such alternative sources newsprint supplies can only be increased by the use of timber resources which have until now been regarded as too inaccessible for economic use. This would mean higher costs and another sharp rise in price to newspaper users.

Meanwhile all other production costs including wages have risen sharply. The newspaper strike of April 1955—the only major strike in the history of the British press—inflicted heavy losses on all national newspapers: according to the Annual Report of the Beaverbrook Newspapers published in November 1955 this and the railway strike cost that group alone around £560,000. The cost to other large newspaper undertakings was of the same order.

Although precipitated by one small group of employees the newspaper strike may in retrospect come to be seen as marking the end of an era for the British press. The wage claims that led up to it were inspired by the knowledge that the war and post-war prosperity of the newspaper industry was coming to an end and that if the unions did not press their claims quickly the opportunity might have passed for a long time. The employers resisted because as easy conditions of trade ended they were trying desperately to hold off rising costs in the one field, that of labour, where they believed themselves still able to exercise some control.

This period of rising costs coincides with an ending of the long period of expansion in newspaper sales. For the first time in their history the market for newspapers may be at or near saturation point. The frontier can be pushed no farther.

Close on 88% of the adult population of these islands now reads at least one morning paper during an average day according to an analysis made by the Hulton Readership Survey in 1956. When this figure is set against that of the $12\frac{1}{2}\%$ of the population rated in surveys of national intelligence as educationally subnormal and able to learn to read only with considerable difficulty, if at all, it seems clear that, failing a considerable increase in the habit of reading more than one newspaper, we are very close to saturation point if not already there. Gains of the order of the last decade and a half cannot be repeated. On the contrary the evidence suggests that newspaper readership has at last begun to take a downward turn. The circulation achievements of the powerful are likely in the future to be increasingly at the expense of the weak.

Such conditions are serious enough for many established newspapers. They make virtually impossible that constant refreshment of the press that came in happier times when costs were lower from the competition of new newspapers.

Sixty-odd years ago it was possible for Northcliffe to launch the *Daily Mail* on a capital of £15,000 and although he subsequently drew on the resources of his periodicals for its development the total amount involved in establishing it at a high level of profit was probably well under £100,000. Twenty years later Beaverbrook acquired the *Daily Express* with a circulation of 230,000 for £57,000 (£15,000 for the shares, the balance to meet a bill owing for newsprint). He had to pump more money into it to put it on its feet but he was able to put it on a sound economic foundation and also launch the *Sunday Express* without putting any very serious strain on the private fortune of 5,000,000 dollars he had made from company promoting in Canada and brought to London with him. Twelve years later, such had been the change in the structure of the press in the interval, Odhams Press was forced to sink more than £2,000,000, close on double the entire personal fortune commanded by Lord Beaverbrook when he bought the *Daily Express* and launched the *Sunday Express*, in the effort to turn the *Daily Herald* with its circulation of 250,000 into a popular national daily. It was able to draw on important reserves of goodwill in a large political movement and had the resources of a great printing works behind it. Yet at the end of this vast expenditure the paper was still making a loss.

The Royal Commission on the Press expressed the view that the cost of launching the *Herald* as a popular paper could not be regarded as relevant to others because the speed of the transformation involved quite abnormal expenditure. Other new popular journals could, it suggested, be started more cheaply. But in fact the frantic speed at which Elias sought first a million and then a two million circulation was forced upon him for the very reason that he was producing a 'popular' paper and that unless a very large circulation and the advertising revenue that went with it could be quickly won there was no means of escaping a ruinous loss.

Similar but even worse conditions would face any new newspaper seeking to break into the mass market today. The costs to be met in the initial period are far greater than they were then— newsprint alone has risen sixfold in price. To the established mass-circulation newspaper there is compensation for this enormous increase in running costs in the vastly increased rates for advertising space. But a new paper could not expect to benefit from these unless it could produce circulation figures to justify them. So far from £2,000,000 being an over-estimate an investment of around double that sum would probably now be needed to launch a new national popular morning paper.

A sum such as this would almost certainly be required if it were necessary for the new paper to build its own printing plant. The Royal Commission took the view that adequate facilities for printing new papers under contract could be found without affecting old ones. It is doubtful whether that was the case even then. It is still more doubtful now. The *Daily Mirror* had originally intended to build its own plant in Manchester to print its Northern edition. It found that it would take five years to do so. The death of the *Daily Dispatch* with its fifty-five years of history and its close on half a million circulation was the result.

There may be printing plants in London on which a small-circulation morning newspaper or possibly an evening paper could be printed under contract. The *Daily Recorder* was printed on the *News Chronicle* presses during its brief life, the *News Chronicle* itself unfortunately not using all their capacity. The Co-operative Press plant which prints *Reynolds News* at the weekend is far from fully engaged the rest of the time. But any attempt to launch a new popular daily of large circulation would certainly be hampered at the outset by the need for a heavy capital investment in plant on which no early return could be anticipated. Under present conditions the costs and the risks are too great.

It is true that in another field of mass communication the independent television programme companies have each embarked upon an enterprise comparable in scope to that of starting a new daily newspaper. But in their case the heavy initial capital investment in the radio equivalent of printing plants—transmitters— is covered by the Independent Television Authority. Running costs are high but the prospect of a big new advertising market is considered sufficiently attractive financially to justify the risk. Anyone wishing to start a new popular national daily would have to meet much heavier costs than the television contractors and do so not in the expectation of a new market to exploit but the certainty of ruthless and severe competition in an already crowded one. It is not an attractive prospect. So long as costs stand at their present level any breach in the monolithic structure of the national daily press is so unlikely as to be for all practical purposes non-existent.

Costs are smaller for Sunday papers but the outlook for new development even in this field is not encouraging as the experience of the *Sunday Star* shows. In June 1956 Hulton Press, owners of *Picture Post* and other successful periodicals, had completed plans for the first full colour Sunday newspaper in Britain and very possibly in the world. It was to sell at 4*d.* and the first print order was for more than 1,000,000 copies. Editorial staffs had been working on the paper for some months, printing arrangements employing a new and in some ways revolutionary colour process were completed. For the first time since Beaverbrook founded the *Sunday Express* at the end of the First World War a new Sunday paper was promised. Instead the project foundered before the opposition of the Newspaper Proprietors Association and the National Federation of Retail Newsagents: both bodies much concerned in the advantages offered by a rigidly controlled newspaper industry. From the N.P.A. Hultons received an ultimatum. The new paper would not be allowed to share in N.P.A. distribution facilities or be carried by the newspaper trains which are essential for speedy overnight delivery unless it were handled by newsagents on exactly the same discount terms as existing Sunday newspapers. From the Federation of Retail Newsagents came a second ultimatum. The two were mutually exclusive. For the Federation demanded better terms than newsagents were getting from N.P.A. members, and informed Hultons that unless these improved terms were given newsagents would be instructed not to handle the *Sunday Star*. Hultons thus found themselves in a wholly impossible situation. Unless they accepted the Federation's demands the new paper would not be sold by the majority of newsagents. If they did the N.P.A.

would refuse to allow it on the newspaper trains. After vain attempts to break the circle they postponed publication of the newspaper indefinitely.

Any further attempt to start a new Sunday paper would run into the same difficulties for although the case of the *Sunday Star* was complicated at one stage by some argument as to whether it was a genuine newspaper or a weekly illustrated news feature magazine the Newsagents' Federation subsequently made it clear that the demand for improved terms would apply to any new Sunday paper. This attitude although in part inspired by dissatisfaction with existing terms is almost certainly coloured by the feeling that with a market that has reached or is near saturation a new paper could only get circulation by taking readers from existing Sunday papers so that the newsagent would have more work with no compensating increase in total turnover. In distribution as in production everything points to the continuation of a frozen press structure.

Only in the market for popular magazines does any real opportunity for new development on a national scale still exist. This market has expanded greatly since the war, especially for magazines appealing to women. Indeed it has done so to such an extent as substantially to increase the difficulties of the middle circulation newspapers since these women's magazines are now strong competitors for the national advertising without which such newspapers cannot survive. *Woman*, owned by Odhams, has shot up to a sale of more than three and a quarter millions a week; *Woman's Own*, published by Newnes, has one of over 2,400,000, and the *Daily Mirror's* latest enterprise, *Women's Sunday Mirror*, has quickly established itself at over a million. Apart from women's papers, however, demand seems to be slackening even in the popular magazine field. Sales of such national weeklies as *John Bull, Illustrated, Picture Post* and *Everybody's* have all fallen recently, in some cases very sharply, and the attempts of the *Mirror* and *Express* to catch readers young by publishing junior editions both turned out disastrous failures.

Nor do conditions in provincial journalism hold any hope of

new daily newspapers. In the past thirty-five years the number of provincial morning newspapers has fallen from forty-one to nineteen, six have died since the end of the war, four in the last two years. So far from there being any likelihood of their number increasing we shall be very fortunate if all of those now in existence manage to survive through this new era of rising costs. Fifty-three cities in Great Britain, apart from London, have a population of over 100,000. In only five of them have readers now any choice between locally published daily newspapers, whether morning or evening, in separate ownership. Twelve have no local morning or evening newspaper of any kind whatever. In each of the remaining thirty-five there is a complete local monopoly in newspaper ownership. And although the Royal Commission on the Press was assured in 1949 that plans for several new provincial evening papers were in preparation all have since been abandoned because of rising costs.

Throughout a large part of the modern press we are thus faced to a degree which would have appalled those who fought for press freedom over the centuries by monolithic structures that show every sign of becoming more instead of less tightly knit and restrictive.

It can be argued that in this, as so often in the past, the press merely mirrors the state of our society. This is the age of mass movements. Mass taste, mass buying, mass thinking govern our lives. Mass entertainment draws the crowds, mass political parties attract their allegiance: indeed politically the 2d. newspapers mirror the life of our times with astonishing fidelity—on the right the *Daily Express*, *Daily Mail*, *Daily Telegraph* and *Daily Sketch* together deploy a total circulation of some 8,000,000; on the left the *Daily Mirror*, *Daily Herald* and *News Chronicle* are within a hundred thousand or so of the same strength. The minority man is out of key with the century: he would do better to stop complaining and thank his lucky stars that there is still as much variety in the press as there is.

So it can be argued. That a largely new reading public should demonstrate a good deal of sameness of taste is, in fact, no matter for surprise. It did so even more when the public discovered by Northcliffe gave the *Daily Mail* so massive a sales predominance over all others for so long. What is unnatural—or at least would seem so in the light of previous experience—is that the serious middle public with a long settled habit of newspaper-reading behind it should be able to support so few newspapers compared with the number that catered for a comparable but much smaller group, forty, fifty or a hundred years ago. The paradox may, however, be more apparent than real. It may be that such papers are losing ground precisely because they appeal to too many people. They have been forced by the economic pressures in the newspaper industry to adopt a pattern contrary to their real function. Instead of seeking to satisfy a particular public they find themselves forced to follow the purveyors to the mass in a fanatical search for an amorphous readership of millions. As a result they neither get those millions nor satisfy the smaller public that is naturally theirs.

This is partly due to the fact that even after two successive price increases in the last five years most British newspapers are still seriously underpriced—demonstrably so when compared with those in most other countries and especially in the United States.

Those who complain of the inadequacies of the popular press— and such complaints come particularly from those in the middle and professional groups—must bear a good deal of the blame themselves unless they are ready to pay more for their news-papers. If serious popular newspapers were able to sell at a price that would at one and the same time do away with their present excessive dependence on advertising and their excessive pre-occupation with circulation it would be possible to produce papers much closer to the real tastes and needs of this middle reading public than is now the case.

This public would almost certainly be better served journal-istically—and with much more satisfaction to the separate groups within it—by four or five national newspapers with sales of a million or even less than by three, each of which must try desperately after a circulation of between one and a half and two millions to keep commercially afloat. The journalistic tragedy of our time is that the risk of trying something new has become too great to be taken. This is bad for society which in the field of news and ideas above all others needs the fertilisation of many rivers if it is to be kept healthy, bad for the press which thrives best on the clash of competition, and bad for the individual journalist whose opportunity of employment is restricted and who may, should he be a journalist of opinion, find himself permanently bereft of any regular opportunity of usefully employing his pen if he should happen, for whatever reason, to relinquish his foothold on one particular platform.

We are at a stage in the industrial development of the press that bears some resemblance—although an incomplete one—to that in the mid-nineteenth century when a frozen industrial structure contributed to the monopoly position of *The Times* by making it virtually impossible for any new newspaper to print quickly and cheaply enough to capture a popular market. The immense burst of activity in the founding of new newspapers in London and the provinces that came in the 1850s owed almost as much to technological developments in printing, paper-making and distribution as to the ending of the Stamp Tax. Psychologically the end of the tax was no doubt immensely important. It was an earnest of a totally new attitude to the press on the part of Government and public. But in itself the tax no longer represented so serious a barrier to new enterprise as did the slowness and high cost of newspaper production. It was the technological revolution in printing, in distribution and in communications that enabled the new papers to meet the demand for a popular press. In the very different conditions of the mid-twentieth century the need is hardly less urgent for a comparable technological revolution. It may well be that only by such a revolution can costs be brought down to a level at which it will once again be economically possible to publish general-interest national newspapers with an optimum circulation of a million or less, increase the viability of independent provincial journalism and bring within reach new evening papers in areas where all competition has ceased to exist.

No such large-scale technological revolution is yet in sight. If it were it would probably be resisted by strongly entrenched interests on both sides of an industry that is remarkable for the fact that except for a few isolated spurts it has evolved so slowly and that the basic processes employed have remained so very much the same for so long. In the end it may be that the application of electronic engineering to the printing industry will add up to such a revolution. The development of magnetic printing processes, photographic composition instead of mechanical setting, and electronic engravers capable of producing half-tone plates in plastic direct from original photographs at half the cost of conventional half-tones begins to point in that direction. Synthetic substitutes may ultimately also bring the price of newsprint to more manageable levels.

Nor can even more far-reaching changes be regarded as beyond the bounds of possibility. A facsimile transmission system by which text or photographs or both can be printed by radio was developed as long ago as 1926 and has since been so improved as to transmit printed matter at a rate of five hundred words a minute from high-frequency stations. Nine years ago the Radio Corporation of America using television transmission for a refinement of facsimile known as Ultrafax transmitted and reproduced in printed form the 1,049 pages of the novel *Gone with the Wind* in two minutes twenty-one seconds—an awe-inspiring thought. With the use of facsimile transmission it would now be perfectly feasible for a newspaper reader to come down to breakfast, switch on his television receiver, tune in to the right wavelength, press a button and receive into his hand an up-to-the-minute, fully illustrated newspaper printed on electro-sensitive paper impervious to light and as easy to handle as ordinary newsprint as it unrolled from under a printer blade in a recorder built into the set in much the same manner as a record player. Technically, in fact, there is no reason why we should not all have our favourite newspapers delivered direct to our living rooms whenever we feel like it without the blessing of composing room, printing press or newspaper train.

Facsimile newspapers have been experimentally transmitted in the United States by the *New York Times*, the *Philadelphia Bulletin*, the *Philadelphia Inquirer* and the *Baltimore News Post*. They cut out the whole of the involved and costly process of printing and distribution other than the actual setting of pages in type. Although such a newspaper would be somewhat different in form from those we are accustomed to—it would probably for example be made up of single sheets, not folded pages, and be smaller in size—there is no reason why in general make-up and content it should not be very much the same.

The facsimile process requires high-frequency radio or television transmitters but in principle there seems no reason why such newspapers could not be transmitted from existing television stations in the morning hours when no television programmes are sent out. Originally one possible objection was that newspapers so transmitted would have to depend for revenue entirely on advertisements—in the same way as commercial television programmes do—and would thus be in the hands of advertisers to an extent that an independent newspaper obtaining a considerable part of its revenue from sales is not. Past experience of give-away newspapers paid for by advertisements and distributed without charge does not create much confidence in such productions.

There seems now, however, no technical reason why this difficulty could not be overcome simply enough by building into the television set along with the facsimile recorder one of the various 'subscription' devices for 'pay as you see' television which have been perfected in the United States. With a combination of facsimile transmission and 'pay as you see' the newspaper reader would simply switch on his set, tune to the wavelength on which his favourite journal was being transmitted at that hour, drop his coppers in the slot to unscramble the transmission and pick up the morning paper. He would get it hot from his own private printing press with news several hours later than if it had had to be printed on giant presses at a newspaper office, dispatched by van and train, and delivered to his door by a newsagent. At the other end it would be necessary merely to set up single copies of each page, put them in a frame that would flick each page rapidly in turn before a television camera, and leave them to be received by any number of readers during the scheduled transmitting period.

The main difficulty—although broadcasting found it possible to get over one inherently similar in its early days—lies, of course, in the fact that it would not pay to transmit a facsimile newspaper, or to take advertising space in it, unless a sufficient number of television receivers were first adapted to receive it; and no viewer is likely to spend money on having a built-in facsimile recorder in his television set unless there is already a newspaper for him to receive, and probably not even then so long as he can get his newspaper in the ordinary way without trouble and expense. Not unless the ordinary television set sold at the radio dealers were to have the necessary equipment built in as standard would facsimile newspapers be likely to find a public of any size: not until facsimile newspapers had created a demand for themselves would radio manufacturers be likely to build such sets. We are back to the old problem of the hen and the egg. However, should commercial television fail to attract sufficient advertising revenue on the appeal of programmes alone it is always just possible that some of those concerned in it might think it worth while to finance a pilot experiment in order to offer the advertiser the additional inducement of a repeat of his advertisement in the more permanent form of print.

All this is speculation for the future. Yet even when launched prematurely on a world unready to alter its established commercial ways to meet their challenge technological revolutions have a habit of refusing to die: they crop up again when times are more propitious. Remote though it may seem it would be overbold to dismiss quite out of hand the possibility that one of these days we may get our newspapers, like so much else, from a television aerial on the roof.

XVII

WHAT KIND OF FREEDOM?

IT is useless to criticise the press without relation to its trading
position. But terms of trade are not all. The freedom of the
press does not exist in order that newspaper owners should
grow rich. It is not a possession of newspapers or their proprietors
or editors but of the community, won by many who were not
journalists, as well as many who were, during that long struggle
for freedom of religion, opinion and association and for the
independence of Parliament, judiciary and press on which our
democratic society rests. Those responsible for a newspaper are
in a different position from those responsible for a business who
may properly govern their activities by what is commercially
advantageous to themselves, their employees and their shareholders: they have inherited other calls on their fidelity. A newspaper must sell to live, but it cannot claim that what sells most is
by that fact alone justified. It has other obligations: obligations
to the past, for newspapers would never have known independence
if earlier men had not been ready to sacrifice themselves for
principle; obligations to the present and the future, for the press
is as much a custodian of national freedom and the qualities of
civilisation as Parliament or the courts. It cannot turn its back on
these obligations without reducing its stature, for it is on them
that its stature depends.

Those who control or write for newspapers have no more right
to claim immunity from the historical responsibilities of their
office on the excuse that these responsibilities come between them
and commercial advantage than have Members of Parliament or
judges: the positions of all three in our society are analogous.

just as the independence of the press was won in the same struggle
as that for a free Parliament and an independent judiciary. The
journalist is not buttressed as they are by constitutional safeguards;
his status and the principles which must govern him in the
exercise of his duties are less firmly rooted in acknowledged
tradition and less clearly defined. Unlike them he is a hybrid, a
Janus with two faces, a two-purpose beast. He has commercial
obligations they do not have. But he has obligations to society
not less important than theirs. It is by the manner and degree in
which these dual demands are reconciled that the press is properly
to be judged. The nature of the reconciliation is not the same for
every age, nor is it the same for all newspapers. But its compulsion
exists for all and at all times.

Recognising this special relationship of a newspaper to its
readers the owners of some have voluntarily made over their
property to non-profit-making trusts, others have deliberately
imposed restraints upon themselves or their heirs in the matter
of a sale.

The control of three national newspapers, the *News Chronicle*
(with its companion evening paper, the *Star*), the *Manchester
Guardian* (with its evening companion, the *Manchester Evening
News*) and the *Observer*, is vested in non-commercial, non-profit-
making trusts, the *Daily News* Trust, the Scott Trust and the
Observer Trust. These trusts are required to devote their income
firstly to development and secondly to charitable and educational
purposes so that there shall be no question of their newspaper
properties being run purely for the profit of individual shareholders or proprietors, now or in the future.

The Times is under ordinary commercial ownership but its
future is similarly safeguarded by articles of association which
require that any transfer of ordinary shares (at present held in the
proportion of nine to one by Lord Astor of Hever and Mr. John
Walter) shall be subject to the approval of a committee consisting
of the Lord Chief Justice, the Warden of All Souls, Oxford, the
President of the Royal Society, the President of the Institute of
Chartered Accountants and the Governor of the Bank of

England—a truly formidable and diverse body. In giving or withholding approval this committee is required to have regard to the importance (a) of maintaining the best traditions and political independence of *The Times* and national rather than personal interests and (b) of eliminating as far as reasonably possible questions of personal ambition or commercial profit. The sale of shares to a Corporation is prohibited.

Safeguards of similar effect are contained in the articles of association of both the *Economist* and the *Spectator*. Restrictions on the transfer of shares to prevent any basic change in the character of the paper also operate in the case of a number of important provincial journals, among them the *Yorkshire Post*, the *Liverpool Daily Post* and the *Birmingham Post*; indeed the present owners of the latter paper and its evening companion, the *Birmingham Mail*, are required by a trust deed established when they bought the property in 1944 and effective until 1965 to conduct the two papers on substantially the same lines and with substantially the same policies as under the previous owner, the late Sir Charles Hyde. In particular they are required under this trust (1) to provide a full and impartial news service with only such comment as is fair and free from bias and (2) to preserve the independent and local character of the newspapers and their freedom from control by any political party or trade association or any London newspapers or any combine or syndicate of newspapers.

Although very far indeed from being universally accepted, the principle that commercial considerations wholly proper in the general conduct of business are not so in the conduct of newspapers is thus formally recognised by several newspapers to whom the influence the press can exert seems more important than profit.

What is the extent of this influence? Contrary to some expectation there is no evidence that it has been diminished by broadcasting or is likely to be much affected by television. The difference between the two mediums is too great. This difference was well set out by Sir William Haley, editor of *The Times* and former director-general of the B.B.C., in his Clayton Memorial Lecture to the Manchester Literary and Philosophical Society on 'The Public Influence of Broadcasting and the Press' three years ago. I am grateful to him for his permission to quote from it. Comparing the influence of press and broadcasting he asked his listeners to bear in mind the limitations of broadcasting before coming to any judgment. The first of these limitations he suggested was its inaccessibility.

'This may,' he went on, 'seem surprising, but ubiquity and accessibility are not the same thing. Broadcasting is geographically the most pervasive means of communication yet devised. Simultaneously it can enter millions of homes: be available to everyone in the land. But that simultaneity is also one of its greatests drawbacks. If you are not available to hear the broadcast then you cannot recapture it. A newspaper can be read during any hour of the twenty-four, a broadcast (I am not speaking primarily of news bulletins, which are repeated) must be heard when it is made. . . . The effect is made all the worse by the vast area of interests that broadcasting has to cover. A day's broadcasting, even in the spoken word alone, ranges far more widely than any newspaper (or indeed than all newspapers combined). But again whereas in a newspaper the reader can turn from one column to another, or from one page to another instantaneously—and read whatever he chooses at whatever pace he wishes—the listener can only go from subject to subject as they are offered over long stretches of time, and then cannot take any broadcast faster than it is delivered. Only the completely leisured, bedridden, or fanatically single-minded listener can get from his wireless set as comprehensive a service as he gets from his newspaper. . . .

'Further there is the limitation—and this applies above all to the news bulletins—of the space factor. (In broadcasting space is time.) The fifteen-minute news bulletin contains under 2,000 words—that is less than two columns of the *Manchester Guardian*. In that compass everything from world events to Parliament and sport has to be compressed. It is good discipline in concentrating on essentials but it has its drawbacks.'

Broadcasting has it is true some strengths that newspapers do not have. The first, as Sir William Haley pointed out, is immediacy, not merely in time but in contact: the ability, particularly where television adds vision to sound, to bring events to the listener or viewer in the home when they are actually taking place. As Sir William Haley said, 'When it comes to great occasions, historic events, or even sporting encounters then broadcasting comes into its own. The heart can be lifted or depressed, the profoundest emotions can be stirred. Some broadcasts live in the memory for ever, as no newspaper report can hope to do.'

Yet this being said the balance is still heavily on the side of the press. 'Newspaper production,' as Sir William Haley went on to point out, 'is an infinitely simpler and more flexible operation. It is therefore capable of far greater adaptability. On a matter such as the Budget, or devaluation, or some scientific revolution, the press can at once provide a wealth of information, opinion, discussion, illustration that would take days to assemble at the microphone (and then be physically unmanageable on the same scale when it got there). In political matters the press is far freer and less inhibited. This has nothing to do with the B.B.C. monopoly; similar limitations affect American broadcasting. Because its output can be comprehended—I am using the word in the sense of being all-embraced and not merely of being understood—by each individual reader, a newspaper can have an impact which no broadcasting station can have.'

Sir William Haley's paper was read before Commercial Television had come into operation in Britain, but I doubt whether he would feel it necessary to alter much of what he had to say on that account. This is not to discount the impact of television. No one who has appeared regularly on the television screen and found himself hailed as an old friend by strangers in bars and restaurants, on buses and trains and in the street, and precipitated into scores of discussions on the various subjects dealt with in his programme is likely to do that. Television and sound broadcasting clearly have an immense and pervasive influence on social attitudes and social values.

So far as the most popular programmes of entertainment and family interest are concerned this influence tends to be directed to sustaining mediocrity as the most acceptable social value. But it can hardly be doubted that in their more serious documentary and discussion programmes broadcasting and television open windows on the world for many people and stimulate a good deal of interest in public affairs that would otherwise remain dormant. Yet for the reasons given by Sir William Haley this influence, although often more direct and sometimes more profound than that of the press, cannot compete with it in total extent.

Nor is television likely to rival the press in the field of news itself for the truth is, as Sir William Haley pointed out, that 'a great deal of news, particularly the most significant and important news, has no visual quality'. In most instances the nature of the medium is bound to be at war with the real values of the news. This is not, of course, true in every case. The impact made by a television reporter who brings to the microphone in front of a television camera Jews and Arabs in the Middle East, there to express in bitter broken English their hatred of each other and of Britain and their longing for war as a means of salvation, is likely to be much greater on those who see it than a dozen newspaper dispatches warning of crisis. But over the whole range of news the television camera cannot compete with the newspaper.

On the premise that he who pays the piper calls the tune it is the newspaper owner who is now generally regarded as possessing this great influence. It would not have been thought so in earlier times. It was Barnes, not John Walter II, whom Lord Lyndhurst dubbed 'the most powerful man in the country', and J. A. Spender, as recorded in an earlier chapter, felt it incumbent upon him as editor to disabuse his chief proprietor, Sir Alfred Mond, of the idea that a proprietor had any right to use his paper for the expression of his own opinions—even in its letter columns. Lord Northcliffe is frequently thought to have altered all this. But in fact he did so only as regards a part of the press—and that the least politically influential.

The influence that C. P. Scott of the *Manchester Guardian*

exercised—and it was infinitely greater than that of Northcliffe—was exercised as an editor, not as a proprietor, although the fact that he inherited his uncle's financial control of the paper naturally helped him immeasurably in making it what he wanted it to be, as many another editor struggling against proprietorial caprice has woefully reminded himself. Moreover even when Northcliffe owned *The Times* the influence exercised by its editor, Geoffrey Dawson, was infinitely greater than his own. Northcliffe, as Dawson himself wrote in a letter to Lord Knutsford, quoted in Sir John Evelyn Wrench's admirable and revealing *Geoffrey Dawson and Our Times*, was a master of publicity whose ability as such 'enables him to associate himself, and to be associated by others, with political movements and events with which in nine cases out of ten he has hardly the remotest connection'.

He indeed had a genius for identifying himself so completely with the *fait accompli* in politics that in the eyes of the uninformed he became the person responsible for it. In fact in most instances his part was small; absurdly so compared with that of Dawson. This was due in part, no doubt, to the fact that Dawson had an infinitely greater understanding of the real nature of political power and a much more subtle comprehension of the springs of political action than Northcliffe had. But it was also due to the very nature of their functions as proprietor and editor.

The influence exercised by a newspaper derives from the nature of the medium—from the fact that it arrives daily before its readers as an ambassador from the outside world conveying to them news of events as seen through the eyes of its staff, docketed and assessed in importance and interest by men working daily at high speed, interpreted and commented on by men required by the nature of their task to make immediate judgments. The character of a newspaper may be set in a certain mould by its proprietor—in the way that Northcliffe created the *Mail* in his own image and Beaverbrook has done the *Express*. But even with such a newspaper the selection of news and features, the twist and turn given to the reporting of events, the total flavour of the daily dish put before the public, reflect, and cannot help but reflect to a very large degree, the personality and judgment of the man who does the daily job of producing it—the editor. The proprietor may inspire the big political campaigns. They seldom, experience indicates, have much influence anyway. It is the editor who makes each daily issue what it is.

It is curiously the case indeed—although some newspaper proprietors and managers do not even yet appear to have got around to the fact—that the commercialisation and popularising of the press so far from diminishing the importance of the editor has in many ways enhanced it—even by the standards of commercial success themselves. That great newspapers are made by great editors the whole of newspaper history shows. But it is also the case that popular papers depend for their success upon their editors to a degree not always sufficiently appreciated for their own good by those who profit from them. Lord Northcliffe was aware of this fact although his brother Lord Rothermere was not. To Rothermere editors were expendable. He did not, he said, believe in strong editors. The progressive decline of the *Daily Mail* and the *Daily Mirror*, both in prestige and circulation, under his control was the result. Northcliffe stamped the *Mail* with his personality—he remained from the beginning to the end its presiding genius, acting virtually, indeed, for most of the time as its editor-in-chief in daily control of all that was done. But having, after some preliminary fun and games, appointed a strong editor, Thomas Marlowe, he had the good sense to hold on to him. Other papers might switch editors. Marlowe remained in charge of the *Mail* so long as Northcliffe lived. Its success was due to him second only to Northcliffe.

There is indeed nothing like a good editor for a newspaper. Whatever may be the level of journalistic success to which they aspire, only those newspapers that hold their editors seem to succeed. The correlation between stability of tenure in the editor's room and a newspaper's success, whether in prestige or circulation, is so close, in fact, as almost to provide the basis for a mathematical formula for the guidance of ambitious newspaper proprietors.

This is obviously so in the case of the more serious newspapers: no one has ever disputed the importance of its editor to *The Times* or the *Manchester Guardian*. Similarly the *Observer* has been made by two editors, the first that great journalist J. L. Garvin who created serious Sunday journalism, the second David Astor who, coming to the editor's chair young and with little political experience, so that many regarded him as no more than his father's—and mother's—son, has shown himself an editor of great courage and ability, giving to the paper new life and vigour.

The *Sunday Times* has been equally sparing in its use of editors. It has had two only in the period of its great modern revival. So also has the *Telegraph*, which owes its amazing progress over the last twenty years to the fact that the first Lord Camrose disposed of all other daily newspaper interests when he acquired it, and became not, as its previous proprietor had been, its manager, but its editor-in-chief, attending daily at the office to conduct its journalistic affairs, even to the reading of all proofs. As for the serious weekly reviews who can think of the *New Statesman and Nation* without Mr. Kingsley Martin or imagine that the *Economist* would have won its immense war and post-war prestige without Mr. Geoffrey Crowther?

It is, however, when one turns to popular journalism where the unimportance of the editor compared with the proprietor is now sometimes accepted as a proven fact that the principle demonstrates itself in the most surprising way. There are no doubt a number of reasons for the success of the *Daily Express*, the biggest of all being Beaverbrook. But one of the most important is that it has had only three editors in its more than fifty-five years life and that its present editor, Mr. Arthur Christiansen, has now been in undisturbed possession for close on a quarter of a century.

At least this seems a natural conclusion to draw from the experience of other popular newspapers. The *Daily Mirror* staggered down the road to bankruptcy when the first Lord Rothermere's policy of no strong editors ruled. Only when Bartholomew seized the chance to grab complete editorial control of the firmest sort was the spell of doom broken. The chequered circulation careers of the *Mail*, the *Herald* and the *News Chronicle* over the past quarter of a century keep step in each case with constant changes in editorship which compare strikingly with the history of editorial stability on the *Express*. For years the *Daily Sketch* fumbled from disaster to disaster under a succession of editors so numerous that it was difficult to keep account of their names: only when a large degree of authority and independence was given to its present editor Mr. Herbert Gunn did it—whether one likes his methods or not—begin to increase its circulation at a phenomenal rate.

The same is true of popular Sunday newspapers. The *Sunday Express*, like the *Daily Express*, owes its success in no small part to Lord Beaverbrook's readiness to appoint an editor and keep him for a long time: in this case Mr. John Gordon. Under the impact of the first Lord Rothermere's conviction that editors were something you got rid of the *Sunday Dispatch* had eight editors in six years. Its circulation fell to less than 700,000 in the process. Since it has been content with one its circulation has risen to over 2,500,000. When the *People* experimented with numerous editors, some good, some bad, it could not pay its printers' bills. With an editor who stayed 'for keeps' its circulation rose to over 5,000,000. The *News of the World* is known throughout Fleet Street as an old faithful that keeps its editors 'for life'. It has the largest circulation in the world. In the post-war period the *Sunday Chronicle* dispensed with editors at a speed that rivalled even that of the old *Daily Sketch*. It died in November 1955.

In fact although the industrialisation, commercialisation and popularisation of the press have done a good deal to alter the face of journalism they have done nothing to impair the basic journalistic fact that newspapers are made by journalists. This was first demonstrated a century and three-quarters ago when the *Morning Chronicle* fell in circulation by two-thirds as soon as Perry, whose editorship had raised it to greatness, left. It is the daily impress of an editor's personality that gives a newspaper character whether the character be grave or gay, austere or scandalous.

Moreover, the importance of the editor which seemed at one

stage in the commercialisation of the press to be in so much danger of being diminished seems likely to become not smaller but larger as time passes. The age of the strongly individualist newspaper proprietor who himself impressed an editorial personality on his paper is almost over: we are moving into the era of the administrators. Only Lord Beaverbrook remains of the old breed. And even he although he has no difficulty in controlling his newspapers by telephone—or telepathy—wherever he happens to be is growing old. The first Lord Camrose is dead, Lord Kemsley's empire shrinks around him. The second Lord Rother-mere shows (fortunately for his properties) none of his father's passion for using newspapers as platforms for personal publicity. Lord Southwood has been succeeded by a committee, the ebullient Bartholomew by the business-like Mr. Cecil Harmsworth King. As for Lord Northcliffe there never was anyone to replace him.

Large circulations and greater costs have increased the capitalisation of newspaper companies, making it more difficult, especially in an age of heavy taxation and high death duties, for one man to own a newspaper and virtually impossible for even the richest to dream of starting one. The characteristic pattern of newspaper ownership in the national press, although less so in the provincial morning press where family ownership still persists, is now becoming that of the large public corporation in which many commercial interests have to be taken into account.

The ownership of the *Daily Mirror* with a readership greater than any other on earth so far from being in the personal possession of one single proprietor, or even of a small group of proprietors, is so widely spread over so many shareholders, many of them small shareholders, that it is quite impossible to give any specific answer to the often repeated question 'Who owns it?' The largest single block of shares, some 22%, is held by the *Sunday Pictorial* Limited. As, however, the *Mirror* is in its turn the only large shareholder—and at that a minority holder— in the *Sunday Pictorial*, and as the rest of the *Pictorial* shares are spread as widely among the ordinary investing public as those of the *Mirror*, this does nothing to concentrate ownership in one group of hands. The *Daily Mail* is owned by a public company, Associated Newspapers Ltd., which now also has a controlling interest in the *Daily Sketch* and is itself controlled by the Daily Mail and General Trust, whose shares are similarly widely spread, although a single block of some 21% of the total is held by Lord Rothermere. The *Daily Herald* is owned by the Daily Herald (1929) Ltd. in which commercial control (although not that of political and industrial policy) is owned by Odhams Press Ltd., a public company in which no individual shareholder or group of shareholders has a controlling interest. The *News Chronicle* as described earlier is controlled by a non-profit-making trust. So also is the *Manchester Guardian*.

Only three national newspapers still remain in private ownership in any complete sense: *The Times* in which Lord Astor of Hever holds 90% of the shares and Mr. John Walter 10%; the *Daily Telegraph* in which the Berry family hold all the ordinary shares; and the *Daily Express* of which Lord Beaverbrook's absolute mastery has never been in any doubt—even although he did announce in 1929 that he had given his controlling interest to his eldest son, the Hon. William Maxwell Aitken, and in 1954 that he had given the same controlling interest to the Beaverbrook Foundation, a British Empire Educational Trust.

The age of the press lord moves into history to be replaced by that of the big business administrator.

The substitution of ownership by public corporations for ownership by individuals does not of course mean, any more than it does in other industries, that effective managerial control is not in fact vested in the hands of a very few people. In this industry, as in others, the control over very large capital enterprises can be exercised with masterful ease through voting control over minority blocks of shares—at any rate so long as things are going well. But it does make it less likely now than in the past that newspapers will become the personal vehicles of dynamic personalities and more likely that their commercial control will pass increasingly into the hands of high-grade salaried executives.

The managerial revolution came to Fleet Street somewhat later than most other places but it is by now firmly entrenched there.

As for the consequences, they may turn out both good and bad. The vast conglomerations of press power in a few individual hands which seemed likely to become the most characteristic feature of newspaper development in the 'twenties and 'thirties obviously had greater potentialities of public mischief, although the danger, like the political influence of the press lords, tended to be over-exaggerated by the nervous. To that extent the extension of ownership by public corporations is to be welcomed.

But although there may be risks in a newspaper becoming the personal mouthpiece of one man there are dangers of a different kind in its becoming simply a business. The great press lords made fortunes out of journalism, but all of them—even the first Lord Rothermere although to a lesser extent than the others— were prepared at times to put both profit and circulation second to the advocacy of what seemed to them important. Lord Northcliffe's attack on Kitchener in the First World War may, as Geoffrey Dawson for instance claimed, have come long after Kitchener had been entirely discredited in governing circles and may have had the effect of making it not more but less easy to get rid of him. But it was conducted by Northcliffe in a spirit of patriotism that did not count the effect of public reaction on the *Mail's* circulation. The *Daily Express* is as brilliantly entertaining and unpredictable a newspaper as it is because Lord Beaverbrook has always been ready to use its profits to make it a better one, spending large sums to give real news more promptly and sometimes more fully than its competitors and following a policy of ploughing money back into development at a rate that his successors may find both difficult and unattractive.

The real danger facing a good deal of journalism today, in fact, is not, as it seemed to be a generation or two ago, that much of its historic duty of public information may be twisted to serve the propaganda purposes of powerful individuals but that it will be pressed into a pattern that denies it all purpose other than the purely commercial one of attracting the largest number of paying customers by whatever means comes most readily to hand.

The responsibility of journalists, and especially of those in editorial authority, will become especially great if this should prove to be the case. The defence of journalism as more than a trade and greater than an entertainment technique—although a trade it is and entertaining it must be—is properly the journalists' and no one else's. It is they who are the legatees of history in this respect. They have both a professional and a public duty to look after their inheritance.

This is not, of course, to suggest that the interests of editor and publisher are necessarily antagonistic. They are far from having proved so in many famous partnerships of the past: they are very far from being so in many instances today, indeed it is difficult to see how any newspaper can succeed at the highest level except when they are identical. Nor is it to suggest that the proprietor and publisher is necessarily likely to be less concerned with the truest interests of the press than is the journalist; this has certainly not proved so on many occasions since the days when Henry Sampson Woodfull, the owner of the *Public Advertiser*, gladly risked prison in order that 'Junius' should have a platform for his views. Nevertheless the guardianship of journalistic values rests primarily with the journalist: *c'est son métier*. He cannot disassociate himself from this responsibility without ceasing, in a fundamental sense, to be a journalist. Nor is there any final excuse for him in the claim that he is, after all, simply a hired man who must do as he is bid. He must be ready, as must all men when issues of principle arise, to stand up and be counted.

The relationship between editor and publisher can never be simple—unless indeed it is so simple as to make the editor no more than a paid servant. The Royal Commission on the Press was content on the whole to accept this simple version as the correct one—especially in relation to popular newspapers. But to do so is, in fact, to set aside a good deal of what is most important in the history of the press and to overlook the fact that the freedom of the journalist—freedom not only from censorship or intimidation by the State but from censorship or intimidation by anyone including his own employer—is an essential part of press freedom.

This freedom involves the right of individual reporters to report facts honestly even if they prove inconvenient to the fancies or prejudices of editors or news editors, it involves the freedom of foreign and political correspondents to report and interpret the evidence before them according to their independent judgments and journalistic conscience, even if to do so is awkward for the policy of the paper that employs them, and it most certainly involves the degree of independence possessed by an editor in his relations with his publisher. Such independence clearly cannot be absolute. Whether a newspaper is owned by an individual, a joint stock company or a trust the right to decide the kind of newspaper it is to be, the sort of public it is to aim for, and the policies it will in general support must rest mainly with those who own it.

Mainly but not entirely, for a newspaper is more than a piece of property, it is a living personality with a character and tradition deriving not only from those who own or edit it but from its readers, from the interests it has historically served, and from the community of which it is a part, a fact, as earlier shown, recognised by some proprietors through the formal instrument of trust deeds and articles of association. This double responsibility is especially true of those newspapers that serve a specific local community, nourished, as C. P. Scott said of them, 'by its resources, reflecting in a thousand ways its spirit and its interests', so that they 'in a real sense belong to it'. To alter the character of such a paper for reasons solely of increased profit, or to buy and sell it as though it were no more than a piece of merchandise without regard to the purposes and policies that have won for it its special place in the community, is an abrogation of the true responsibilities of newspaper ownership, although one which some of those who have made large profits out of newspapers have found by no means uncongenial.

Free enterprise is a valuable bulwark of a free press. But the freedom of the press differs from, and ought always to be recognised as greater than, the simple freedom of an entrepreneur to do what he pleases with his own property. A journalist has commitments to the commercial interests of those who employ him. But he has other loyalties also and these embrace the whole relationship of a newspaper to its public.

This is equally so whether the character of a paper derives from the authoritative discussion of public affairs or from its power to interest and entertain a wide variety of readers whose concern with public affairs is limited and intermittent. The influence of a newspaper on its readers derives not only from its expressed opinions but from its daily selection of news, the honesty of its reporting, the weight of its headlines, the values it emphasises in its features, the whole picture of the world and what is important in it that it daily presents to those who read it. By the very nature of daily newspaper production these depend more upon the editor and his staff than on anyone else. The editor is legally responsible for all that appears in the paper he edits; his moral responsibility is not less. He ought not to be allowed to escape it. But he ought also to be put in a position to sustain it in the public interest no less than his own.

The correct working relationship between a newspaper editor and his proprietor or publisher is not easy to define. It has been much discussed, although less so in Britain that in some other countries. In Norway the leading journalists' associations have defined the correct relationship as one that, within the broad framework of policy laid down for a paper by its owners and mandatory on it by reason of its traditions, gives the editor 'complete freedom to maintain his own opinions even though they may not in some cases be shared by the publisher or management', and that places upon him 'the entire responsibility for the editorial content of the paper'. 'He must not', according to this definition, 'allow himself to be influenced to uphold opinions which are contrary to his conscience and conviction. He directs and accepts the responsibility for the activity of his editorial staff.' This definition has been largely accepted by influential

Norwegian public opinion and has been reflected in the constitution of the leading newspapers.

Much the same is true in Sweden. Thus although the editor of the leading Swedish Liberal paper, the *Dagens Nyheter*, is required under the terms of his appointment to consult with the chairman of the board on major political matters it is also stipulated in the paper's constitution that it is the view of the editor and not of the chairman that shall be decisive in such matters and that political questions shall not be discussed at board meetings but shall be determined by the political staff of the paper. Approximately the same procedure rules in the chief Swedish Conservative paper, *Svenska Dagbladet*. A number of Dutch papers have similar provisions in their company-statutes requiring that so long as he holds office the editor shall have absolute independence in his decisions on the editorial contents of the paper.

In Britain independence in the control of editorial policy is similarly guaranteed to the editor of the *Manchester Guardian* under the Scott Trust and also to the editor of the *Manchester Evening News*. Although formally the articles of association of *The Times* vest control of policy in the chief proprietors in practice the independence and authority of the editor is virtually absolute. That of the editor of the *Observer* is specifically safeguarded in its articles of association.

Such independence is far from belonging to the editors of most great commercial newspaper enterprises. Nor, since their purpose and the relations they have with their readers are so different, would it be wholly appropriate. Yet although the relationship between editor and publisher necessarily differs on a popular mass-circulation newspaper from that on a journal of opinion the diminution in the status of the editor to no more than a paid servant of proprietorial interests, the mere tool of other men's whims and financial appetites, that has accompanied a good deal of the commercialisation of the last half century or so runs dangerously counter to the public interest and is contrary to the traditional role of journalism in public life.

The journalist is at once freer and more vulnerable than the barrister, the solicitor, the doctor. Freer because he belongs to a more open profession that recruits men and women of diverse experience through many different doors and must be able to do so if it is to maintain its true character; more vulnerable because he is a wage-earner dependent for the most part on one employer. Yet his professional responsibilities to the public are not less than theirs. The obligations imposed upon them in their relations with the public and supported by the powers vested in their governing professional bodies, the Bar Council, the Law Society, the General Medical Council, are not applicable to him in the same form. Yet the preservation of the strictest ethical and professional standards in the press is no less important to society than in their case. And because he is dependent, to an extent they are not, upon the goodwill of a single employer, the journalist may find himself less able than they to resist pressures that would reduce them.

The journalist ought to accept and ought to be required to accept standards of professional integrity morally not less mandatory than those of the barrister, the solicitor or the doctor. But what is required in their case to safeguard the public against professional malpractice is required in his case not only for this reason, important though it is, but also to provide the journalist himself with a safeguard against those pressures to which one who is dependent upon a single master may find himself vulnerable: a professional power to set against, and if necessary act as a counter-balance to, the immense and growing power of financial control in the newspaper industry.

It is possible that the Press Council will provide such a counter-power: indeed there are already some signs that it is beginning to do so. At the time of its foundation I took the view, as did several members of the Royal Commission out of whose recommendation it was born, that there would have been great advantage in establishing the Council as a statutory body with powers analogous to, although not identical with, those of the General Medical Council. Such a statutory body would from the beginning have entered the field able to provide a valuable counter-balance to the massive power of commercial interest, which ought not to be left to decide alone the standards by which popular journalism is to live. Yet it is possible that a voluntary Press Council may in the end succeed in doing this no less effectively. The moral pressures it can bring to bear, both on proprietors and journalists, are considerable. Its specific judgments may be overridden, but they can serve to create a general climate of public and professional opinion that cannot be ignored so easily and whose effects may be pervasive and far reaching. To create such a climate is the most important of all the responsibilities that rest upon the Council. It is a responsibility to which it is applying itself with considerable courage and in which it needs all the public and professional support it can get.

Yet whatever the Press Council may do it is upon the individual journalist that the ultimate responsibility rests. He is the legatee of a great tradition. He cannot abdicate. He has loyalties greater than to his pay packet and they should be paramount.

XVIII

IN NO MAN'S SHADOW

WHEN all is said that has been said in the previous chapter we are still left with the final question: what in this day and age, does the influence of the press, far-reaching and pervasive as it obviously is, really amount to— and what ought it to amount to?

That it has changed enormously in character and scope during the past hundred and fifty years, and even during the past fifty is clear. It is wider but less profound: no modern editor can hope today to exercise such direct influence on Government and public policy as Barnes or even Delane did, although Geoffrey Dawson came very near to it during his editorship of *The Times* between 1912 and 1941.

What gave *The Times* of the first half of the last century its immense influence was the restricted field of its impact; that and the fact that by a combination of editorial and business circumstances it was the only paper worth bothering about. No other newspaper can ever again occupy quite this position, not only because the structure of the press has completely altered but because the structure of society has altered also. Even in Delane's last years the unique authority of *The Times* was already passing.

The Times of Barnes and Delane was able to exert the influence it did on those who governed Britain because they were a small, compact group that could be reached by one newspaper; they read virtually no other, and they held in their hands all the strings of political power. Moreover this influence was exclusively directed to one field of human activity, politics, to an extent that is not true of any newspaper today. Right up to the end of the nineteenth century, indeed some way into the twentieth, when men talked of the influence of the press they meant political influence exclusively. That is no longer true.

Direct political influence is still, of course, an important part of the influence a newspaper can exert, particularly in the case of serious journals of opinion. But it is only a part, not the whole, and in the case of the mass-circulation press it is usually the smallest part. The impact of the press is now far wider but much less deep, and it has taken on many new forms. If the twentieth century can hardly expect to see another Barnes or Delane it is equally true that the modern newspaper editor may hope to influence an infinitely larger section of society over a much wider range of its activities than Barnes or Delane ever did and in ways that were not open to either of them.

The last editor who can properly be compared with Barnes and Delane is Geoffrey Dawson. Superficially the comparison, indeed, is very close. In circumstances very different from those ruling in their day he exercised during his quarter of a century's editorship of *The Times* (from September 1912 to September 1941 with a four-year break from February 1919 to January 1923 in the last four years of Northcliffe's life) an influence on great events hardly, if at all, less than theirs and certainly far larger than that of any other newspaper editor, or proprietor, of modern times.

There is, however, a real sense in which Dawson's influence although bolstered by his position as editor of *The Times* did not derive from it as that of Barnes and Delane did. In some respects, and these vital ones, it was not a journalistic influence at all, as theirs was wholly. Indeed so far from having its roots in the principles that guided them, and that ought always to guide a great editor in the practice of his craft, it was in important particulars alien to these principles, and in the event dangerously so.

Barnes's influence was rooted in the conviction that a newspaper is 'not an organ through which the Government could influence the people but an organ through which the people could influence the Government'. He held, as *The Times* said of him in a leading article published on the centenary of his death, 'that honest writing needed not to carry, and could not carry, any weight but the weight of the argument'. This led him not only to a belief in the anonymity of journalism but also to the certain conviction that the influence of a newspaper must, of its nature, rest on open argument in its own columns. *The Times* was his life. He rarely sallied far beyond it. Even his hair was cut for him by a compositor while he sat at his desk and he dined most evenings in the editor's room, usually off tripe. In its columns he argued and thundered, constantly reinforced by the stream of information as to opinion in the country which came to him from his agents. If any man wanted to see him, however eminent, he could come to see him in Printing House Square. He did not seek statesmen out to whisper advice in their ears; his hammer blows were all struck in the open.

Delane dined out constantly. He knew everyone, picking up secrets 'by sticking to the centre of them'—'as quick on news as a toad's tongue on a fly'. But all his activities were centred on his one consuming interest, *The Times*. The world and what went on in it excited him only in so far as it demanded report and comment in his newspaper. He studied the play of politics, no man more closely. But he stayed disengaged. He moved among the great, but remained uncommitted. Like Barnes, a greater editor than he, the only commitment he acknowledged was to journalism itself.

But Dawson was a committed man. He entered journalism almost by accident in South Africa. Milner, whose private secretary he was, arranged for his transfer from the 'Kindergarten' to the editorship of the *Johannesburg Star* so that that paper should support the Milner policy after Milner had returned to England. He remained committed all his life—to Milner, to the 'Kindergarten', to All Souls, to the Athenaeum, to Round Table 'moots', Grillon's dining club, the Travellers; round and round from one to the other he went talking with Milner, and Lionel Curtis, with Leo Amery, Lord Brand, the Marquess of Lothian,

Lord Halifax, Lord Altrincham and F. S. Oliver, round and round and back again, talking and planning, drawing up memoranda, drafting letters of advice, dropping words in the ear of this statesman or that, lunching privately with Prime Ministers and Foreign Secretaries; always active, always concerned for the best; the Secretary-General, as Sir Robert Boothby has called him, of the twentieth-century Establishment.

It was an honourable commitment and a high-minded one, for Dawson was an honourable man. So were they all honourable men, this small group of powerful people whose writ ran so large and in the event so disastrously in the years that led to war.

It was an honourable commitment, but it was not a journalistic one and in the end it led Dawson into courses contrary to the principles that should sustain journalism at its highest levels and that had sustained Barnes and Delane.

One may follow the manner of Dawson's activities through the pages of his diary and memoranda: the Group meetings that decided as early as November 1916 that Asquith must be replaced by Lloyd George and that Lloyd George must have Milner (at that time hardly known to the general public in Britain) at his right hand in the War Cabinet; the talks with the King's secretary in the 'twenties on the desirability of a National Government; the 'heart to hearts' with MacDonald at Chequers; the private chats with Baldwin, the Archbishop of Canterbury and Lord Hardinge before the Abdication; the *tête-à-têtes* with Chamberlain in the years that led to Munich ('Prime Minister in excellent form and stood pat on appeasement'); the 'interesting talks' with Sir Nevile Henderson about getting Göring to come over for the Grand National and with Lord Halifax about Mr. Chamberlain's visit to Berchtesgaden. As one follows all these what comes to impress one most is not only Dawson's ceaseless activity (however did he find time to edit his paper as well as he did while keeping his eye on so many irons in so many fires?) but the extent to which he directly involved himself in the policies and even the political fortunes of his friends, friends chosen always, it must be said, from the highest motives. One is impressed, too, by the extent to which, 'always conscious', as Bishop Headlam said of him in the Commemoration Service at All Souls, 'of having tried to do what was right', he identified himself and the group of which he was a part with the State and in so doing crossed the line that Delane had said should always separate the purposes of journalism from those of statesmanship.

'We cannot admit', said *The Times* of Delane, 'that its [a newspaper's] purpose is to share the labours of statesmanship or that it is bound by the same limitations, the same duties, the same liabilities as that of Ministers of the Crown.'

Because his purposes, and to a great extent his methods also, were essentially political and not journalistic Dawson came to accept these limitations and those duties. Barnes had conducted himself *vis-à-vis* Cabinets as though he were in truth a Fourth Estate; Dawson conducted himself *vis-à-vis* Prime Ministers as though he were a superior Civil Servant, a confidential adviser. The influence that a great editor exercises should lie in the open. Much of Dawson's lay behind the scenes. It should derive from the width of his knowledge of opinion in all classes of the community, the readiness of his newspaper to reflect it. Dawson knew little or nothing about the mind or mood of most of the ordinary people of Britain as his almost total disregard of the problem of mass unemployment throughout most of this period shows. Imprisoned in his 'circle' he seems, for example, to have been almost totally ignorant of, or wholly uninterested in, the trade union movement and completely unconscious as he moved from contact to contact of the eruptive force that such a man as Ernest Bevin was to bring to national and world affairs. The only trade union leader mentioned in his diary is J. H. Thomas, whose 'robust imperialism and misplaced aspirates' are noted with condescending affection.

The influence properly exercised by the editor of a great newspaper ought, in the words of that famous leading article of *The Times*, to rest on the conviction that the duty of the journalist 'is the same as that of the historian—to seek out the truth above all things and to present to his readers not such things as statecraft would wish them to know but the truth as near as he can attain it'. Dawson was too much committed to statecraft for that journalistic compulsion to hold his fidelity. Instead he could write self-approvingly to a friend in 1937, 'I do my utmost, night after night, to keep out of the paper anything that might hurt their [the German Government's] susceptibilities'; and in the interests of appeasement could drive Norman Ebbutt, the distinguished *Times* correspondent in Berlin, to despair by so emasculating his truthful dispatches as to destroy their purpose in reporting the extent of Nazi atrocities and ambitions. And he could force its Parliamentary correspondent to resign by doctoring his report of the reception given to Duff Cooper's resignation speech in the House of Commons after his protest against the Munich agreement.

Dawson exercised great influence in the affairs of Britain for more than a quarter of a century and did so, although with dire consequences in some instances, from the purest motives and the highest sense of duty. But although his position as editor of *The Times* contributed enormously to this influence it was not essentially a journalistic influence. It is not comparable to that of Barnes or Delane or to that of C. P. Scott in his own times. He quarrelled with Northcliffe because he saw him as seeking to make *The Times* the instrument of a personal policy; yet although he spoke and thought much of what he liked to call the 'Company' of *The Times* whose individual personalities were lost in the personality of the paper there is a sense in which he himself did exactly what he accused Northcliffe of trying to do. He made *The Times* the instrument of his personal policy rather than himself becoming the instrument of a newspaper recognising fidelity to no other cause than that of serving in its columns the 'enlightened force of public opinion' with absolute independence of all other interests or Governments.

The influence that a great journal of opinion ought properly to exert in these modern times has been described more modestly than Dawson understood it—or perhaps than he himself always exercises it in practice—by the present editor of *The Times*,

Sir William Haley, in the Clayton Memorial Lecture to which I have already referred.

Comparing the influence possessed by the greatest newspapers and journalists of the past to that which may even now be seen on very rare occasions when an almost unanimous press clearly reflects public opinion on some particular issue, he went on to say : 'But the deeper, and the subtler influence—and I believe the healthier one compared with the old days—is the formative and interpretative power of the press today.'

Faced, he suggested, with the manifold political and economic complexities of our time, the great masses of the people eschew opinion ; they leave it to their representatives, and judge, as best they can, by results.

'It is the power of the press, particularly the serious press, to inform those representatives on these hosts of matters which is now important. Such newspapers have a mass of news, background information, and advice pouring into their offices. They also have experts on their staff who are giving whole-time study to some individual country or group of domestic problems. . . . These papers have sources both of information and of informed judgment which are in total not available to the ordinary Member of Parliament and can often supplement even the knowledge of Ministers. That, and their power at the same time to present legislators with some idea of serious public opinion, is a powerful influence. It may have little of the old dramatic effects obtained in Barnes's day. It can be far more constructive, widespread, and continuously in operation.'

But if this applies to the serious quality press, daily and weekly, national and provincial, and also, as I think it does, to the more serious of the popular newspapers which in some measure may also claim to influence 'the intelligent opinion of all classes in industry, in the universities and schools, the professions, the churches and the arts and all walks of life', what of the rest: the great-circulation newspapers which, working day by working day and Sunday by Sunday, seek to contribute to the entertainment and education not of 'informed public opinion' but of the other nine-tenths of the iceberg, the great mass of the people who, to an extent never remotely true at any previous time in our history, now account for the great bulk of newspaper readership?

Sir William Haley, who holds no very high opinion of the mass-circulation press, suggested in his lecture that it is especially in regard to such newspapers that we must now consider the influence of the press in much wider than political terms. This is undoubtedly true. It may well be the case, as he said, that not for many years has the popular press played any decisive part in the result of a particular General Election—although the influence of the *Mirror* on the 1945 election, particularly on voters in the Services, cannot be written off too lightly. It is certainly the fact that over recent years 'the political structure of the Kingdom has tended to move more and more into two more or less equally balanced, monolithic blocks, loyal to their Party above all else' and that 'the rank and file membership of these blocks is recruited rather from an attitude of mind than from a belief in a particular political philosophy or Party programme'. It is in shaping these broad attitudes of mind that the popular press exerts its major influence.

But what of Sir William Haley's further judgment? 'Is the national temper what it was?' he asked, and went on to declare that in too many minds today there had come to overlay the innate good nature of the British people 'an attitude of cynicism, jealousy between class and class, of suspicion, of jeering at standards and disregard for institutions, of respecting nothing and believing in nothing, of taking it for granted that the individual should have everything he can desire and that he owes the nation nothing in return. . . . There is a general feeling that someone is doing the ordinary man down, bilking him, misleading him, jeopardising him, getting at him in one way and another, and generally being responsible for the fact that he is not able to be a carefree, continuously entertained uninhibited lotus-eater.'

'One cannot help noticing', Sir William Haley went on, 'that these are identical with the values and attitude of some of the popular press. It is necessary to qualify. Much of the popular press is admirable ... it deliberately appeals to and seeks to foster the true interests of the British people, their tolerance, their sense of enterprise, their imagination, their courage.... But there are some papers which do none of these things and are a disgrace. Often they are humbugs enough to pander to evil by making a show of attacking it. Dailies and weeklies, they have huge circulations. Naturally they go to the less discerning and discriminating sections of the community. In a direct way they can be said to have no political influence. But indirectly, cumulatively, they are building up an attitude of mind in the new generation which can be disastrous unless it is counteracted.'

These criticisms were repeated even more strongly nearly two years later in a leading article in *The Times* of 31 July 1955. They are no doubt very widely held among much of the public *The Times* caters for.

'What', asked *The Times*, celebrating the centenary of the repeal of the Stamp Duties, 'will be the future of the press?' It answered: 'It can safely be said that if it continues its present course it will regain neither status nor authority. The race for mammoth circulations has led in some cases to a disgraceful lowering of values. The baser instincts are being pandered to, not only in lasciviousness—the influence of this can be overrated —but in social attitudes and conduct as well. Envy, jealousy, intolerance, suspicion are all too often being indirectly fostered. Irresponsibility is rife. The tone of voice is a perpetual shriek. So-called brightness is all. By no means all popular papers are thus (it is in fact deplorable that some of the worst examples should be classed as newspapers at all), by no means all the journalists on even the worst newspapers wish them to be thus. But the turning of the press into predominantly a business enterprise, the fact that in the present state of newspaper economics readers have to be fought for by the million to make popular journalism viable, have engendered forces greater than the journalists.'

Although most of those dependent on the suffrage of the people are (Mr. Aneurin Bevan dissenting) more polite—or

careful—than this in what they say about the popular press
many leaders of the churches and universities and others pro-
minent in one way or another in public affairs have said much the
same. They agree with Sir William Haley: 'Politicians, particularly
Ministers, often tell us the British press is the finest in the world.
Much of it is. Serious newspapers, some of the great national
newspapers, the provincial newspapers are admirable. But take
the press as a whole and such encomiums simply are not deserved.
Foreign visitors here are often appalled at the levity and false
values of many British newspapers. They have moved into the
entertainment industry—and not very high-grade entertainment
at that.'

In its second annual report the Press Council felt it its duty to
defend the popular press against so wholesale an attack. It argued
that although mass-circulation daily and Sunday papers might
well, like other human institutions, suffer from some of the faults
catalogued, these should not blind critics to their very real
virtues and values. These virtues were eloquently described in
the following terms:

'To expose injustices, to right wrongs, to give advice, to
befriend the friendless and help the helpless—these are among
the services which these newspapers are constantly rendering to
people who could not otherwise obtain them. They take up
causes and run "campaigns" which would naturally not see the
light of day in the staider section of the press because that is not
its purpose. They are invariably on the side of patriotism and
legality, of courage and chivalry.'

The defence, like the criticism, runs to excess. But both have
a core of truth. It is no good looking to the mass press for the
qualities one admires in small-circulation serious newspapers.
But it is equally the case that it brings to light a great deal of
petty bureaucratic tyranny that would otherwise pass unchecked
and that many small but important injustices, and even some
major ones, are set right by the vigorous onslaughts of the mass-
circulation papers.

Much of the criticism directed against those newspapers with the largest circulations can be shown to be justified in particular instances, a great deal that fills their pages is likely to be found superficial, trivial, ill-balanced and boring to those brought up on older traditions of journalism. But the *Mirror* and *Sketch*, the *People*, *Sunday Pictorial* and the rest are not written for readers of *The Times*. To criticise them by its standards is a waste of time. It indicates a failure to understand, or perhaps to face, what is happening in the world.

In his paper to the Manchester Statistical Society on 'Newspaper Circulation 1800–1954', to which reference has been made in an earlier chapter, that distinguished journalist and historian the late Mr. A. P. Wadsworth, then editor of the *Manchester Guardian*, remarked that the history of newspapers in the first half of the nineteenth century is to be explained by the conviction of the influential classes that 'the lower orders were not to be trusted'.

I suspect that a good deal of the criticism now directed against newspapers that the mass of the people in our own times have made their own is, consciously or not, inspired by something of the same feeling. It is a feeling sharpened, no doubt, by the fear that, for good or ill, the masses are no longer so willing to be told what is good for them by their social and intellectual betters as they once were and are therefore likely to prove a greater threat than in the past to many traditional standards and institutions. Certainly one cannot help but notice a significant parallel between much of the criticism of the popular press made by *The Times* and its readers and that directed against 'the lower-priced papers' by the distinguished economist J. R. McCulloch in the middle of the nineteenth century: 'Such papers are, speaking generally, addressed to the lower and poorer classes of the community; and their writers find it more to their advantage to flatter the prejudices entertained by their readers, and that espouse their peculiar views howsoever inconsistent these may be with the interests of society in general, than to inculcate sounder though less popular principles.'

All men, even the most liberal, tend to identify the interests of the State with the standards and values that find approval in their own circle; and sometimes, of course, they are right. If they are of good will and hold authority they need to be constantly reassured in their consciences that their possession of it is in the common interest and that the principles by which they govern are respected even by those who disagree with them. They are impelled by a loyalty to the trade of authority that comes in some measure to embrace all who are in it.

The inescapable bi-partisanship forced for a time upon the political parties over a large field of foreign and economic policy by post-war circumstances, the political vacuum brought by the general acceptance of the major principles of the Welfare State, all these have tended in the last decade and a half to increase the sense of homogeneity among men of authority and influence. So has the impact of the B.B.C. which has felt itself impelled by its sense of responsibility as a monopoly public service to minimise not maximise the differences in public life. The ideal picture of the British way of government has become one in which public men arguing before a microphone or a television camera demonstrate that however much they may disagree on small matters they are basically of the same mind, serve the same common good and rest their actions on the same general premisses.

In this cosy world the Federation of British Industries and the Trade Union Congress cuddle together like the lion and the lamb and coo the same tune and the two great monoliths of party politics, protesting how much they dislike each other, reserve their venom for the heterodox in their own parties. The Twentieth Century Establishment spreads wider and farther than that of previous centuries as the acceptance of the duties of authority brings into its orbit new social and administrative groups, each impressed by events into a common pattern of responsibility, each accepting a common language of moderation, each anxious above all things to reduce areas of discord to ever smaller and more manageable proportions.

This, no doubt, is admirable. Much of it in any event is inevitable. Without it Britain could hardly hope to find a way through the economic forest. But it is a great deal more interesting for those who do the administering than it is for those whose modest lot it is to be faithful members of the rank and file. Many of the great issues that stirred ordinary men and women in the past are now ended. The fight for political freedom is won. It has left in the mouths of millions comparatively recently enfranchised the dry taste of political boredom as they vote apathetically for one or other of the two great political machines, each so confident of its ability to tell the ordinary man and woman what is good for them, each so like the other in so many ways, each busy proving that co-existence is possible. The yawning gap between the privileged and the unprivileged of earlier decades has been reduced to a series of irritations, sharp enough in some instances, but less capable of mobilising great emotions of courage and loyalty to put them right. National homogeneity has had its reward: we are better fed, better clothed, better housed, better educated, better cared for than at any time in our history.

'Public opinion', said Sir John Seeley, 'is necessarily guided by a few large, plain simple ideas. When the great interests of the country are plain, and the great maxims of its government unmistakable, it may be able to judge securely even in questions of vast magnitude. But public opinion is liable to be bewildered when it is called to enter into subtleties, draw nice distinctions, apply one set of principles here and another there.'

That is true—and a great deal of political life has now been refined down into subtleties. The Establishment has grown new heads. These heads talk in different accents but they grow from the same body. They argue one with the other, but do so in the language of those whose disagreements are rooted in a vast common agreement. When they turn their faces to the crowd the same admirable sentiments, the same calls to unity, the same insistence on discipline and hard work, the same promises of better times tomorrow if only we are all good today fall from their lips and the same smile of benevolence suffuses their features with ineffable goodwill, with the consciousness of duty done, with the highest moral rectitude and the most disinterested sense of public service. They stand for important standards and values—who would deny it?

But, and here is the rub, the values and standards they preach come down from the top. They draw their strength from the closed convention of established authority—not less closed in its essential pattern because deriving from a wider constituency than formerly. No doubt they are fit subjects for admiration and emulation. But they ignore many of the conflicts that still exist in society; the exasperations, illogicalities and irritations, the sense of being pushed around, the anger at some specific result of all this high-minded official benevolence and bureaucratic tidiness. It may be, indeed, that they overlook something even more fundamental, a profound resentment against the restraints of a social mould deriving from the values of an earlier age which those at the bottom had little part in shaping.

The popular press does not overlook such things. It exists to reflect them, to give them a voice; to shout, protest, expose and play hell. Naturally the process is hardly agreeable to those conscious of more solemn obligations. The administrators of society always find it difficult to understand the resentments of the administered, especially when they are conscious that they mean so well by them. Only the most cynical of governing classes fails to think itself the custodian of the values essential to a good society. But the medallion of authority, even when made of the very best metal, tends to look very different according to which face is turned towards you. It has always been the function of the popular press to look at the face of authority from below; to be dangerous to those who govern, even when their intentions are of the best; to subject the standards and values of the Establishment of the day to the vulgar realities of common life and to turn upon what Cobbett, the greatest popular journalist of them all, called 'The Thing' all those resources of wit and indignation, invective, derision and hammer-headed obstinacy to which common men have gone throughout the ages to preserve themselves against the mould into which authority would press them. Even good Governments need to be constantly reminded that the governed also have a point of view and that when the shoe pinches it is the wearer not the cobbler who feels the hurt.

This is as much the real job of the popular press today as it ever was: indeed it becomes more so as the area over which bureaucracy reigns grows wider and the power of political machines that have grown in strength and rigidity for nearly a century accumulates. If those who edit and write for the popular press are told, as they frequently are, that it is the duty of responsible journalism to guide public opinion and not merely to follow it they can reply as Barnes did to Lord Brougham's secretary that 'whether he guided or followed it was very much the same to him so that his paper enjoyed the credit, which he always claimed, of being the guardian of it'.

Let us, however, look at the case against the popular press and particularly the tabloids and mass-circulation Sunday newspapers a little closer. One part of this case is that as regards a large proportion of their contents they are not newspapers at all but mere entertainment sheets. This, of course, is true. But since when has entertainment ceased to be one of the functions of journalism? Addison and Steele would certainly have been surprised to hear that it was not, or that the only proper journalism was that which dealt with serious public affairs. Between them they helped to change the social atmosphere of an age by dealing almost exclusively with those matters to which men and women turn when neither business nor public affairs claims them.

In truth the conception of the newspaper as properly concerned only with large matters of public interest is almost entirely Victorian, a solemn interlude in two and half centuries of boisterous existence. It did not rule earlier, it does not rule in any newspaper, however serious, now; even *The Times* has recently introduced a women's page and taken to publishing rather strange feature articles on its social page. The development of the newspaper as a daily magazine is not an invention of the modern popular press or even of Northcliffe (a great student of newspaper history) but a reversion to an earlier pattern. The gossip column is at least as old as Bell and Perry and Stuart, the crime story much older.

One may deplore the quality of some of the entertainment. But it is not a reflection of original sin on the part of journalists or even proprietors—though some of both show no great anxiety to resist temptation when it comes their way—but of the straits to which an industrial mass-society has brought millions of its members. For the most part this entertainment is neither worse nor better than that offered to eager patrons by the film industry, by the purveyors of literature to the masses through the cheaper commercial circulating libraries, or by the producers of mass-audience programmes on sound radio and television whether transmitted by the B.B.C., Radio Luxembourg or the programme contractors of I.T.V. It deserves no more praise. It may make one a little sad that so many of one's fellow citizens should find satisfaction in so unutterably boring a picture of the resources open to the human spirit at this stage of civilisation. But anyone who thinks that the mass-circulation press is guilty of depraving public taste is ignorant of what public taste has evoked in its service in most other forms of mass-entertainment.

But however considerable their entertainment content all newspapers must accept some, at any rate, of the obligations of the journalist in the field of public affairs. The charge brought against much of the mass-circulation daily and Sunday press is that it misconceives its duties in this respect to such a degree as to muddy the waters of public life and distort the whole idea of what a free press ought to do and be in this modern age.

This case was well set out by *The Times Literary Supplement* of 18 November 1955 in a leading article, 'A Free Press', based on an essay on press freedom in a collection of papers *The Road To Justice* by Lord Justice Denning. In this leading article *The Times Literary Supplement* suggested that two contradictory ideas as to the assumptions on which a free press should operate now exist. The first is held by responsible people outside the profession. The second is held by many journalists themselves.

The first it described in the following terms: 'It [the press] exists to supply the information which the public needs to make political decisions; to enable public opinion to judge the impartiality of the courts; to praise virtue and condemn corruption in high places, and to amuse by satisfying harmless curiosity. Given these standards, a man can judge when the press is using and when it is abusing its freedom; sometimes, though here the calculation of advantage is always extremely complicated, the law can prohibit the abuse of freedom and recompense those who suffer from it. In general, however, the proper use of freedom will depend upon the individual and composite sense of responsibility of members of the profession themselves.'

But there is, argued *The Times Literary Supplement*, a second view, 'commoner among journalists themselves', which has a more romantic and less utilitarian colour. It is from this that the trouble comes.

'It springs', said *The Times Literary Supplement*, 'from the conception of the press as a "fourth estate" in perpetual and necessary collision with the other three; it assumes that the business of the press is essentially criticism and that newspaper offices are the natural temples of the spirit of radicalism. The business of the pressman is to put the cat among the pigeons, which cat among which pigeons is frequently held to be a matter of little importance. The sovereign test of efficient journalism, on this view, is its power to make an impression and to command attention. Its philosophical justification, if one were required, would have to be the theory that public opinion, however carelessly informed, is always the best arbiter, and that the value of an opinion to society can be accurately measured by its power, when skilfully presented, to attract adherence.'

Expressing a judgment undoubtedly shared by many in positions of influence and authority, *The Times Literary Supplement* argued that this second, journalistic, view of the freedom of the press as an instrument for the radical criticism of society has now been outdated by events. It derived from an age of oligarchic government when the structure of society was intensely hierarchic and when everything was weighted in favour of the established order. Such conditions no longer exist. In earlier circumstances it was fitting that the press should be regarded as an instrument of opposition with a disruptive function intended to check complacency in the powers that be. It is no longer so. We are a democracy. The whole direction of government is decided by public opinion. The press should now 'no more think of itself as an instrument of opposition than as part of the mechanism of government . . .

'Now the press has a judicial role and the philosophy of rebellion upon which it was nurtured has accordingly become out of date . . . newspapers should outgrow the phase of knight-errantry and concentrate . . . on performing a function as useful to society as the daily delivery of milk.'

As regards journals, and journalists, of opinion for whom what matters is that 'formative and interpretative power' described by Sir William Haley in the Clayton Memorial Lecture I quoted from earlier there is no doubt a good deal in all this, so long as it is not pressed to the point of insipidity. Yet even for them, or rather for their readers, there are risks. The judicial role is a difficult one to sustain without the power and discipline of the law to support it. If this role is claimed without such safeguards as operate in law to ensure that those who deliver judgment have given due and impartial weight to all relevant evidence, and only to what is relevant, it may contain greater potentialities of mischief than a dozen openly partisan statements. It calls for an absolute quality of disinterestedness: such a quality of disinterestedness as Geoffrey Dawson, for instance, found it impossible to achieve when he suppressed the evidence from his own correspondents that might have weakened support for the causes to which he and his closest confidants had committed themselves or when he threw the great weight of *The Times* behind policies the evidence for and against which he had deliberately refrained from putting impartially before the jury of its readers.

The journalist who claims a judicial role for himself and his paper ought to do so only if he can be completely sure of his power to empty his mind of all prejudice, even the most worthy, and free himself of all interests and associations, however public spirited, that might cloud impartial judgment. He must be concerned with nothing but the facts and be confident of his ability to give to those that affront his dearest principles the same weight as to those that reinforce his most cherished opinions. To claim such judicial objectivity requires formidable self-assurance. To sustain it calls for qualities not easily come by even in the highest minded. There may be such men. But it seems to be straining credulity beyond reasonable bounds to expect to find them in the office of every popular newspaper.

Nor even if it had the resources to sustain a role so far outside its natural inclinations would the popular press be right to accept it. The world observed from the offices of *The Times Literary Supplement* in Printing House Square differs a good deal from that seen from the shop floor of an engineering works in Sheffield, the cage of a pit in South Wales, the driving seat of an all-night truck on the Great North Road, the girls' rest-room in a plastics factory on the Great West Road, the kitchen sink of a back-to-back house in Leeds, a dockside in Liverpool, or even a clerk's desk in an office in the City.

It is well enough, and valid enough, to say that 'in a democracy the whole direction of government is decided by public opinion' and in the larger sense this is, of course, true. But except at General Elections, even if then, it does not particularly seem so to millions of the governed. The public will, no doubt, is paramount, but the administrative machine is vast and anonymous: it grinds on its way regardless. Public opinion determines the general direction of government, it is true, but most of the issues by which a Government, when elected, sets its course are subtle and complicated. They involve arguments on means and costs and the balance of advantage that require an expert knowledge and experience of the practical in government beyond the reach, or inclination, of the majority.

The ordinary man and woman must judge as best they can by results; and in major matters the results may come too late and be too final for their judgment to have much effect. In small matters, in personal matters, in matters that affect a man or his neighbours or people of his own sort directly, or that affront his sense of what is right and fair and true to common justice, his power to influence is larger because his direct knowledge is greater and his emotional response more immediate. But even then this influence is likely to be small unless it can become part of a wider protest, find a voice that even the largest administrative monster will hear above the grinding of its own machinery.

It is in the providing of such a voice and not in the fulfilling of a judicial role for which it has neither the resources nor the capacity that the popular mass-press fulfils its true function in public affairs. Its role in society is not that of a judge but that of a minefield through which authority, great and small and at every level of policy and administration, must step warily, conscious always that a false step may blow it up. The estate of journalism is a dangerous one. It ought to be so both for those who work in it and those they scrutinise. It exists as a force in society to remind all those who govern that systems are made for men and that the standards ruling in Whitehall and the Athenaeum may look very different in Streatham, Whitechapel, Bootle or Moreton-in-the-Marsh; it must remind them also of the untidy, incalculable forces of public approval and resentment that they must take into account in their deliberations and the strength of emotions that move unseen beneath the surface of public affairs. And it must make them remember, too, that they live and rule in a changing society in which social, moral and legal values are not fixed and absolute for all time, to be passed like an entailed estate from one generation to the next and from one order to another, but are subject to the constant erosion of the tides of human feeling, so imprecise, so incoherent, so fallible, yet so powerful and compelling.

If this is, in fact, the true role of the popular mass-press in all its forms it is not a small one. Nor, although lacking in the austere dignity of the judicial role, does it carry with it lesser responsibilities. The popular press fails in its fidelity to those journalistic principles that ought to command its allegiance not when it refuses to undertake tasks that do not properly belong to it but when it sets aside the values that its real functions involve.

These values belong much more to the advocate than the judge. They do not call for impartiality, but they do for honesty; honesty to those attacked as well as to those defended. They do not require that all that can be said on either side shall be set out with equal weight in every newspaper and that in a partisan world the popular press alone shall be non-partisan. But they do require that facts shall not be distorted to bolster up a bad case or make a good one stronger, and they do require that what is said shall be said with both courage and fairness.

It is when it betrays these values—and no one who consistently reads all daily and Sunday newspapers can deny that they are often betrayed—that the mass-circulation press abdicates from the real role it should play in a modern society. The challenge it makes on behalf of common men, the defence it offers against the pressures of the administrative State and of the powerful and ubiquitous public and private corporations and associations that march so authoritatively through modern society, the eruptive force it can bring to bear upon the self-regarding societies of the powerful and authoritative who, serving the public according to their lights, yet sometimes forget in the close-knit loyalties of their joint interest what rights the public have—in all these its effectiveness is crippled when it lays itself open, as it too often does, to charges of misreporting, malice, unfairness and gross exaggeration. It can with confidence withstand the attacks of those who, true to a pattern with a long history behind it, distrust it because it is popular; it need not worry if it is thought vulgar, noisy and disreputable. All these are in its nature. What it cannot afford to do is to open the gates to its enemies by itself providing them with evidence that it is biased, malevolent and ill informed and ought not to be taken seriously.

The function of the popular press is too important to be jeopardised by disregard for values of truthful reporting and honest comment that should be common to all journalism, whatever the public it serves. The defence of these values, although shared by all who have to do with newspapers, lies primarily with the journalist. It rests on his shoulders with the weight of history.

The press changes as society changes. It finds new publics, develops new techniques, responds to new demands. It is not necessary to allocate virtue between different kinds of news-papers: each must make do with its own. The great journals of information and opinion are secure in their position. The informative and interpretative power they exercise is vital to civilisation. They exert an influence on thought and decision not easily to be calculated, since it permeates in some measure every aspect of national life. The great mass-circulation newspapers with their very different functions to perform command their millions, and they, too, reflect and influence in their fashion the shape and colour of our society. Only the middle group of serious popular papers is in serious difficulty and that not so much because of any journalistic defect as because trading conditions impose upon them with increasing severity a pattern un-characteristic and uncongenial. Their decline is as much a public tragedy as a journalistic one, for such newspapers perform a service no others can provide. In so far as their position reflects the current pattern of society and the forces powerful within it it is not one in which we can find either pride or satisfaction.

Despite all changes in the structure of the press and in the number and kind of newspapers the basic commitment of journalism remains, however, the same as always. It is identical for all. It is to report honestly, to comment fearlessly, and to hold fast to independence. The profession of journalism is known to possess its cynics. Why should it not? They have much to be cynical about both in their own trade and in what they see of the world and its inhabitants as they move about their business. But those who serve journalism serve one of the great professions of the world. The allegiance it properly commands is absolute.

Those who give it that allegiance need stand in no man's shadow.

INDEX

A

Aberdeen, Fourth Earl of, 90; on *The Times*, 87

Addison, Joseph, 14, 19, 22, 28, 145, 284; and *The Spectator*, 23

Advertisement Supplements to *The Times*, 82

Advertisement Taxes, 29, 81

Advertising: early economic independence through revenue from, 50–1; use of revenue from, 60, 146–7; relation to circulation, 77, 179; display, influence of, 171ff., 179; loss of revenue in economic crisis, 177; rise in rates today, 179, 207, 242; cost of attracting, 179–80

Advertising World, 176

Ainsworth, Harry, 187

Aitken, Hon. William Maxwell, 262

Almon, John, 50

Altrincham, Lord (Sir Edward Grigg), 273

Amalgamated Press, sale of to Berry brothers, 177–8

America, early position of press in, 111–12

American Civil War, 92

Amery, Leopold, 272

Anne, Queen, 13, 15; death, 19

Answers, 136–7, 138, 141, 145, 146

Anti-Jacobinism, 67

Applegarth, Augustus, 132

Arbuthnot, Dr. John: *John Bull* pamphlets, 15

Aspinall, Professor: *Politics and the Press 1780–1850*, 31, 50; on restrictive legislation, 67

Asquith, H. H. *See* Oxford and Asquith, Earl of

Associated Newspapers Ltd., 262

Associated Press of New York, 120

Association of Proprietors of Daily Provincial Newspapers, 120

Astor, Hon. David, 259

Astor, Colonel J. J., 182

Astor, Viscount, of Hever, 252, 262

Athenaeum, the, 102

Athenian Gazette, 16

Athenian Mercury, 16, 131

Audit Bureau of Circulation, 237

Authority, popular press attitude to, 283

Aviation prizes, 149

B

Bagehot, Walter, 101, 102

Baghdad, the press in, 33

Baldwin, First Earl, 160, 273

Baltimore News Post, 249

Bamford, Samuel: *Passages in the Life of a Radical*, 69

Baring, Thomas, 88

Barnes, Thomas, 9, 65, 72, 97, 145, 148, 171, 175, 256, 284; early days on *The Times*, 73; chosen editor, 73; making *The Times* voice of public opinion, 74–5, 79; revolutionises home reporting, 75; support for Queen Caroline, 76–7; and Parliamentary reform, 77; successful catering for public demand, 78; and the middle classes, 79, 81, 96; anonymity of, 85; and provincial opinion, 107; his influence, 270, 271–2, 275

Bartholomew, Harry Guy, 196, 259, 261; joins *Daily Mirror*, 224–5; becomes editorial director, 226; standard of popular journalism, 226–7

Bartlett, Vernon, 190.

Bauer, Andreas, 121

Beaverbrook, Lord, 159, 160, 165, 180, 184, 229, 261, 262; and the circulation war, 202–3; on propaganda, 214; interest in power, 214–15; desire for political power, 215, 217–18; his life, 217; lack of subtlety, 218; and purchase of *Evening Standard*, 175; takes over *Daily Express*, 218–21, 241, 251; attitude to editors, 259, 260; use of *Daily Express* profits, 263

Beaverbrook Foundation, 262

Beaverbrook Newspapers, cost of strike to, 239

Beeton, Samuel, 102

Beggar's Opera, The, 16

Bell, Clive, 15

Bell, John, 60, 61, 145, 285; *Apology for the Life of George Anne Bellamy*, 53; and the *World*, 54; and the *Oracle*, 54

Bell's Life in London, 102

Bell's Weekly Messenger, 54–5, 102

Bellamy (House of Commons doorkeeper), 57